Clangers™

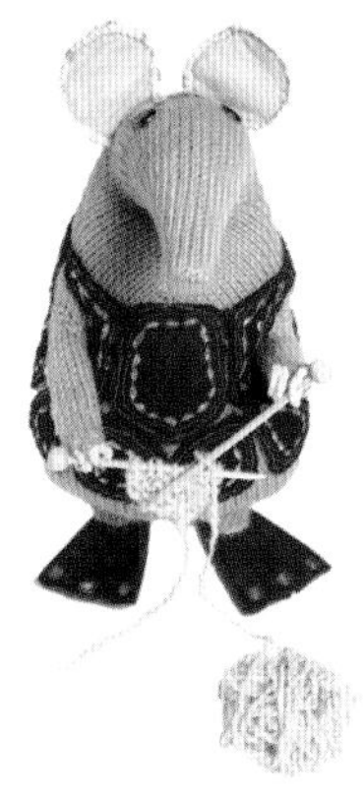

The Complete Scripts 1969–1974

OLIVER POSTGATE

with Daniel Postgate

unbound

First published in 2022

Unbound
Level 1, Devonshire House, One Mayfair Place, London W1J 8AJ
www.unbound.com

Text design by carrdesignstudios.com

A CIP record for this book is available from the British Library

ISBN 978-1-80018-198-4 (hardback)
ISBN 978-1-80018-199-1 (ebook)

Printed in Slovenia by DZS

1 3 5 7 9 8 6 4 2

For Prudence Postgate
and Joan Firmin

Contents

Foreword

by Michael Palin

Of all the children's television shows I watched with my children, *Clangers* was the most special.

Peter Firmin and his wife, Joan, created a visually imaginative, cosily reassuring world where children felt safe and at home, but what I enjoyed, as a parent, was the tone of Oliver Postgate's storytelling. There was always a touch of gentle severity, a slight hint of impatience as the characters went about their business. The children, Tiny and Small, were impulsive, Major was well-intentioned but basically hopeless, and Granny spent a lot of time asleep in her chair. (Mind you, as a grandfather myself, I absolutely recognise this portrayal.) Mother was the only one of the family allowed to display consistent good sense.

Loving and supportive as the Clangers were, their adventures were told without a trace of sentimentality, which to me was another great quality of Postgate's writing.

He was the creator of their world yet managed to portray himself as someone who was never absolutely in control of it. Despite that, or perhaps because of it, he had enough authority to sell us a convincing relationship between a human being and a family of pink knitted creatures.

The episodes were a series of neatly constructed, beautifully paced playlets. In the space of ten minutes seemingly insurmountable problems came up, caused general mayhem and were ingeniously solved to everyone's satisfaction. You never left the Blue Planet without knowing that all had turned out just fine. Which was a comfort to children and a great relief to parents.

For me, the secret of the Clangers' appeal lay in the mix of the exotic and the everyday. The Blue Planet may have been far, far away in a remote corner of space, yet when you got there Major was in his den and Granny was knitting.

The Blue Planet, or the Blue Universe around it, was not full of bug-eyed, green-skulled space men zapping each other, but obliging clouds that would come and water your plants and frogs on springs and chickens made of scrap iron. There were dragons on the Blue Planet but they made soup.

The Narrator was important but he wasn't all-powerful. With his catchphrase – 'Oh dear!' – he was frequently as confused as everyone else. He never out-guessed the Clangers, sometimes running to keep up. 'Oh, that *was* a good idea, Mother!' or 'That *is* clever, Tiny.'

The ethos of the Clangers' world was the same as William Goldman's oft-quoted judgement on Hollywood: nobody knows anything. Or perhaps in the Clangers' world: nobody knows everything. Which is why the Blue Planet had to be a world in which everyone needed to help everyone else. It was an egalitarian world, where everyone, at some time, supplied the solution to the problem. It was a world sustained by cooperation.

It's also a world of saving and recycling. Long before this became an essential part of our lives, the creators of the Clangers made a point of making the most humble piece of equipment, the discarded nut or bolt, the most mundane piece of metal, into the hero of the hour. After all, the Clangers lived under dustbin lids.

In this aspect Postgate and Firmin anticipated by some fifty years the simple, unsensational formula that made *The Repair Shop* such a success.

There was another show that came out long before *The Repair Shop* which shared the same quirky, subversive, anti-establishment tone as *Clangers*, and at its birth in the same year, 1969, was also unlike anything that had gone before.

It was called *Monty Python's Flying Circus*.

And one of its writers was a very big Clangers fan.

Enjoy the scripts. And marvel at the craftsmanship that produced these little gems.

Michael Palin

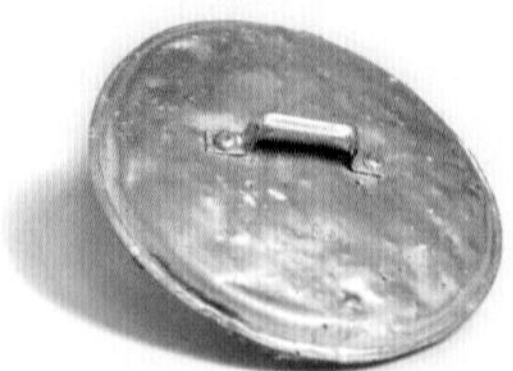

Foreword

by Maggie Aderin-Pocock

Hello and welcome to this book.

My name is Maggie Aderin-Pocock and I am a space scientist and science communicator, and I was inspired to become a space scientist by *Clangers*.

Let me explain. You see, I was born in 1968, and in 1969 the first Moon landing happened. This is when Neil Armstrong and Buzz Aldrin stepped out onto the Moon surface. I was too young to remember it happening, but it had a big effect on me. From a very early age I decided I wanted to go out into space. But what sealed the deal for me was watching *Clangers*.

The Moon landing made me think that getting into space was a good idea. But it was the Clangers that

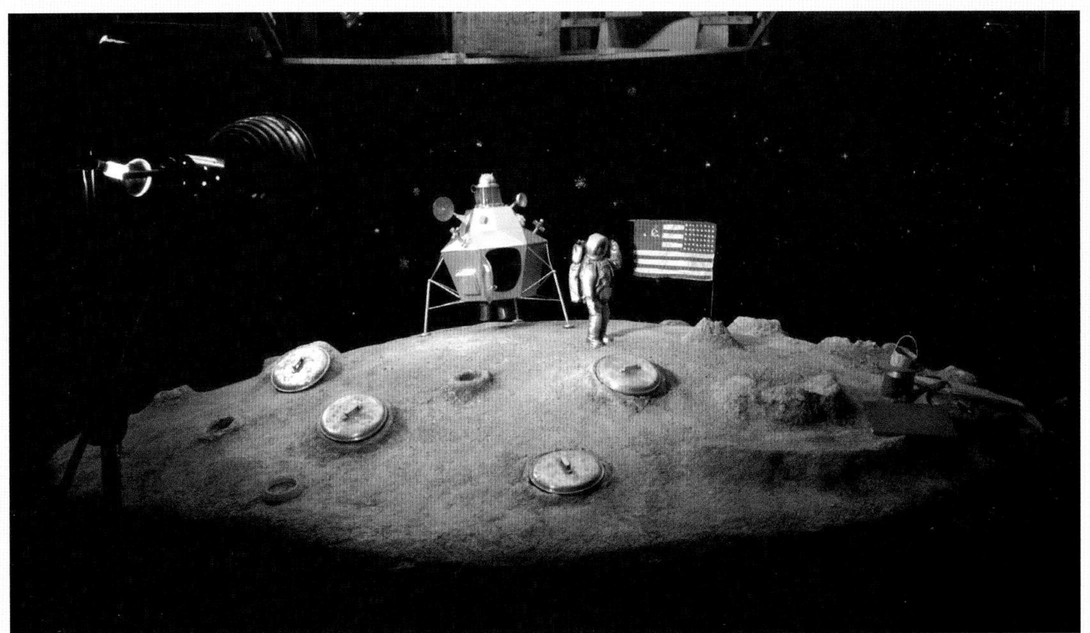

The Clanger-planet set with astronaut and sellotape.

gave me my reason for wanting to get into space. You see, I wanted to meet them all. These small, wonderful aliens captured my imagination. They lived on a planet orbiting a different star – what we would call an exoplanet today. They had amazing adventures and were part of a wonderful community. A community I wanted to join.

I wanted to play with Tiny, Small and Baby Soup Dragon, knowing that even as children we have ideas that matter and make a difference. I wanted to invent things with Major Clanger in his workshop, trying out new gadgets and investigating any space junk that might come our way. I wanted to visit the Soup Dragon's volcanic den, mining the blue-string soup wells to feed everyone. (I am still trying to find a good recipe for blue-string soup.) If after my adventures I wanted some quiet time, I would sit peacefully in Mother Clanger's garden, perhaps lending a hand to tending to some of the exotic plants. But my favourite thing would be to sit with Granny Clanger, chatting while quietly knitting and having a snooze if needed.

It turns out that the Clangers also introduced me to the wonderful world of science fiction, where we look at current ideas in the scientific world and expand them beyond. Just like imagining a community of aliens living harmoniously on a small planet out there in space.

As an astronomer it is also marvellous to see what started off as a brilliant bit of imagination, a simple story for children and adults alike, of creatures living on a very different planet going around a different star. Now, some fifty years later, we are detecting these exoplanets, even if we have not found the aliens yet.

Just as they did when I was a child, the Clangers provide some much-needed peace in a very hectic, sometimes overwhelming, world. With this book we can see how the magic was created with original scripts, sketches and pictures.

Each and every one of us needs a Clanger moment in our day. With this book these moments are now available 24/7.

Enjoy.

Maggie Aderin-Pocock

The Chromatic Awakening of Smallfilms

As Daniel Postgate has noted, in his companion essay featured in this book, it was the BBC who, when commissioning *Clangers*, demanded Oliver Postgate and Peter Firmin venture beyond the black-and-white frame that had defined the look of Smallfilms' work up to that point. Writing in his autobiography, Oliver recalled: 'In 1968 the BBC issued a decree which put paid to our ambitions to make any more *Pogles' Wood* type films. In future all bought films were to be in colour – not only "in colour" but "colourful". They wanted something completely new and quite astonishing.'[1] While the BBC had been experimenting with colour broadcasting on BBC2 for over a year prior to this instruction, the unequivocable nature of the BBC's steer is reflective of the concerted effort being made by both the BBC and ITV to gear up for a complete transition to colour broadcast by the end of the 1960s. In fact, and in a fitting loop of fate, the debut broadcast of *Clangers* (16 November 1969) formed part of the first weekend of widespread colour television broadcast in the UK.

However, the ability to actually watch *Clangers* in colour as intended was impaired by the limited number of colour television sets sitting in homes at the time of its broadcast. As Iain Logie Baird, grandson of John Logie Baird, notes, colour TV sets 'did not outnumber black-and-white sets until 1976, mainly due to the high price of the early colour sets', and that by the end of 1969 only 200,000 sets were in use in the UK.[2] Sales data confirms Baird's assessment of the steep price differential between colour and monochrome at the time of colour's introduction, while also showing how colour television deliveries overtook monochrome deliveries for the first time in 1973.[3]

While Oliver and Peter would have known that not every member of the audience would get to see the dazzling colour of the Clangers' world when it was first broadcast, this didn't curtail their visual ambition. Beyond the iconic pink of the Clangers, the first two seasons offer up, to name just a few of the most prominent examples: a green Soup Dragon, blue Sky-Moos, orange Froglets, the silver and gold Iron Chicken, brass Hoots, an orange television set, a brass music boat, and red and yellow Glow Honey. By embracing colour technology in such an emphatic way, *Clangers* secured a lasting place in the popular imagination.[4] Even at a time when many other shows were being produced in colour, the colourfulness of *Clangers* stood out. This is confirmed in the promotional mailer produced by Roy Williams, Oliver and Peter's marketing agent, which emphasised, in uppercase, that the show was 'IN COLOUR', while also referring

to the fact that they lived in 'a labyrinth of yellow caves' inside a 'blue planet'.[5] Evidently, right from the outset, the colour production of *Clangers* was seen as an active ingredient, and not simply a reflection of new broadcast expectations.

A particularly virtuoso use of colour can be seen in the episode 'Goods' (BBC1, 22 February 1970). This episode debuted at a time of increasing environmental concern in Britain, with the first edition of *The Ecologist* magazine being published in July 1970, while the British branch of Friends of the Earth was established in September 1971. The episode's opening monologue sets the scene, noting how 'complex and convenient' the lives of the people who live on Earth have become, before reflecting upon how this reality is not visible from the vantage point of those looking down from outer space:

> One can see no factories, no roads, no cars or railways, no toothbrushes, no plastic mixing bowls, none of the millions of articles that man manufactures to comfort his short life. By comparison, we can imagine how dull and empty must be the lives of beings on other planets, which do not enjoy the benefits of a modern, industrial civilisation.[6]

With these words of dullness and emptiness still ringing in our ears, we cut to an image of the Clangers, colourful and certainly not dull, providing a moment of playful juxtaposition, before the sound of a falling object prompts the Clangers to take cover. Hearing a crash, the Clangers emerge to discover many colourful broken pieces littering the surface of their Moon. Working together, the Clangers quickly piece the object back together, revealing a machine (clearly made of Meccano, of course) that, after the spin of a control dial, can fabricate plastic items.

This sequence is rich with comedic reversals, as the descriptions provided by Oliver's narration frequently mischaracterise the objects, which is then followed by the Clangers' misappropriation of some objects, thereby adding a further layer of whimsy. For example, we see 'a plastic teapot' (which is clearly an orange plastic watering can), which Tiny Clanger then attempts to play as if it were a saxophone; 'a pretty hat' (which appears to be a red plastic cup); and then another hat, but this time 'a hat for Major Clanger' (which appears to be a white plastic thimble). After this initial flurry of fabrication, the Soup Dragon retrieves a key that appears to belong with the machine. After using the key, the machine begins to operate at high speed, producing dozens of plastic cookie cutters (coloured red, yellow and blue), plastic flowerpots, plastic boxes, plastic buckets, plastic toy cars, a plastic toy dog, a plastic spade and what looks like a plastic net from the 1960s board game Mousetrap. These objects emerge from the machine so rapidly that the Clangers' cave is quickly filled with plastic detritus.

Ultimately, the Froglets come to the Clangers' aid, by providing a magic top hat that can make the objects vanish when dropped into it. With the cave clear, the Clangers and Froglets go to bed, leaving Oliver, through his narration, to have the last word: 'The place is going to look a bit empty without all those plastic things, but you know, I think the Clangers may be better off without them.'[7] By offering this closing statement, he provides clear confirmation of his overarching goal: to critique our obsession with and reliance upon mass-produced plastics. In this episode we can see how Oliver and Peter's layered storytelling is supported – and enhanced – by the exaggeratedly colourful nature of the episode, with the strong primary colours of the plastic objects contrasting garishly with the softer tones of the Clangers' cave, thereby reinforcing the destabilising impact of plastic mass production to the natural order. In this moment, we can see how colour television technology played a profound role in shaping both the production and reception of *Clangers*.

Chris Pallant

[1] Oliver Postgate, *Seeing Things: An Autobiography*, Sidgwick & Jackson, London, 2000, p. 271.

[2] Iain Baird, 'The Story of Colour Television in Britain', Science + Media Museum [blog], 15 May 2011. Available at https://blog.scienceandmediamuseum.org.uk/colour-television-britain (accessed 10 June 2021).

[3] Ibid.

[4] Chris Pallant, *Beyond Bagpuss: A History of Smallfilms Animation Studio*, BFI, London, 2022, pp. 246–47.

[5] 'Clangers promotional mailer', *c.* 1966, File WW3/23/1, 'Clangers (The) – Owners Rights – Oliver Postgate & Peter Firmin', BBC Written Archives Centre (WAC), Reading, UK.

[6] Author's transcription from *Clangers* episode 13, 'Goods', viewed on DVD (Dragons' Friendly Society).

[7] Ibid.

Genesis of the Clangers

London 1936: it's George Lansbury's seventy-seventh birthday and the Lansbury clan are gathered en masse to celebrate. An occasion somewhat shaded by recent events – George has been mauled by Ernest Bevin at the Labour Party Conference. War is looming and apparently this is not a time for the fancies of pacifism. George, a man of peace, had little choice but to step down as the leader of the party he was so instrumental in forming.

A young boy named Oliver Postgate bustles through the chattering crowd clutching his box of tricks, recently bought from Hamleys, with the intention, before bedtime, of cheering up his old granddad. After the trick is assembled, George is relieved of his gold pocket-watch and it is placed in an ornate goblet. With some deft movements and stirring incantations, the contents of the goblet are transformed into hot, foaming liquid! The magician has heightened the effect by adding a piece of soap into the mix to get the froth really going. The room falls silent. The soap turns in the foam, its yellow hue easily mistaken for the gold of the watch itself. George's eyes grow wide: he has weathered many challenges to his stoicism over a long and esteemed career in public life but this is something entirely new. Protestations erupt: the watch was a gift from the people of Poplar and his most cherished possession.

After a dramatic pause, the watch re-materialises unscathed and Oliver is bustled away by his grim-faced mother. But for a moment the otherwise unremarkable little chap had caught the attention of his elders and betters… with MAGIC.

Fast-forward some thirty years or so and Oliver's box of tricks is now a triad of outbuildings on what was once a farm but is now the home of the burgeoning Firmin family. While living in London, Peter Firmin had worked with Oliver on a variety of quirky TV programmes. Now he has relocated to the peace of the Kent countryside to pursue a career in the fine arts. However, Oliver has come after him with other ideas...

Little does Peter realise that soon he and Oliver will be waltzing in the yard, trying to work out the physicality of a new puppet show: how Mr and Mrs Pingwing would dance together. The television company Smallfilms is formed and Peter is Oliver's glamorous assistant for the next twenty-five years, creating all that is seen in their tender and wistful films.

Oliver and his own large family ensconce themselves in an erstwhile public house, a short walk from the farm through woodland, but a day's journey for a Pogle. Oliver dreams up his stories in what was once the pub's snug, perching at his father's roll-top desk, next to a very large hatbox – always overflowing with scrunched-up paper: his discarded ideas. He writes in the morning, pecking away at his typewriter; then, after lunch, he clambers into his Citroën 2CV (or as he says, puts it on) and heads up to the Firmins' farm. As a very young boy, I have the idea that he writes a story in the morning and films it in the afternoon. Although not quite that simple, it isn't too far from the truth. My earliest memories of my dad are of someone always busy, always in a hurry. His gait is one of barrelling forward only to break his fall at the last moment with the next outstretched leg.

Scenes from the book Noggin and the Moon Mouse*, published in 1967.*

Woe betide anyone unfortunate enough to escort him on a mission to the shops or even a dog walk, especially if only three-foot high. He lives as he strides – launching into unknown territories with a sort of anxious recklessness. Frankly, it sometimes seems he has the very Devil at his back. I once ask him what he wants for Christmas. He looks me up and down with tired eyes and asks for an extra week.

To be honest, to begin with, I don't have a clue what he's up to. On my occasional visits to the farm I am bewitched and bewildered. The big barn, with its ancient oak beams far above and darkness beyond, is rich with the spectre of musty magic. The pig shed is even darker, and windowless; converted in height to accommodate Oliver, who is, by his own admission, a tall pig. It has an old battered car seat as the only spare chair, and it's so supremely comfortable I wonder why we don't have them as furniture at home. Perhaps I find it so luxurious because I'm in the very centre of my dad's snug kingdom – on his throne. Curiously, there is also a woodland scene on legs: the stump of a tree with a pleasantly rustic door in it. If you flick the right switch the darkness is banished and the scene is bathed in bright light. I understand it is the woodland house of the Pogle family from a kind of fantasy which is a serious business for my dad. If I clamber up and gently push open the wooden door I don't see the Pogles' home inside; instead it's empty and perfunctory, with the odour of sawdust and wood glue. I'm very slightly disappointed, but also excited. I feel I've mischievously trespassed into the workings of an elaborate dream.

Oliver's Bolex camera, made stop-frame capable with Meccano.

Towards the end of the 1960s the call comes from on high. No more tales of woodland folk. The BBC are after something altogether new, colourful and snazzy to show on the colour TVs people are getting now. What to do? Luckily, about this time my brother Simon tells Dad of something far-fetched but useful. A giant named Edward lives on the dark side of the Moon. He wears armour to protect himself from falling meteorites and keeps himself warm by sucking soup up a straw pushed through to the Moon's soupy interior. Then there is the story of the creature who crashes its spacecraft into a medieval horse trough, which finds its way into Oliver and Peter's book *Noggin and the Moon Mouse*. All such information is gathered together and built upon.

Eventually, what is rustled up is certainly new and adventurous, and yet also comfortably similar to what has come before. It has a sort of superposition, simultaneously comforting and strange. The viewer can never fully settle on what it really is and, as such, will remain constantly curious. This alchemy is the hallmark of the Smallfilms' worlds and one of the things that guarantees their longevity. But no one knows that yet.

Smallfilms studio: the pig shed.

Stanley Kubrik has made his science fiction epic *2001: A Space Odyssey*, David Bowie is finally finding his voice with *Space Oddity* and the US have the Moon in their sights. Space is very much in the air, and Oliver and Peter join in, with their heady neighbourhood of oddball characters centred on a species of mouse-like aliens. 'Clangers' are named after the *CLANG* noise made by their dustbin lids. They are literally a close-knit family – with some uncles and aunts to make up the numbers – who live in the warm interior of a blue planet lost in the yawning void of space. Any inch of such a place would kill a human in a minute, but for the Clangers it's home.

Oliver intends the Clangers to speak in whistles – the most approximate sound the human ear can understand of the nuclear-magnetic resonance they apparently use in the airless environment of deep space. However, their moods and intentions need to be communicated in a coherent fashion so scripts are prepared in the Queen's English to be freely interpreted by Oliver and his old college friend Stephen Sylvester, who previously collaborated on *Pogles' Wood*, voicing Tog and the Plant and writing stories. They use a variety of swannee whistles, the smallest of which is made from the shaft of a Bic biro. The exchanges are kept short and crisp; no need for anyone to ramble on. The initial idea is that the viewers will understand what the heck is going on by the whistles and action alone, but the BBC reasonably decide that this isn't such a good idea. They suspect the children's attention could drift. So a voice-over is introduced with an unseen observer remarking on what transpires throughout the episode.

Once the BBC give the whole crazy idea the go-ahead, the Smallfilms machine fires into action. The kettle is boiled and tea is made. Joan Firmin, Peter's wife, knits Clanger skins while Peter builds the planet's surface and the realms below. He dresses the caverns, nooks and crannies with other-worldly flora: copper trees, cotton-ball trees, drinking-straw plants and bright yellow tulips that can stroll around. Visually, the Firmins capture the bright boiled-sweet aesthetic of the swinging Sixties with aplomb. Meanwhile, Oliver scribbles instructions by way of wiggly lines and blocks next to his typed script for the composer, Vernon Elliott, to get a general idea of what's needed for incidental music. The whistles and narration are recorded first for Oliver to animate to, marking out the segments of animation time in seconds. Oliver mutters the numbers – like a distracted bingo caller – for a captured child, armed with pen and clipboard, to jot down. With two large families, there are many children to choose from, and their labour is cheap, if not free. The opening narration and the trip across space, with its earnest tone and invitation to 'listen', bear an uncanny similarity to the beginning of *A Matter of Life and Death* by Powell and Pressburger, another duo who produced films that resonate with a kind of romantic, wistful Britishness. Alas, this association only occurs to me later down the line, when Oliver's no longer around to be asked about it. Vernon Elliott's compositions come in, music of sublime strings and staccato glockenspiel. Warm and sweet then suddenly fresh and discordant. Its modern classical style couldn't be more appropriate.

Oliver and Peter discuss Clanger designs while the Pogles look on.

A chicken of Meccano lays a metal egg, inside are music notes. If you plant them, they grow into trees – music trees with more notes which you can pick and use for flight. In your new flying machine you go 'fishing' – you catch a top hat, inside are Froglets… and so on. We've all been there.

The ecosystem of the planet is made sturdy and believable. There will be no winks to the camera to suggest this is all make-believe. Peter and Oliver are sticklers for ensuring their worlds have, as one critic observed, 'conceptual integrity'. One can imagine the lives of the puppets continuing as usual even after the cameras have stopped rolling and the camera crew have returned to Earth. The nature of this integrity, at least in the case of the Clangers, is another matter. It seems to come from that no man's land of indeterminate length that happens before sleep, when we loosen our grasp on the real and let the fancies of our dreams creep inside. Or, to put it another way, it has a keen-eyed logic wrapped in the imaginings of a child.

Clangers is a serial, each episode building on the one before, introducing new characters to the unfolding events, and they all fit together to play their parts in the story matrix. A reader of the *Daily Mail* once took the trouble to remark that the Clangers 'are not Christian', and although, strictly speaking, that's true – for one thing Clangers certainly don't feature

Oliver at his editing suite.

in the Bible – they do have the qualities of kindness that any faith would be proud of. Whoever comes out from the vast darkness to visit their small blue planet can expect a warm welcome. And although, as you'd expect with such larger-than-life characters living in such close proximity, there is a certain amount of agitation from time to time – the Soup Dragon can be volatile, the Iron Chicken brittle – generally everyone gets on surprisingly well.

Oliver films the action slightly from above, partly to give the whole thing a wildlife documentary feel, and partly to save his back from all the bending over to look in the camera eyepiece. Oliver animates fast, especially by today's standards, moving his puppets directly from one gesture to the next. Only the 'flying' scenes can slow things down somewhat. The music boat, which appears to float in space, is attached to a makeshift crane device by painted catgut, and must be left to swing to a standstill between each shot. Otherwise, apart from the planet's surface being set on fire when a spaceman leaves in his rocket (fortunately a bucket of water is at hand), the filming goes well.

The farm has an ecosystem of its own, and every now and then hot sustenance is brought out to the studios. Not soup from a dragon, but tea and biscuits from one of Peter's many daughters. Later on, people ask me if Oliver and Peter used mind-altering substances to help them think up this 'far-out' creation – it was the Sixties after all. But the mundane truth is they got by on tea and biscuits.

The world of the Clangers is set in the big dark barn, sharing the space with swallows who – with no respect for children's television – poo onto the planet's surface, and mice who, by night, scurry amongst motionless puppets, bringing with their presence a

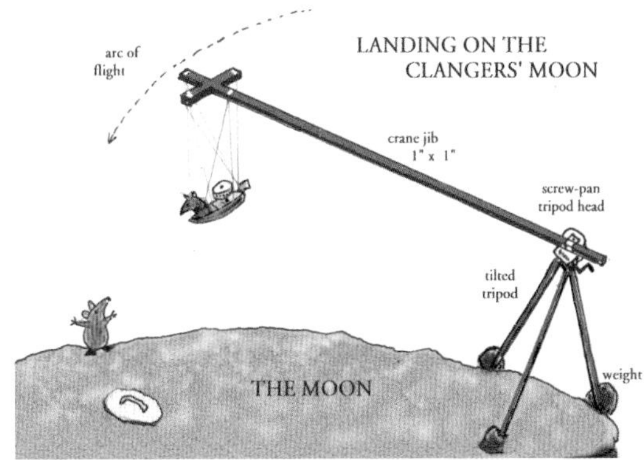

Oliver's sketch of his special-effects crane used for flying scenes.

whole new level of surrealism. On my visits I peer into the barn with trepidation. I'm terrified of the Pogle Witch who, quite rightly, was banned by the BBC from appearing in further Pogle films for being far too frightening. Now she perches high up on an ancient beam and glowers at me with her beady eyes, daring me to enter. But when the filming is finished and the Clangers are no longer needed, Peter lets me take them and scamper off into the safety of the yard, to set up my own tableaus, snap them with my Instamatic and make up my own story of the Clangers' visit to an old farmyard in Kent. I'm even allowed to take a Sky-Moo home and I play with it until it falls apart.

Ultimately, the planet and its underworld are broken up and tossed onto the bonfire behind the barn. Room must be made for the next world: a shopfront for a certain plump, sleepy cat. But the planet and its inhabitants endure, both in the hearts and minds of children – now grown up to be responsible members of society – and, for a few years after, as pale blue chunks of space debris unearthed by Peter's daughter Emily while turning over the soil on the Firmins' vegetable patch.

Daniel Postgate

The Bible

the CLANGERS

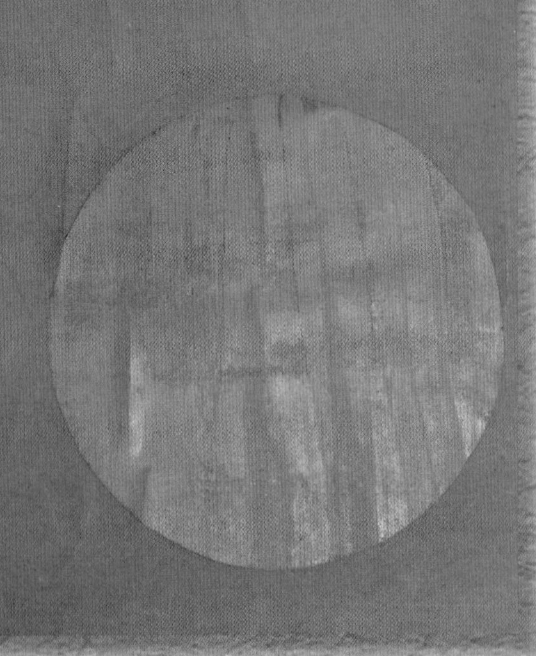

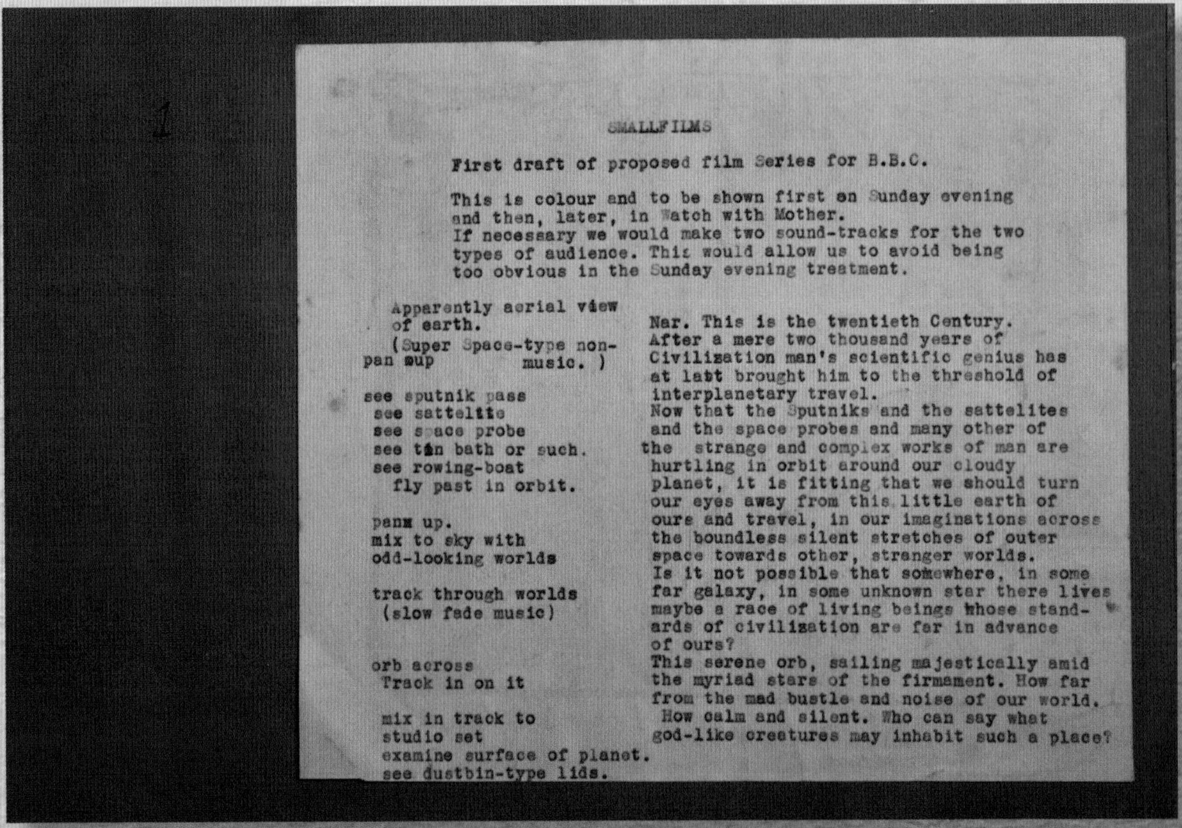

1

SMALLFILMS

First draft of proposed film Series for B.B.C.

This is colour and to be shown first on Sunday evening and then, later, in Watch with Mother.
If necessary we would make two sound-tracks for the two types of audience. This would allow us to avoid being too obvious in the Sunday evening treatment.

Apparently aerial view of earth.
(Super Space-type non-pan up music.)

see sputnik pass
see sattelite
see space probe
see tin bath or such.
see rowing-boat
fly past in orbit.

pan up.
mix to sky with odd-looking worlds

track through worlds
(slow fade music)

orb across
Track in on it

mix in track to studio set
examine surface of planet.
see dustbin-type lids.

Nar. This is the twentieth Century. After a mere two thousand years of Civilization man's scientific genius has at last brought him to the threshold of interplanetary travel.
Now that the Sputniks and the sattelites and the space probes and many other of the strange and complex works of man are hurtling in orbit around our cloudy planet, it is fitting that we should turn our eyes away from this little earth of ours and travel, in our imaginations across the boundless silent stretches of outer space towards other, stranger worlds.
Is it not possible that somewhere, in some far galaxy, in some unknown star there lives maybe a race of living beings whose standards of civilization are far in advance of ours?
This serene orb, sailing majestically amid the myriad stars of the firmament. How far from the mad bustle and noise of our world. How calm and silent. Who can say what god-like creatures may inhabit such a place?

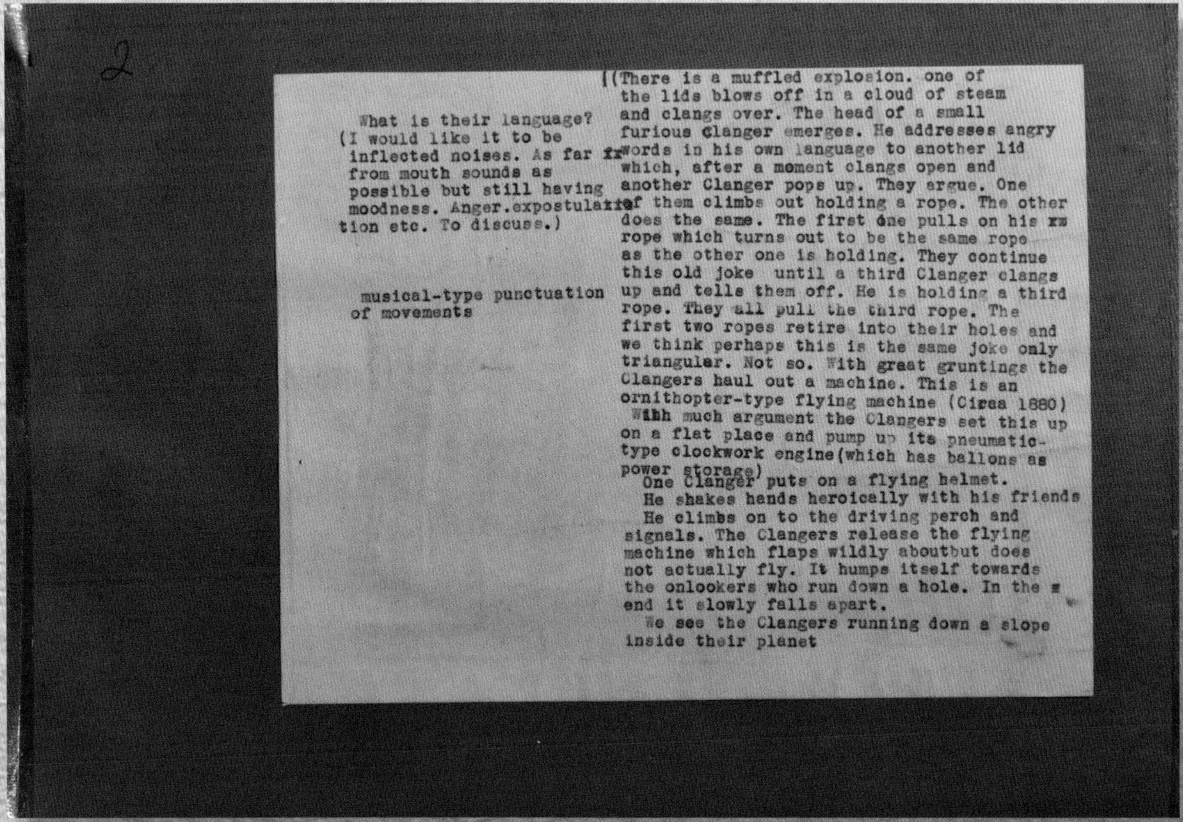

2

What is their language? (I would like it to be inflected noises. As far fr from mouth sounds as possible but still having moodness. Anger.expostulaxxa tion etc. To discuss.)

musical-type punctuation of movements

((There is a muffled explosion. one of the lids blows off in a cloud of steam and clangs over. The head of a small furious Clanger emerges. He addresses angry words in his own language to another lid which, after a moment clangs open and another Clanger pops up. They argue. One of them climbs out holding a rope. The other does the same. The first one pulls on his xx rope which turns out to be the same rope as the other one is holding. They continue this old joke until a third Clanger clangs up and tells them off. He is holding a third rope. They all pull the third rope. The first two ropes retire into their holes and we think perhaps this is the same joke only triangular. Not so. With great gruntings the Clangers haul out a machine. This is an ornithopter-type flying machine (Circa 1880) With much argument the Clangers set this up on a flat place and pump up its pneumatic-type clockwork engine(which has ballons as power storage)

One Clanger puts on a flying helmet.

He shakes hands heroically with his friends

He climbs on to the driving perch and signals. The Clangers release the flying machine which flaps wildly aboutbut does not actually fly. It humps itself towards the onlookers who run down a hole. In the x end it slowly falls apart.

We see the Clangers running down a slope inside their planet

3

(We have our first sight of the inside of the planet which is where the Clangers live. It may be a labyrinth of translucent caves with houses carved in the expanded polystyrene rock. There may be forests of copper trees with copper ~~in~~ leaves. The Clangers are metal-workers and most of their equipment is made from copper sheet and rock. They have a scource of power which we do not have which is that the berries of ~~the~~ some of the trees have the faculty of generating steam-like pressure when enclosed. This means that they have some rather basic cars and power-tools.)

We follow the people down the corridor to where some other Clangers are waiting. They stop and,pointing back, tell what has happened.

The aeronaut Clanger comes disconsolately down the slope, dangling his helmet.

(He is, incidentally our father-figure. The story now becomes less general.)

He sits in his chair and looks sad. Mrs. Clanger dabs his brow and murmurs words of comfort. She suggests that he might like a bowl of soup. He nods. Small Clanger(our hero) is despatched to fetch a bowl of soup. He takes the copper can and gets on his bike thing Tiny Clanger(our baby heroine) is distraught at his departure and demands to go as well. She jumps on the back of the bike and they ride ~~x~~ away to the forest where the soup-wells are.

The soup-wells are little pointed hills or stalagmites. Small Clanger and Tiny Clanger ~~sh~~ sniff about like Bisto Kids until they smell the flavour soup they are after. Small Clanger unscrews one of the hills and looks in. There is a shout of rage from inside and he replaces it hastily. He unscrews another hill and speaks civilly to the soup-keeper inside. He passes in the jug to be filled. Tiny Clanger leans too far over and falls in. There is a great noising inside the well and she is pitched out again rather soupy. The soup-keeper hands out the can of soup. Tiny Clanger is told to pick a flower from the copper tree. She does this and tosses it into the well. The soup-keeper is heard to ~~x~~ receive it with delighted sounds and he chews it up with relish. ~~small Clanger runs back the hilltop small~~ The Clangers turn to go. The Soupkeeper calls to them(to shut the door)

Small Clanger runs back and screws on the hill-top. They ride home. Deliver the soup to Mum.

Pop drinks the soup. Scratches himself. He settles down for a nap,puts a circular newspaper over his face and snores.

4

Small Clanger puts on the flying helmet and pretends to fly. Tiny Clanger is on the slope. She whistles to him and they run up to the hatch-way and out into the open. They examine the failed flying machine. They play with it. Tiny Clanger punches one of the balloons for fun. It detaches and shoots up into the air on its own blast. They do this to another balloon. Tiny Clanger is delighted but Small Clanger is moved to thought. He sits and thinks. Then he has an idea and picking up one of the balloons in one hand and Tiny Clanger in the other he runs into the planet. He jumps on to his bike and they ride to the soup-wells. They pick many flowers from the trees.

Theyunscrew thetop of the soup-well and are greeted uncivilly by the soup-keeper. They throw in flowers and he is mollified and is persuaded to blow up the balloon for them.
The Clangers tie off the balloon with string.
Tiny Clangersits on Small Clanger's head,back or shoulders (depending on the anatomy) and they leap home in long bounds hanging from the balloon.
They arrive home and other Clangers,small and large are amused. They dance around the bouncing pair.
Suddenly the string around Small Clanger's middle comes undone and Tiny Clanger is on the balloon all on her own. She slowly rises.
Pandemonium.

Tiny Clanger rises to the roof of the cave and bounces against it among the copper leaves.
The Clangers are alarmed. They wake up Mr.Clanger and point out what has happened.
He climbs a tree. It bends.
They try to form a pyramid .It colapses.
They fetch a ladder but there is nothing to lean it on and it topples.
Tiny Clanger whimpers.
Mrs. Clanger brings out a blanket. She tells them what to do.
The Clangers bounce Small Clanger trampolinicallly in the blanket until he bounces high enough to catch hold of the string of the balloon. Theydescend. Tiny Clanger is handed to Mum. Small Clanger is very pleased with himself. He dances on the table recounting his exploits...Until he catches sight of Mum and Dad's stern faces. His story slows down and stops.
He takes off the flying helmet and ingratiatingly gives it back.
Their faces are stern.
He slinks away droopy and hides under the table.
Mr. and Mrs.'s faces are stern but they look at eachother and cannot keep them straight. They start to giggle. They laugh
Small Clanger looks out. Mr. and Mrs. lift him up. All the Clangers laugh and sing and dance.

SEASON 1

Episode 1

Flying

For the very first time we drift across the twinkling infinity of space, or in this case Christmas baubles hung in front of black cloth. And while a disembodied voice earnestly invites us to untether our imaginations, our eyes finally settle upon the 'serene orb' of a small blue planet. As we ease towards the planet's cratered surface, the voice poses a question: what sort of 'people' may live on a star like this? It is time to eavesdrop. The prospect of life on such an arid place seems unlikely. But we are in luck! Not only is there emergent life, but we find it at a moment of great importance.

It is Sunday, 16 November 1969. Two days earlier David Bowie released his eponymous album featuring the track 'Space Oddity', and humanity launched its second audacious mission to the Moon. As the Apollo 12 Lunar Module is still in transit, we find Major Clanger just about to launch his own ambitious flying machine. A quick handshake with his daughter and he's good to go. The balloons are tight and plump and the copper blades readily flap to life.

Meanwhile, back on Planet Earth, Oliver Postgate looks on with nervous concern as Major's attempted launch goes haywire. The machine cavorts about the planet and tumbles to an undignified halt.

Such are the best-laid plans of mice and men.

Postgate's worry is real, extending beyond the fate of his whimsical creation. Will our own adventure, still in progress, end in calamity, too? And, of lesser importance of course, will the first episode of *Clangers* be remembered, as Postgate described it, 'as a sick joke'? Only time will tell.

With the luxury of hindsight we know the human trip ended well. But what of Major? His eccentric machine was supposed to whisk him up into the darkness of space, but instead, in failure, it merely drew him into his own internal darkness. However, a simple mug of hot soup, freshly fetched from the soup wells, is enough to make him cheerful again… because, on the whole, the Clangers' planet is a cheerful place.

The Clangers Cl/1

Episode 1. Flying

Commentary track		Music and Effects track
Narrator This is the planet Earth. It is a small planet, wrapped in clouds but, for us, it is a very important place, it is home. But supposing we look away from the earth and travel, in our imaginations, across the vast starry stretches of outer space. Then we can imagine other stars, stranger stars by far than ever shone in our night sky...and planets too. This calm serene orb, sailing majestically among the myriad stars of the firmament. Perhaps this star too is home for somebody. Can we imagine the sort of people who might live on a star like this? Let us go very close. Let us look and listen very carefully and perhaps we shall see.....and hear....		Introductory music
		(clang as dustbin-lid comes off)
	Cl.	Hi. Where's Charlie?
That is a Clanger		
		(clang. Another dustbin-lid)
	C2.	I'm over here. I've got the rope.
And that is another Clanger		
	Cl.	I've got the rope.
	C2.	No this is it, look!
They seem to have a piece of rope.		(he pulls his rope)
	Cl.	Hi, look out. (he pulls his rope) (C2. is pulled in)
	C2.	What do you think you're doing. (C2. pulls)
And now they seem to be having an argument about their rope		
	Cl.	All right then! (Cl. pulls)
	Cl. + C2. ad- lib	(You rotten rodent! (This is the rope (No it's mine, this is the one! (I'll drag you down! (Let go you horrible thing!
	C3.	Stop! Stop! Oh you bad Clangers
Hmm! Quite right too. That's no way for Clangers to behave.		You are bad! bad! Come over here at once and help us work (They walk out)
	Cl.2. +3.	Pull! pull! pull! etc. (They haul out machine) (pumping sound)
Ah, now, that is Major Clanger with his flying machine. All set, ready to fly up into the sky.		
	Mj.C.	Ah. yes, there it is...good, all ready. Well, good luck. (shakes hands) (Mj.C. climbs up)

C3. Contact
Mj.C. Right, let her go!
Cl. Up, up and away
(The flying machine leaps about. The flying machine falls apart)

Oh dear!

(All Clangers run indoors shouting)
All Eek, Eek
It fell to pieces
It fell to pieces and ran away
You should see the mess!
(Sad music as Mj. Clanger enters very dejected and sits down)

Oh, poor Major Clanger, he has had a very hard day.

Mrs.C. Oh you poor old Clanger, you have had a bad day...soup?

What he needs is a mug of hot soup.

(she dabs his forehead)
Mrs.C. Hi, Small Clanger. Take this and fetch soup.

Small Clanger will fetch it.

S.C. All right
T.C. Me! Me! Me! I want to come

Tiny Clanger wants to come too.

S.C. All right, come then.
(Music as T.C. jumps on to the trolley and they pole away to the soup-wells)

So Small Clanger and Tiny Clanger are going to the soup-wells to find the soup-dragon and ask her for some soup.

S.C. Here we are..now which is the one

Well, here are the soup-wells, but where is the soup-dragon.

sniff, sniff, sniff
T.C. How about this one?
(S.C. pushes off lid of 2nd well)
S.C. Hallo, anybody at home? (echo)
D. Hallo, what do you want?
S.C. Soup, please

There she is

D. All right, pass in the can
(bubbling)
here you are
S.C. Thank you
T.C. And here's a flower for you
D. Ooh, Oh thankyou very much
(munch, munch)
(she eats the flower)
S.C. Bye bye
(they walk away)

off

D. Door! Door! Door!
T.C. Oh sorry!
(she pushes back the lid and walks out)
(They carry the soup home)
S.C. Here you are then, soup.
Mrs.C. Here's your soup dear
Mj.C. Soup, Ah yes, soup.

Ah, soup, delicious soup

(Mj. C. drinks soup, swallows)
Ooh yes, ooh, ooh.

and Small Clanger and Tiny Clanger could go outside and play while he has a rest

(he settles for sleep)
(S.C. looks at flying helmet. He tries it on.)
T.C. Wheep?
S.C. All right then
(They run outside)

T.C. Oh what's all this stuff?
S.C. Bits of flying machine.
T.C. Oh aren't they funny?
(she looks at them)

Theres an interesting thing. The remains of the flying machine

T.C. Hmm...yes...what's this?
(she pushes a balloon, it flies up)
ooh! yes! that's good
Look, Small Clanger, it went
Up, weeep! up and away
S.C. Yes
T.C. But that was good, wasn't it... wasn't it?
S.C. Shut up, I'm thinking.

Small Clanger is busy thinking. I expect he is inventing a flying machine

T.C. Oh all right
(S.C. thinks)
S.C. That's it, come on.
(They pick up the balloon and run in)
(They run to the soup-wells)
D. Now, for goodness' sake, what do you want?
S.C. Please, please, will you blow up our balloon for us?
D. All right
(puff, puff, puff)
D. There you are.
(S.C. ties a string to it)
S.C. Come here, Tiny Clanger.
(S.C. ties the string to Tiny Clanger's armour, and then to his armour. She climbs on his back.)
S.C. Up, up and away!
(musical sequence)
(They dance home)

Yes, well it is a flying machine, ...of a sort!

T.C. Eek, eek, eek, eek.

Oh, poor Tiny Clanger, bouncing on the ceiling.

Mj.C. What's going on?
C1,C2, C3. ad-lib Look up there! Tiny Clanger in the sky. Can't you see, she's come adrift!
T.C. Me! Me! Me!

They must get her down

(Mj. C. climbs a tree, it bends)
T.C. Me! Me! Me! Me!
(Clangers make a pyramid, it collapses)
T.C. Me! me! me! me!
Mrs.C. Here, get hold of this
Jump on Small Clanger
(Clangers toss Small Clanger in a blanket high enough to reach T.C., grab her, pull her down)
Mrs.C. Oh you poor Tiny Clanger

Poor Tiny Clanger! Safe at last but very frightened.

T.C. (muffled) meep, meep, meep!

Small Clanger seems very pleased with himself. He made a flying machine and it really worked.

S.C. I'm the clever one
I went and fetched the balloon
I let it go up there and then
I bumped and bumped and
er...
I...

But his parents are angry. They think it was a dangerous game. Well, it was dangerous wasn't it

This is your flying helmet isn't it?
I just borrowed it
and..
oh dear..
...I'm sorry

Mj.C. (giggles)

But in the end they have to laugh, and once they start laughing they laugh and laugh and then they can't be angry any more.

Mrs.C. (giggles)

All Clangers (giggle)

(all Clangers dance out)

(End music and Captions)

Episode 2

The Visitor

As the Clangers' planet borders, at a full 360 degrees, the vast unknown, the possibility of the arrival of something unexpected is always on the cards. And, for us, what could confound expectation more than the immediate and familiar? In this case, the very thing we are gazing at: within our television, another television!

The episode finds the narrator in a candid and sober mood. A small orange TV, an object so well known to us but so exotic to the Clangers, inexplicably turns up from 'surely the most troublesome' of worlds. The issue is twofold. Firstly, we have the object itself: junk – 'expensive rubbish' – cast off into a pristine Universe. And secondly, where it is from, or rather who it is from: Humanity – you and me – the very reason that this distant, tainted world whence this object came is so troubled in the first place.

The second point is hammered home by what's actually on the box. A loud and proud despot (Oliver Postgate himself) puffed up with self-importance delivers a bombastic speech. However, surprisingly, despite their natural humility, or perhaps because of it, the Clangers find him somewhat impressive. If the box were to stay, would they be seduced by such a tyrant? It's a thought too terrible to contemplate. Luckily, the TV's content suddenly changes to something at the other end of the spectrum: raucous, reactionary rock and roll (enthusiastically performed by Oliver's stepson Krispian Myers)! This taste of the swinging Sixties doesn't go down so well. The Soup Dragon is appalled by the racket and promptly shuts down her soup kitchen in protest. In order to placate the alarmed dragon, and so save their delicate ecosystem, the Clangers have no choice but to jettison the TV back into the infinity of space.

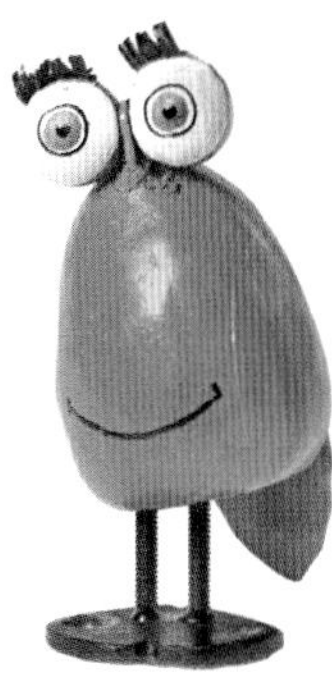

The Clangers C2/1

Episode 2. The Visitor

Commentary track		Music and Effects track
Narrator		
Of all the stars and moons and planets that shine in the sky, by far the most troublesome of all is surely this one. This small cloud-covered planet is our earth, the home of the human race. From a distance it looks harmless enough, just a coat of mist and clouds hiding the land and the sea. The trouble is, that the people there, mankind, us, are not content to stay in one place but are constantly hurling objects into space. Some of these objects come back to earth, but others, sattelites, spent rockets, and other unwanted articles litter the orbits of the earth beyond. Who can say where some of this expensive rubbish may ultimately arrive as it hurtles aimlessly through the universe?		Introductory music
		Introductory music ends
	S.C.	What's that?
That is Small Clanger		
		yes there's something there
and he has heard something		
		ooh I wonder what Here it comes again
Here it comes again		
		yes, there it goes I must fetch the others (he opens lid. Major Clanger looks out)
	Mj.C.	Ooh look
	S.C.	There it is, come on. (The Clangers run out, pan down and see them run past upside-down. Pan up again) (They run into shot on top and stop)
	Mj.C.	What do we do.
	S.C.	Let's get somebody to bring the see-saws.
	Mj.C.	Oh all right then
	S.C.	Hi there below
Well of course that's right, the only thing to do is set up the equipment and try to catch it.		
		Come up with the see-saws!
	T.C.	All right, they're here catch hold of this
	S.C.	Right, ooh I've got it (He hauls out a see-saw)
	T.C.	And this one
	Mj.C.	Right, I've got it (He hauls out a see-saw and carries it away. C2 jumps out, followed by T.C. who is carrying a butterfly net)
	S.C.	Come on dear, stand in your place (T.C. stands on see-saw 2)

(S.C. stands on see-saw 1)

S.C. Right!

T.C. Go!

(Music as they leap)

T.C. Got it.

S.C. What is it?

(T.C. tips out a television set)

All Oooh! ooh!

(They approach it warily. T.C. touches it.

TV Set Hooray, Hooray, Hooray

(The Clangers run and hide)

(T.C. walks up to the set again)

T.C. It seems all right again

(The others approach, one of them touches it)

TV Set Roar, Rum, Rum, Roar!

(They run and hide)

(The Clangers look at the set)

T.C. walks bravely up to it.

T.C. Now you're a nice little noise-box.
Now we all love you
Oh you are a good good box, good box!

(She pats the TV Set. It plays gentle music)

T.C. See, all it wanted was a kind word

(The others approach)

S.C. Nice tune. Shall we dance?

T.C. Yes

(They dance)

(They pick up the box and dance indoors with it.)

(They meet Mrs. Clanger with the trolley. They put the set down on the trolley. It is silent again.)

Mrs.C. Oh, it has stopped

Oh, it has stopped

T.C. Come on, sing some more pretty music.

S.C. Perhaps it doesn't want to sing any more.

Perhaps it is tired, or hungry

Mrs.C. Soup, perhaps it wants soup.

T.C. All right, I'll go and fetch some soup.

So Tiny Clanger runs off to the soup-wells to find the soup-dragon and ask her for some soup for their visitor who is hungry.

(She takes small can and runs to soup-well.

T.C. Oh dragon, dragon, dragon!
There's a box of music arrived and it will sing to us if we give it soup.

D. Oooh really.

T.C. Yes, and please can we have lots of soup in this little can to feed it with because it is hungry.

D. Certainly
pouring
here you are

(away) T.C. Thank you oh thank you, see you later

D. What an extraordinary young person. Youth ah youth

mix to houses

(She descends)

T.C. Here you are, here is soup..

Yes, here is the soup, but their visitor doesn't seem to have a mouth. How do they give it soup?

Little singing box would you like some soup?
It doesn't seem to have a mouth.
What shall I do?

S.C. Pour it on top
(T.C. pours soup on it. It splutters and sparks and smokes. Suddenly it shines blue-ly on them).

Telly (Long ad-lib exhortation in incomprehensible french.)
(At the end the Clangers clap and T.C. thanks the box. She pats it).

Telly YAH, YAH, YAH
(All Clangers run, hide.)
(Mj. Clanger creeps up behind the set and dowses it with the big soup-jug, accidentally he pushes the trolley. It rolls away)
(The trolley, can and telly trip over a well and tip over. The telly starts to shout pop again.
The soup-dragon rises.
She decides she likes pop.
She emerges, waves her spoon and is really ecstatic.
The music becomes ecstatic and the soup-dragon grabs the TV Set to dance with it soupily.
It stops, splutters, sparks and shocks the soup-dragon).

D. Oh you horrible OW OW ooh!
Let go
(Bomp. Crunch.)
(She throws it away and goes down, slamming the lid.
The Clangers approach the lid.
They knock on it.)

muffled D. Go away. I'm not sending soup till you get rid of it.

S.C. Soup. May we have soup.

D. No, no soup. Get rid of it.

S.C. Ooh.

All Oooh, ooh.
(They turn to look at the silent TV Set, one of them holds up a net.)
(They creep up on it and net it)

S.C. That's it, come on, run!
(They run out with it)

Mj.C. Put it on here
(They put the set on the see-saw).

Mj.C. Right then! Ready, all set,Go!
(They bump the Telly back into space.)

All There it goes
Goodbye

Yes, it's nice to have visitors, but sometimes it's even nicer to see them go.

Captions

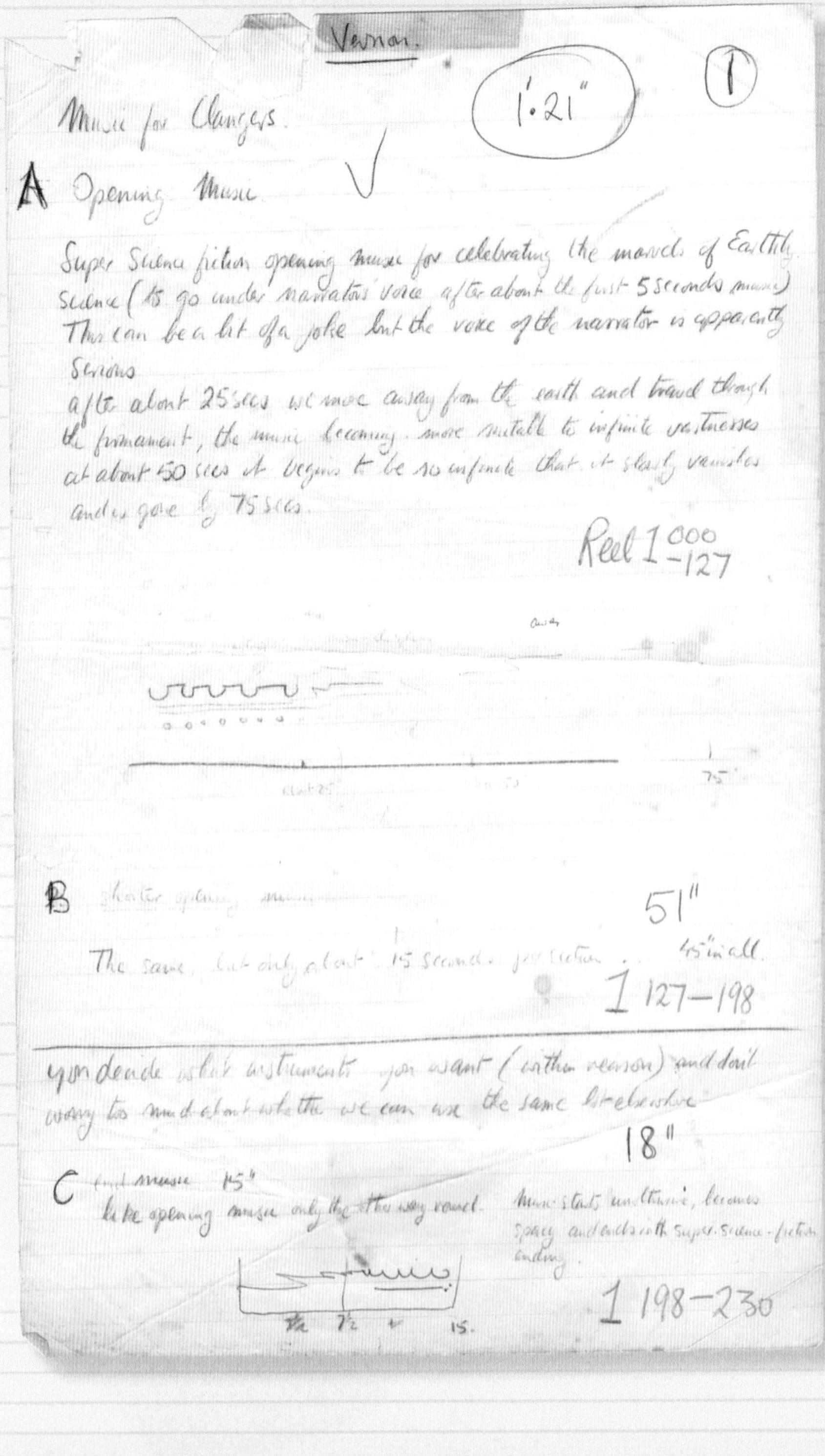

Vernon.

1'.21"

(1)

Music for Clangers.

A Opening Music ✓

Super Science fiction opening music for celebrating the marvels of Earthly science (to go under narrator's voice after about the first 5 seconds music) This can be a bit of a joke but the voice of the narrator is apparently serious

after about 25 secs we move away from the earth and travel through the firmament, the music becoming more suitable to infinite vastnesses at about 50 secs it begins to be so infinite that it slowly vanishes and is gone by 75 secs.

Reel 1 000 -127

B shorter opening music 51"

The same but only about 15 seconds for fiction. 45" in all.

1 127–198

you decide what instruments you want (within reason) and don't worry too much about whether we can use the same bit elsewhere

18"

C end music 15"
like opening music only the other way round. Music starts unearthly, becomes spacy and ends with super-science-fiction ending.

1 198–230

Page 3

Music for Clangers actions

H group. Accompaniment to the Clangers' punt trolley.

1^{600}_{637}

H1 medium speed poling along.

(33)

0 7" 21" 28"

H2. Same as H1 only faster. (shorter time OK) (27) 1^{637}_{657}

H3. Similar only very fast for 10 secs then accelerate wildly to crash at 20 secs.

1^{657}_{678}

0 10 20 (28")

I groups. Clangers build something that falls over

(11")

2^{045}_{077} + gliss 090 I1 build a pyramid, pause at top then gliss until falls.

(6-10)

2^{090}_{120} I2. Same as I1 but smaller (quicker and shorter time) (change tempo only?)

~~I3 … I1 but larger (i.e. slower and longer time) (change key + tempo?)~~

J group. See-saw or trampoline
1st clanger jumps on 1st see-saw, throws 2nd Clanger up who somersaults and lands on 2nd see-saw which throws 3rd Clanger up into the sky. Just glissandi really.

2^{120}_{150} J1

0 1 3 7

Loony. do again

J2. same but …

0 1 3 7 10

Episode 3

Chicken

We find Major Clanger with new contraptions to try out: two large copper rockets. The first one goes up a treat, brightening the sky with its frivolous fireworks. The second, however, hits something with a *CLANG*, and metallic pieces rain down onto the planet's surface. It is, or was, a *being* of some sort, now wrought asunder. It's an entrance much like that of the eponymous hero of Ted Hughes' children's book *The Iron Man*, written about the same time as *Clangers*. In this particular case, though, the being doesn't turn out to be a colossal metal humanoid full of primal desire, but a chicken – an *iron* chicken. This perhaps begs the question: which came first, the chicken or the Id?

The episode goes on to demonstrate how abruptly chaos can arrive, even in the most settled of places. The architecture of society is upheld by mutual storytelling. Tales from identities whose very existence relies on, and is maintained in, the self-same stories. It is a vital but fragile thing. The identity of the Meccano fowl is spectacularly undone in a moment, and when reassembled – as though with a taste of something from beyond the horizon – she seems to have 'lost the plot'. Switched off to that around her, she literally walks through any cave wall which may stand in her way, noshes on copper trees and, without seeking permission, guzzles on precious soup, totally unfazed by the frantic spoon-beating the horrified Soup Dragon dishes out.

Let's be in no doubt – this is anarchy; this is chaos.

Luckily, Tiny Clanger, wise beyond her years, steps into the breach with a gift: a nice necklace for the chicken. And, more importantly, an acknowledgement of the chicken's identity, which brings the wayward bird back into focus, and back into the circuitry of civilisation.

The episode ends at a tantalising point. Before going on her way, the chicken returns Tiny's gesture with a gift from herself – a curious metal egg, the contents of which will bring about a significant transformation in Clanger culture.

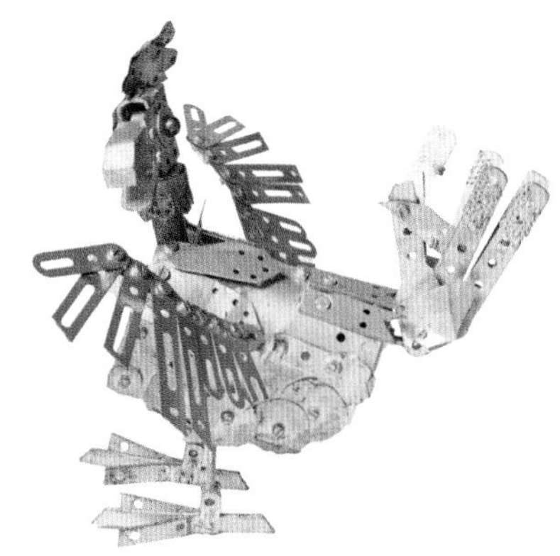

The Clangers

C3/1

Episode 3. Chicken

Commentary track		Music and Effects track
Narrator		
This planet, this cloudy planet, is the Earth. It is our home, the place where you and I live. But supposing we look away from the Earth and travel, in our imaginations across the vast endless stretches of outer space. There we can imagine other stars, stranger stars by far then ever shone in our night sky, and other stranger people too. People perhaps whose civilization, skill and efficiency may be far in advance of ours.		Introductory music
		Introductory music ends. (Doors slowly open. They jam) (The doors jerk) (A Clanger jumps out of a hole)
	Cl.	Oh dammit the B. Thing's stuck again. (He goes up to the door and kicks it) (The doors begin to move again)
	Cl.	All clear
	Cl.C2.	Pull, pull, pull. Pull, pull, pull.
	Mj.C.	There it is, set it up ...oh...over here
That must be a rocket		
		(Clangers set up their space rocket)
	Mj.C.	All right, everybody clear. Up there now!
And that is Major Clanger ready to start the count-down. I wonder what sort of rocket it is.	Mj.C.	8,7,6,5,4,3,2,1,zero. (presses plunger) (Clangers look up, see stars as sky rocket pops)
	All.	Ooh! ooh! Ah! Ah'.
That was the best sort of rocket, a sky-rocket, full of stars... and of course they want to let off another one.	S.C.	That was good, may we let off another?
	T.C.	Yes please, please.
	Mj.C.	All right, one more, just one!
	All	Pull! pull! pull! Pull! pull! pull!
	Cl.	All set
	Mj.C.	Right, stand clear everybody! ...5,4,3,2,1, zero (whoosh) (The rocket shoots up but it hits something metallic in space which squarks loudly.
That one hit something. Look out!	Mj.C.	Look out everybody. (The Clangers dive into holes and shut lids) (Bits of metal fall from the sky.) (The Clangers cower in the holes.) (Mj.C. looks out, looks up)
	Mj.C.	All clear now.

What an extraordinary lot of objects. Well the only thing to do is carry them below and try to fit them together again.

(The Clangers go out and look at the pieces)

Mj.C. Let's collect them all up together and take the pieces indoors.
(They carry in the pieces and put them down in the square)

Mj.C. Look, they fit together.
Come on, help fit it together.
(The Clangers re-assemble the pieces into a large iron chicken)

S.C. Look at that.

T.C. What on earth are they making?

S.C. I don't know what it can be.

Mrs.C. They are putting it together again.

T.C. Oooh

Mj.C. There,that is all done.

There, that is all done. I wonder what it is.

(The Clangers back off, revealing the chicken. The chicken slowly begins to move. It stretches clankily, creaks.)

It looks like a sort of chicken.

Ch. (yawns)
(yawns again)
(rattles its limbs one by one)

Ch. Oh, how d'ye do Mj. Clanger. You've done a very good job of re-assembly.

Mj.C. Oh not at all, not at all, sorry you have been inconvenienced.

Ch. Thankyou very much.

Ch. Thankyou very much.

Ch. Thankyou very much.
goodbye goodbye.

away

(The chicken turns and walks away)

And so it says goodbye and walks away and it's nearly time for Small Clanger and Tiny Clanger to fetch the soup for the Clangers' tea.

(The Clangers watch it go, then they turn to go about their business.)

Mrs.C. Teatime in five minutes small Clangers, please will you fetch me some soup.

S.C. All right, come on Tiny Clanger

T.C. All right.
(S.C. and T.C. pole away on trolley)

S.C. Hi, look

T.C. What

S.C. Over there.

What have they seen? Oh it mustn't do that! It is eating the copper trees. That is not allowed.

(Chicken is walking along the soup-dragon set, eating the flowers off the trees.)

S.C. Come on we must tell the dragon

They must tell the soup-dragon

(They roll to soup-well)

S.C. Hi, dragon, dragon!
The chicken is eating the flowers.

D. The what is what?

S.C. Look, here it comes.

(Chicken approaches, looks at them, opens lid of adjoining soup-well)

Ch. Good morning all

Oh look! It's drinking the soup straight out of the soup-well. It mustn't do that!

(chicken puts its head into well and sups soup noisily)

D. Here, you can't do that!
Come out! come out I say.
(She beats the chicken with her spoon)
Come out!
Come out!
Come out!
Come out!
(chicken raises its head)

Ch. Ah!
Delicious, capital soup, very nourishing.
...well, goodbye all
goodbye
goodbye

And it just walks away again. Whatever will it do next?...

(The chicken turns and walks straight through the wall)

It's walking through the wall! It walked straight through the wall

S.C. Cooo!

S.C. We must go home at once and tell the others.

D. Don't forget the soup

S.C. Oh yes, here you are!

Oh yes, don't forget the soup.

(dragon fills the jug)

D. Here you are

S.C. Right, come on Tiny Clanger
(They set off for home)

And home they go to tell Mother Clanger what they have seen. I wonder if she will believe them.

(Mrs.C. is setting the table)

Mrs.C. Ah, there you are. I wondered what had happened.

S.C. That chicken was eating the soup.

Mrs.C. Ooh was it?

T.C. Yes and it walked along and walked straight through the wall.

Mrs.C. Never, I don't believe you.

S.C. Look up there!
(They look up)

Mrs.C. Something coming through the roof.
Look out.
(The clangers hide)
(The chicken breaks through the ceiling, dropping clouds of debris and flaps down to the Clangers' table. It stands on the table and eats their food.

Ch. Hmm, bacon and fried bread
my favourite

Now its eating their tea, look, Major Clanger won't like that!

(munch munch munch)
hmm very delicious
(munch munch munch)

Mj.C. And just what the blazes do you think you're doing?
You blasted a hole in the roof up there! You littered the place with pieces everywhere!
Now you are eating our tea.

Ch. Your tea?

C3/4

Mj.C. Yes, our tea

Ch. Oh how sad
how sad
everybody is always cross with me.

Oh dear, now she's upset. She's going broody

Mj.C. Will you please go away!

Ch. Isn't it terrible to be unwanted.
(she settles down on the tea-table broodily)

Mj.C. Oh I don't know!
(he stumps away)

Well, she doesn't understand, somebody should be friendly and explain things to her.

(Tiny Clanger is making a necklace of golden leaves, she takes them to the chicken)

T.C. We love you little chicken

Yes, Tiny Clanger will do it and she has brought her a present.

It's just that you make rather a mess. Here, wear this, it's a present

Ch. Oooh

T.C. You see we live here

Ch. Oooh?

T.C. And we eat the food or would do if you weren't sitting on it.

Ch. Oooh do you?

T.C. Oh yes, yes we do. But we love you all the same.

Ch. Oooh so do I, how nice. Stand clear while I lay you an egg.
cluck

Now, whatever is she doing?

cluck
cluck cluck Cluck!

An egg!

"ping"
(She lays an iron egg)
There we are, that's for you.

And it's a present for Tiny Clanger.

T.C. For me? a real egg. Thankyou

Ch. Shall we go now?

T.C. Right-ho.
(T.C. and the chicken walk up the ramp to the great outside)

Ch. Bye bye then

T.C. Bye-bye chicken

All Bye-bye

And away she flies back to her spiky nest somewhere in the sky.

Captions

SMALLFILMS 10.11.69

The Clangers I MUSIC CUE SHEET Episodes 1 to 8

Episode 1. Flying

3'41" Instrumental Background The Clangers Suite
by V. Elliott.

Episode 2. The Visitor

2'42" Instrumental Background. The Clangers Suite
by V. Elliott.
0'42" "Visual" Instrumental. Vilia (waltz) by
Franz Lehar.
0'27" "Visual" Instrumental. No Smoke by Alan Young.

Episode 3. Chicken

1'46" Instrumental Background. The Clangers Suite
by V. Elliott.

Episode 4. Music

2'26" Instrumental Background. The Clangers Suite
by V. Elliott.
2'10" "Visual" Instrumental. The Music Trees by
Vernon Elliott.

Episode 5. The Intruder

2'10" Instrumental Background. The Clangers Suite
by V. Elliott.

Episode 6. Visiting Friends

2'05" Instrumental Background. The Clangers Suite
by V. Elliott.
0'52" "Visual" Instrumental. The Music Trees by
V. Elliott.

Episode 7. Fishing

1'54" Instrumental Background. The Clangers Suite
by V. Elliott.
2'13" "Visual" Instrumental. The Music Trees by
V. Elliott.

Episode 8. The Top Hat

2'05" Instrumental Background. The Clangers Suite
by V. Elliott.

n.b. The Clangers Suite and The Music Trees were specially composed by Vernon Elliott, arranged by Vernon Elliott and played by the Vernon Elliott Ensemble. They are not at present published.
Vilia by Franz Lehar was a recording provided by the B.B.C.
No Smoke by Alan Young is published by the Carter-Lewis Co. Ltd.

Music for
Music tree and music notes etc,
music-powered boats + hoops etc.

page 5

Glockenspiel bell-music, very clear and single-notey. essence of music.

N. faint music (boat theme) from inside the egg (Ep 4). 20 secs.
Nice music for ends etc. 2 150/184.

O. Bundle of odd notes fall on to the ground. (off the cuff) 4" 2 184/326
P. group. (choosing notes for a time)

4 notes P1. 4 separate notes as T/C picks them up and taps them | first time . . . . | 5

4" 4 notes P2. / Same 4 notes but in sequence, can detect a time / 4½" one tenth time from
10 4 notes. / Repeat with more sense of time / 3½ 9 all told
15.

4 notes P3. / play 4 more notes tentatively } 4
22 4 notes. / Repeat with time sense } 9
26 8 notes. play P2 and P3 together = time of 8 notes
34.

4 notes P4 play 4 more notes tentatively — or 4 Better. will not.
40 12 notes. play P2, P3 + P4 together carefully = time of 12 notes
— 50

P5 play time 3 times
12 notes. once. good ordinary
12 notes 59 second time - slowly. very schmalzy, rubato.
+.08 12 notes gaily third time fast. very gay. — last gay 5 2 notes. 11
1.16

P.6 2 sad deep notes left after the dragon has eaten the others.
(1·20) = 1·25"

P.7. Dragon has swallowed the notes — no timing, check this — opens its mouth and instead of noises it plays the notes but in a different time. Last is going it "sings" Goodbye! Goodbye! I sing you a last goodbye!" it goes, pauses, 3 secs, reappears and sings it again. "Goodbye, Goodbye, ..." then it goes again 3 secs, reappears and sings, "Goodbye, Goodbye" etc 2 184/326

| 3 | | 3 | | 3 |

Episode 4

Music

In this episode we learn more about the gift from the Iron Chicken – the metal egg. And as with all eggs, there's more to it than meets the eye.

Eggs are a favourite story device in the Smallfilms' worlds. Idris the dragon emerges from an egg kept red-hot in Ivor the Engine's fire-box; so deeply Welsh he instinctively knows the anthem 'Land of my Fathers'. *Pingwings* starts with young Penny Pingwing being sent off to fetch Mr Pingwing (hanging up to dry on the washing line) because Mother has just laid a brand-new Pingwing egg. Graculus the bird tells Noggin the Nog of a land he has never seen but somehow knows well, from the time when he was an egg. And Mr Pogle finds a snoring bean which grows into a magic, bilberry-wine-swilling, story-telling plant. Well, the last one isn't an egg but you get the idea.

The Iron Chicken's metal egg is the first example of the Clanger world's fantastical biosystem. While Major Clanger's attention is on the nuts and bolts of industry, the sweat and tears of laborious trial and error, the egg hails from an entirely different realm – effortless and mystical. Tiny Clanger finds music notes inside the egg and, in a sequence veering dangerously near to educational, she draws out the lines of a stave on a cave wall, sets the notes onto it and makes them play.

It turns out that if the notes are planted, music trees will grow. But first water is needed. In a rather matter-of-fact way, a cloud is introduced, as if we should expect this incongruous piece of weather to be found so far out in space. What's more, it is sentient and demands good manners from those seeking its help.

The music trees are watered, and when in full bloom they join the Cloud in a charming musical duet. And why not?

Episode 4. Music

Commentary track		Music and Effects track
Narrator If we look out at the night sky, we can see millions of stars and the stars we can't see we can imagine. We can imagine them any colour and shape we like but of course, we cannot hear them. This star for instance, this serene orb sailing forever through the silence of the sky. Does it ring with the music of the spheres? Or is it always silent or is it silent simply because, just now, the inhabitants are inside, safely asleep in their beds.		Introductory music Introductory music ends.
	T.C.	Funny, I can hear music
Funny, I can hear music		yes, listen to that
It seems to be coming from the egg.		ooh, it's coming out of the egg perhaps there is something in it. (She picks up the egg and goes out with it)
That's Tiny Clanger and that's the egg the iron chicken gave her. I wonder what's in it.		(She carries the egg to the music quarry) (She unscrews the egg) (She empties out a heap of notes) bing, bang, bong bong, bing bang
	T.C.	Ooh I wonder what they are (She picks up a note and taps it. Bing bang bong bing)
They are notes. Notes of music!		
	T.C.	Ooh well fancy that! I know! Where is there a black twig? (She runs and picks up a black twig. She draws 5 lines on the wall with it)
	T.C.	There (She puts the notes on their places one by one)
	T.C.	Good (She points to the notes again, they play)
	T.C.	Hee! Hee! Hee! Hee! (She runs to fetch more, and puts up four more. They play as she puts them up.) (Then she points to the four more notes. Then she points to the set of eight notes.)
	T.C.	Hoo! hoo! doodle di doo do! Hoo Hoo Hoo. (She runs and fetches four more notes and as she puts them up they play. Then she stands back and conducts the tune three times.)

T.C. Cor that's marvellous. I'll go and fetch Small Clanger to see it.

away — Coo! coo! coo! (she runs out)

There's the soup-dragon, look. She seems very interested in those notes

(The soup-dragon walks in, looks at the music)

D. Hmm!
(Tiny Clanger shakes Small Clanger.)

T.C. Wake up Small! wake up! come and look at this.

S.C. Come and look at what?

T.C. Come! come! come!

S.C. All right, all right, I'm coming.
(They run and stop dead on edge of quarry)

T.C. S.C. What's that?

She's eating the music

(The soup-dragon is eating the notes of music off the wall. She turns to look at them.)

T.C. What have you done? You've eaten all my music!

D. Sings. (Goodbye Goodbye)
(The soup-dragon moves across to eat the last two notes on the floor.

T.C. No you don't
(She puts the half-egg on top of the notes and guards it)

S.C. You're a bad dragon, go home.

T.C. Yes, go home. Goodbye!

D. (sings goodbye)

T.C. S.C. Goodbye! goodbye!
(The dragon walks away and turns)

D. (sings goodbye again)

S.C. T.C. Oh goodbye! goodbye!
(The dragon walks away over the quarry, it looks back and)

D. (sings goodbye again)
(then it walks out of shot)
Small Clanger and Tiny Clanger look at the two remaining notes.
T.C. picks them up and bangs them.
T.C. and S.C. look at each other and shake their heads, they are very disconsolate.)

Oh dear, only two notes left.

S.C. Ooh

T.C. Ooh

S.C. (jumps up) I know! I know! Come on, bring the egg and the notes.
(They run upstairs and out)

S.C. Let's plant them here!

T.C. Allright
(They plant the two notes)

T.C. Will they grow

S.C. Of course
(They wait)

Well, they have planted the notes. They don't seem to be growing very fast.

T.C. They aren't growing very fast are they?

S.C. Perhaps they need watering.

T.C. There's a cloud over there.

Yes, perhaps they need watering. Perhaps the cloud will rain on them.

(They walk over to the cloud)

T.C. What shall we do?

S.C. I'll lift you up and you can blow it along.

(T.C. climbs on his back and blows at the cloud. The cloud does not move.)

T.C. Oh you horrid old cloud, why don't you move?

The Cloud doesn't seem to be moving. Perhaps it doesn't like being blown at.

(she blows some more)

T.C. Oh come on!

(the cloud bops her on the nose)

T.C. Eek, eek, it bopped me on the nose.

S.C. Now you've made her cry you rotten cloud.
All we wanted you to do was drop a few drops on our music notes over there.

Well there you are. It only wanted to be asked!

(The cloud moves over to the diggings and drops a few drops on each note.)

T.C. Now they will grow.

(The plants begin to grow, the earth splits)

T.C. Look!

(The trees sprout and lift up)

S.C. Look!

(The trees flower, and the flowers fall leaving notes on the branches.)

T.C. Look at that.

S.C. Coo isn't that good.
Come on Tiny Clanger you must conduct a pretty music.

(He gives her a piece of white stick. T.C. bows to him. She bows to the trees. She lifts her baton. She conducts)

(Clapping)

All. Hoo Hoo Hoo Hoo Hoo
Oh very good, very pretty, very distinguished!

(T.C. drops her stick and runs to tell her parents.)

T.C. ...and there were these notes in the egg the chicken left me. The dragon ate some of them and ...

(S.C. holds up the baton, he conducts a stately air.)

(The Clangers all dance.)

Captions

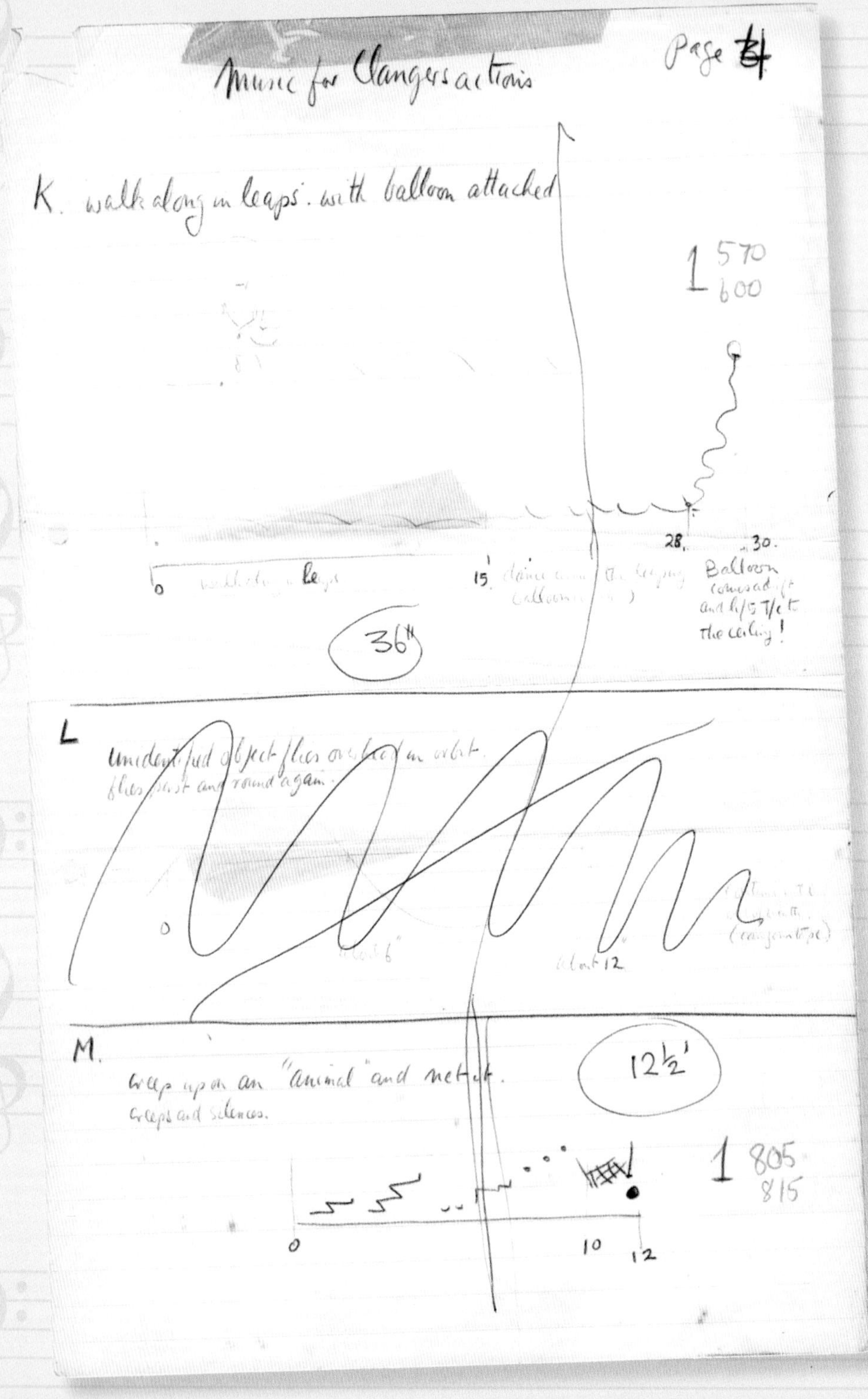

Music for Clangers actions

Page 64

K. walk along in leaps: with balloon attached

1 570
600

28. 30.

0 walk along in leaps 15 dance with the leaping balloon

Balloon comes adrift and floats up to the ceiling!

36"

L

unidentified object flies overhead in orbit. flies past and round again.

0 about 6" about 12

M.

creep up on an "animal" and net it.
creeps and silences.

12½'

1 805
815

0 10 12

A Clanger skeleton: the inside framework of a Clanger puppet.

Episode 5

The Intruder

The narrator quickly warms to a favourite subject. The one about how humanity is so troublesome, throwing junk out into the Universe. But on top of this, it is also meddlesome – sending probes and robots and whatever out into the Cosmos to perform bothersome and 'unwarranted intrusions'. In this case it's a roving robot that has a passing resemblance to the moon-dwelling jobsworth from Nick Park's *A Grand Day Out*. The robot crashes down on the planet, knocking over some sort of Stonehenge construction the Clangers are busy preparing. The intruder quickly gets on with the task of digging up bits of the planet, probably for later analysis to look for evidence of life. The visit is brief but influential enough on Major Clanger to reignite his desire for rocket-making and adventure. This time he has a destination in mind – Planet Earth!

Chekhov's dramatic principle of 'a gun shown in the first act must be used in the third' holds true for this episode. The rover has a telescope attached, which Major Clanger accidentally pulls off in an enthusiastic 'handshake', and sure enough the telescope comes in handy for the denouement…

Just before Major blasts off in his hastily assembled rocket device to learn more about this 'golden planet', Tiny and Small get a good look at it through the newly acquired telescope and call Major's attention to what they find. The view of our Earth, much magnified to the point where New York City is visible, makes it crystal clear that the place is best avoided.

Oliver Postgate had a favourite saying he claimed came from somewhere in the ancient Middle East: 'Seek not, else you discover.' Wise words.

Episode 5. The Intruder

Commentary track		Music and Effects track
Narrator		
Of all the planets in the solar system, of all the stars in the Milky Way, perhaps the most troublesome is this one. This cloud-covered planet is called Earth. Our planet, the home of the human race. People have stood on the earth and looked away into the sky and tried to imagine what life would be like on other planets, other stars,... and they have done more than imagine. They have invented things, complex rockets so powerful that they will blast away from the earth and carry space-probes to invade these distant planets. Robot devices that will land, explore, take photographs and even dig up pieces of the unfortunate planet and make off with them. Who can say what havoc may be caused, what peaceful lives disrupted by these unwarranted intrusions.		Introductory music
		Introductory music ends.
	Cl.	Give me that one
	C2.	All right, here you are.
Look, the Clangers are building a sort of house.		(He passes up a brick.)
	Cl.	Now that goes in there...good There, that's pretty. (They stand back and admire what they have built)
	C2.	Listen
	Cl.	Look up there
They have heard something	C2.	There's something coming Take cover.
	All	Take cover Take cover (They all dive into holes, and clang on lids) Interior shot, crouched in holes. Whatever it is, lands with a crash. The Clangers look out. Their stonehenge is wrecked.
	Cl.	Look at that
	C2.	Oh dear, what a mess.
Look at their building! broken in pieces. Whatever can have done that?		(They climb out, look at the debris)
	Mj.C.	That's terrible, I wonder what can have done that.
	Cl.	There it is, take cover.
There it comes, look out!		(The Clangers dive for cover. The space-probe lumbers into view. The Clangers watch it covertly. The space-probe pushes bricks about, peering here and there with its telescope. The Clangers watch it as it produces a digger and starts to scrape up a piece of planet. Mj. Clanger sees this and is angry.)

C5/2

Mj.C. It can't do that. It's eating our world.
Here! Here! You can't do that!
(He walks up to the machine)

Mj.C. Here I say you can't. That's ours.
(The machine pushes him out of the way)

Mj.C. Who d'you think you're pushing?
(The machine whirrs away, turns and scans Mj. Clanger with its telescope. It approaches Mj. Clanger, raises and lowers telescope.

How do you do?

Mj.C. Oh, how do you do?
(Mj. Clanger shakes hands with the telescope and it comes away in his hand.)

Mj.C Oh, thankyou.. I say this is yours I think.
(The machine backs off, and appears to run away from him.)

Mj.C. Here I say, this is yours.
(He follows the machine about)

Mj.C. I don't want it you know. It isn't any good to me.

Cl. Look out, look out.

Mj.C. What?
(Mj. Cl steps back as the device sets itself up and ignites its rockets.)
(Mj. Clanger watches it go)

Major Clanger thinks it's marvellous! He thinks it is so marvellous that he is making a speech. He is telling the Clangers that they must make a space rocket and fly away to that distant golden planet!

Mj.C. Marvellous, marvellous...
What power! what grace!
(He turns and addresses the others)

Mj.C. That golden planet, Earth, is where that came from. That distant marvellous, lovely world.
That is where we must go!
We Clangers together must make rockets and fly there.
Come below with me and we will make something out of the old firework rockets.

So the Clangers go below to make their rocket, but Small Clanger and Tiny Clanger are more interested in something else.

All All right then, if you say so, I suppose he knows what he's doing.
(The Clangers go below, leaving the telescope behind. Small Clanger and Tiny Clanger approach the telescope.)

T.C. What do you think it is?

S.C. I really couldn't say.
(They examine it)

Funny-looking thing, it looks like a telescope.

T.C. Look, there's a window, I can see through it.

S.C. Let's take it to the music trees.
(They carry the telescope to the music trees).

S.C. Look at this thing.
(Appreciative tinkling.)

T.C. Could you please hold it for us, I would like to look through the window.
(certainly, certainly)

		(T.C. reaches out the telescope to the music tree which holds it for her. She looks through the telescope.)
	T.C.	Ooh ooh look at that oooh
	S.C.	Let me look
	T.C.	That star up there, it's ever so Big!
Oh yes, it is a telescope. There is the earth!		(S.C. looks through the telescope. We see the earth, fairly large.)
	S.C.	Ooh, ooh, ooh.
	T.C.	We must tell the others about this. Come on. (They run indoors.
They must tell the others about this.		All the other Clangers are busy assembling a double rocket.)
	T.C.	Please..er..could I have a word with you.
	S.C.	Er please...I want to talk to you.
	T.C.	Please we've found out something about that..outside.. please?
They don't seem to be taking much notice.	S.C.	Can I please have a word with you? They aren't going to listen.
	T.C.	Come on then!
Ah well, I suppose they are just too busy, making their rockets to listen to Small Clangers.		(They run out again and play with the telescope)
	T.C.	Now let's see yes, yes I think so yes, it's the chicken star.
Yes, it's the chicken's nest.		(She stands aside from the telescope and shouts) Hallo, Hallo, can you hear me?
Well of course the chicken can't hear her. She is much too far away.		(She looks in again. We see the iron chicken on its planet. T.C. pulls the Zoom lever Zoom in.)
	T.C.	Hallo Hallo chicken! (She looks in again, the chicken has not heard her)
It's no good shouting, she can't hear.	T.C.	She can't hear me. I'm sad the rotten thing.
	Cl.	Hi you lot, come and help with this. (They are pulling out a rocket-ship.)
	All	Pull pull pull pull
	Mj.C.	Now we are all ready. I will take my place. That is the planet we are going to That one
	S.C.	That one
That is the planet he is going to		(S.C. runs across to T.C. and tells her which planet to look at, earth.)
	T.C.	Ooh, that one
Tiny Clanger is having a closer look at that planet.		(T.C. looks out at earth)

T.C. Ooh,
(She pulls the Zoom lever.
Mj. Clanger is in place.
The others retire to a safe distance. One of the Clangers starts to count down)
ten
nine
eight
seven
six
five
four
three
two
one
(T.C. is looking at the earth, she pulls the Zoom handle back. T.C. gives a hoot of alarm. T.C. runs into shot and stays his hand on the plunger.)

T.C. No, no, no, you mustn't... come and see.
(The Clanger comes and looks through the telescope.)

Cl. Oooh! oooh! ooh!

Oh I wonder what he has seen.

(He hoots with alarm)

Mj.C. What's going on down there.

Cl. Terrible things going on.

Mj.C. Oh I'll come down and have a look.
(Cl. looks again and hoots with alarm.)

Cl. Oh dear, oh dear, oh dear, how horrifying!

He seems very alarmed about something.

Mj.C. Let me see!
(Mj.C. looks through the telescope.)

Mj.C. Ooh how extraordinary! Well, fancy.

Oh,...oh I see.

(He looks again. We see what he sees, a high shot of Manhattan skyline.)

Mj.C. V.O. ooh ooh revolting!
(He looks up)

Mj.C. What do you think?

Cl. No No

No, No, They don't seem to like the look of that planet after all. Perhaps it would be best to put the rocket away again and stay at home.

Mj.C. No No

T.C. & Mrs.C. No No No

All No No No No No
(No-ing, they push the space-ship back indoors and close the doors behind them.)

Captions.

Page 7.

Music trees, boat etc.

S. very slight blowing away music as the clanders blown away into distance and lands on planet
faint flutter'd flute perhaps, rising notes

3 382-440

T group.

2 387-460

0 T1. collect 12 "random" notes for the boat theme off the floor. 15.

T2. play them over slowly. with 1 note out of place or discordant 25.
T3. play them over slowly with the note corrected. 32.
T4. play the theme middling but get faster over first 3 bars then the wheel comes off its post and goes unbalanced charging wildly about wrecking the place. chased in duet by panicky clangers on foot (flute) ends with clang into tree

clangers chase it flute

37

crash into tree
///clang!

0 3 bars collect
16 bars more or less.
3 secs 42 460

This isn't very good as a picture as I shall alternate [illegible] and chasing clangers so really they go in alternate phrases with one or the [illegible] [illegible] as they chase about.

Time: well, about 50 secs or so see how it works out.

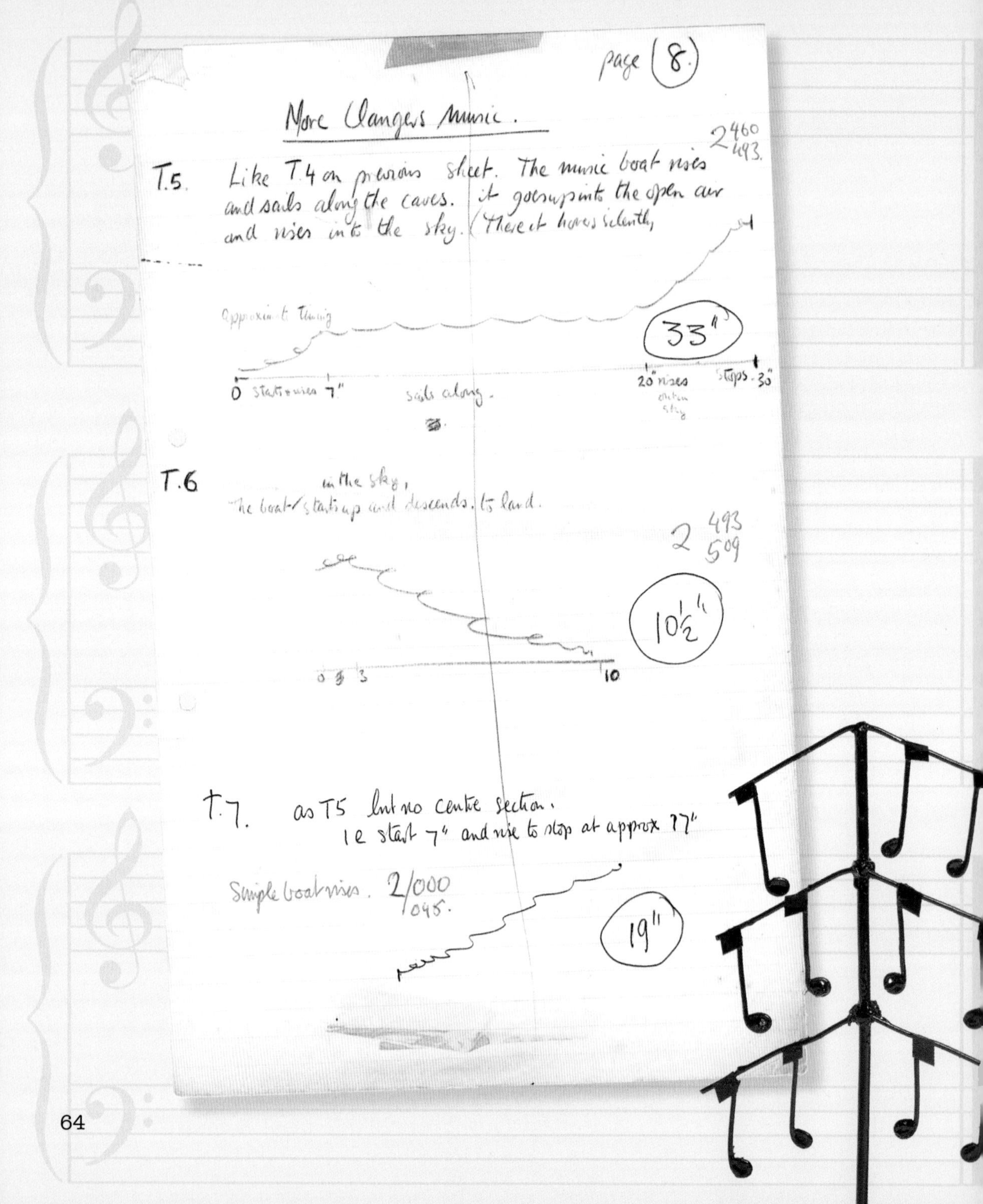
page (8.)

More Clangers music.

2 460 / 493.

T.5. Like T.4 on previous sheet. The music boat rises and sails along the caves. it goes up into the open air and rises into the sky. (There it hovers silently,

Approximate Timing

33"

0 start rises 7" sails along. 20" rises into the sky stops. 30"

T.6 The boat in the sky, starts up and descends. to land.

2 493 / 509

10½"

0 3 10

T.7. as T5 but no centre section. ie start 7" and rise to stop at approx 17"

Simple boat rises. 2/000 / 045.

19"

Episode 6

Visiting Friends

This episode packs a lot into its ten minutes, moving the action along at a brisk pace from pathos to peril to comedy to afternoon tea.

We discover there's more to the music trees' notes than meets the ear. We learn that the Iron Chicken enjoys visitors and offers refreshment from fine bone china. Hardly the uncouth anarchist she first appeared. We observe that Major Clanger's dual-rocket device is, unsurprisingly, not all it's cracked up to be when the rockets head upwards without their passenger. And we take note that this season first aired at a time when sending children to bed early was still a popular punishment.

The Clangers remain planet-bound, much to Major's frustration, but we catch a hint of the changes to come when Tiny takes off in her simple but effective 'hoopicopter' – a hoop from the hoop-plant, powered by the mystical music notes. Again, there is an exchange of gifts between Tiny and the Iron Chicken, thus further deepening their bond of friendship. After some mild peril the Cloud becomes something of a hero, bringing Tiny safely home. Although it must be said that the Cloud is about as passive as it is possible for a hero to be: unable to move under its own effort, it needs to be blown to and from its destinations.

The most endearing moment comes when Tiny makes her bedtime communication with the Chicken by means of her new radio hat – a warm moment shared across the yawning chasm of space. And it's a relief to see a piece of technology actually working for a change.

The Clangers

Episode 6. Visiting Friends

Commentary track		Music and Effects track
Narrator		
This is the planet Earth, the place where we live. It is a small star, one among millions of others in the universe...and it is interesting to look away from the earth and imagine that we have a big telescope which will allow us to look at other stars. Stars like ours but far stranger than ours and perhaps, on one such star somebody is also sitting comfortably with a telescope and is scanning the sky hoping to catch a glimpse of old friends.		Introductory music Introductory music ends
Yes, it's Tiny Clanger, looking through their telescope.	T.C.	Chicken! Chicken! I'm here! I'm here!
	S.C.	She isn't taking any notice She can't hear you from so far. (T.C. runs to a high place)
	T.C.	Chicken! Chicken! look at me Has she noticed?
They are looking at their friend the iron chicken.		
	S.C.	No, she's going away.
	T.C.	Oh it's rotten. I wanted to talk to her! I've got a jewel for her.
Tiny Clanger has found a jewel for her.		
		(Mrs.C. clangs off a lid)
	Mrs.C.	Come on in now, it's teatime. Come on, both of you.
	S.C.	All right, we're coming. Come on Tiny. (He runs in but T.C. does not follow)
	S.C.	Come on Tiny.
	T.C.	All right, in a minute. (S.C. runs in and T.C. follows reluctantly. She reaches the edge of the hole, looks in, looks back at the chicken's planet and waves again.)
	T.C.	Chicken, Chicken!
Poor Tiny Clanger. She never understands that the chicken really is too far away to hear her.		(She runs to the telescope and looks through it. There is no sign of life on the chicken's planet.)
	T.C.	Sniff. (She sits sadly under the branches of the music trees and sheds a tear. She looks at the trees.)
	T.C.	I'm sad. The chicken didn't see me. I have a jewel to go on her necklace, look but she didn't see me. And I can't tell her.
music trees		(Play a short sympathetic tune and drop some notes on the ground in front of her. T.C. picks them up and looks at them.)

Narration		
Poor Tiny Clanger. What she would really like to do is fly all the way to the chicken's nest to give her the jewel she has found and have a nice cup of tea and a chat.	T.C.	They've dropped some notes. (She spins them in her fingers and they play a rising scale).
	T.C.	Ooh I like that.
Ah that's interesting. They rise up.		(She does it again and notices that as she turns, the ring of notes rises.)
	T.C.	Coo! that's good. I like that! (She runs to a hole, jumps in. She plucks a pin from a pin tree, runs out with it, grabbing a ring from a ring-bush.)
	T.C.	There we are, let's fit this together.
Now, what is she making.		(She fixes the ring of notes like a helicopter.)
	T.C.	There we are, let's try it.
Oh, it's a sort of helicopter		(Tiny Clanger swings the rotor. The notes burst into tune and the hoop helicopter plays her up into the sky.)
off	S.C.	Where are you Tiny Clanger.
It flies, It doesn't look very safe though. I hope she isn't thinking of going very far on that thing.		(he dives below)
		(We watch Tiny Clanger fly away on her strange aircraft. The Clangers watch her go.)
	Mrs.C.	Clanger! what shall we do? What shall we do?
	All	What shall we do? What can we do? We'll all rush about madly.
	Mj.C.	No! I know, let's go and fetch out the space rocket. We'll chase her with that.
	All.	All right, all right then.
away		Come on, come on! come and help. (They lug out the double sky-rocket and set it up.)
	All	Pull, pull pull, pull.
	Mj.C.	Right then, point it that way. ..good (He jumps in, puts on his helmet.) Right-ho, contact!
	Cl.	Contact
	Mj.C.	Right then, up, up and away!
	Cl.	Away (Cl. pushes the plunger.) Whoosh, the two rockets shoot up together.
	Cl.	There he goes, there he goes.
	All	Good luck Clanger! Good luck!
	Mj.C.	What d'you mean, good luck? (Pan down and see Mj.Clanger sitting in the centre piece, slightly blackened. The rocket left it behind.)
	All	Oooh, oooh.
	S.C.	It's breaking up. I can see the bits of it falling off.

(We see through his telescope Tiny Clanger's helicopter falling apart.

Oh dear! It's all broken up! Poor Tiny Clanger is floating in space.

The pieces of notes fall away and leave her sitting in her hoop, weightless in space.)

T.C. Me! Me! Me!
Mrs.C. (Looks through telescope) Oh my poor Tiny Clanger.
All What shall we do? What shall we do? What shall we do?
S.C. The chicken has seen her.
Mrs.C. What. Let me look.
(We see through the telescope, the iron chicken rise from its nest and flap up into the sky.)
T.C. Me! Me!
Ch. It's all right dear, I'm coming, I'm coming...
Here, grab my feet
That's right
T.C. I'm there! Up we go
Ch. Hold tight now.
Mrs.C. The chicken has taken her away. Away to somewhere else. Oh dear! Oh dear!
All What shall we do? What shall we do?
(S.C. is talking to the cloud.)
S.C. If we all blew you hard enough do you think you would arrive?

Ah, now, Small Clanger and the cloud have thought of something.

Cloud (Tinkle)
S.C. Right then, I'll set them in line.
Listen everybody, stand in line along here
That's right...all line up
And cloud, I'll blow you over there to that end
(blow)
(The cloud sails to the beginning of the line and hovers.)
S.C. Right! Everybody blow!
The Clangers blow in turn and the cloud is blown faster and faster until a last blast blows it out of orbit. We see the cloud blowing away.
Mrs.C. What are they doing?
S.C. Having tea.
(We see Tiny Clanger and the iron chicken sitting at tea on the chicken's untidy planet, deep in animated conversation.)
Ch. Oh it is good to see you. How nice of you to come.
T.C. Oh I was looking forward to coming to see you, I found a jewel-berry to go on your necklace. Look, here it is. I hope you like it.
Ch. Oh it's delightful.
T.C. Let me fix it on for you.... there!

Oh yes, the jewel Tiny Clanger found. It is a present for the chicken.

T.C. Oh yes, it suits you...very pretty.

Ch. Well thankyou so much, Tiny Clanger. I like that ever so much. I must find you a present.
(She roots below and brings up a sort of helmet with an aerial. It has a torch inside and it lights up faintly.)

Ah she's finding a present for Tiny Clanger

Ch. That's our personal radio. You press the button on the top and my box here lights up. Go on try it.

What an odd-looking thing.

T.C. (Presses button)

Ch. See! it lights up and we can talk to each other.

T.C. Ooh, that's marvellous.

Ch. Hallo, here is another visitor.
(We see the Cloud arriving)

T.C. Hallo Cloud, have you come to take me home?
(The Cloud tinkles and heaves to next to her.)

T.C. Well, it's been so nice. I do hope we shall see some more of you.

Ch. Yes, well, keep in touch, you know. I'll give you a flap of my wings to blow you away.
(She stands up and flaps vigorously. The cloud begins to move.)

And she gives a flap of her wings to help the Cloud on its way.

Ch. Goodbye Goodbye Goodbye!
(We leave her planet and approach the Clanger's planet)

S.C. Here they come! Here they come!

All Here they come, here they come.
(The Cloud lands. T.C. jumps off. Mj. & Mrs.C. grab T.C.)

Mrs.C. You're Bad. You're naughty. You go straight to bed!

T.C. But the chicken gave me a present. Look.

Mrs.C. I don't care. Go straight to bed!

Straight to bed

Mj.C. Bed!

T.C. Bed?

Mrs.C. Yes! at once. Bed.
(T.C. goes indoors. She goes to her bed-hole. Before retiring, she presses the knob on her radio helmet. On the chicken's planet, the box buzzes.)

Ch. Hallo, hallo.

T.C. Hallo chicken, I am home.

Ch. Oh good, I'm glad you got home safely.

T.C. I'm going to bed now. Goodnight.

Goodnight Chicken.
Goodnight Tiny Clanger.

Ch. Goodnight.
(T.C. climbs into her bed-hole, covers herself, and snuggles down for sleep.)

Captions.

Episode 7

Fishing

For centuries science has given humanity a utilitarian type of grasp on the phenomenon of life. In recent years, however, the cutting edge of our investigation has led to a place where the tried and tested mechanics we previously embraced so completely have given way to the necessary recognition of other, more esoteric, goings-on. The cheeky shenanigans in the quantum realm, for example, have thrown a spanner into the Newtonian works and left us humbled before the sheer mysticism of this thing we call existence.

On the Clangers' planet the marriage of technology and the unknown is about to take place. In a move away from rocket science, Major Clanger has overseen the manufacture of a vehicle of entirely new design: a helicopter of sorts. Unfortunately, it fails in its singular task of getting off the ground for any sustained period. Poor Major – he really isn't having much luck.

Fortunately, his children have the presence of mind to take advantage of the magical powers of the extraordinary music notes, happily given to them by the music trees; and, voila, the Clangers are no longer shipwrecked on their small blue world.

Small Clanger takes the adapted music boat on her maiden voyage while the other Clangers look on. Like most of us on Earth, they don't need to know *how* or *why* something works; that it does work is marvellous enough. The next question is the *what*, or rather the *what for*. This is a point often overlooked when something new is devised. For instance, whether the telephone is a good invention ultimately depends on what is said on it.

But the invention is in safe hands. Tiny puts the boat to good use, with a spot of fishing.

The Clangers C7/1

Episode 7. Fishing

Commentary track		Music and Effects track
Narrator		
We can stand on our firm Earth, on this planet which is our home and we can look out at the vast empty spaces of the Universe. We can ask ourselves how empty are these spaces between the stars. Who can say? For years now, men have been busy hurling unwanted objects away beyond the orbits of the earth and of course, who knows what other civilizations on other worlds have also been using the Universe as a celestial rubbish dump. Some enterprising creatures with proper equipment could reap a rich harvest by trawling this vast endless sea.		Introductory music
		Introductory music ends.
	S.C.	Ready Get set Go!
	T.C.	Eek
	S.C.	Got you? what's in the net?
	T.C.	Broken, look.
	S.C.	Ooh, broken
Oh it is broken, look.	T.C.	Ooh, broken.
	All	Oooh (They go indoors)
	T.C.	Look, everybody, the net is broken.
Ah, Major Clanger does not care about their broken net, He has made another flying machine.	Mj.C.	Never mind, never mind. When my boat is finished it will sail up in the sky. Up, up and away. Look, it is nearly finished.
	Mj.C. (calls)	When will it be ready?
	Cl.	It's ready now.
	Mj.C.	Good, come on you two, come and give us a hand to pull it out.
	All	pull pull pull pull pull pull pull pull pull pull
I wonder if this one will work.		
	T.C.	Is it going to work?
	Mrs.C.	No
	T.C.	Oh dear (The Clangers lift the boat onto the outside.)
	All	Pull pull pull
	Mj.C.	Right, all set, wind up the rope. Everybody ready? I'm on board, all set! (The Clangers pull the rope as hard as they can. The flywheel whines up to speed. The screw spins. The boat rises.)
	Mj.C.	It works. Up we go! (The boat rises a few feet, hovers as the flywheel slows down and then slowly and gently descends on to more or less the same spot.
Oh dear, not one of his best machines.		

	Mj.C.	Oh the rotten thing. (He walks away. The other Clangers haul the boat back indoors)
	All (away)	Pull pull pull pull pull pull pull pull pull pull
	T.C.	I've got an idea. Do you remember that helicopter I made.
Tiny Clanger has thought of something.	S.C.	Yes, with music notes. Come on. (They run to the music trees)
	S.C.	Please may we have some notes please.
	music trees	Certainly, help yourselves.
Notes from the music trees. Now what do they want them for.		(They collect a dozen ripe notes and run indoors to the quarry. There, Tiny Clanger lays down the notes on the floor and plays them over once. The soup-dragon appears)
	D.	Oh, more notes for dinner, how nice.
Here comes the soup-dragon. She is particularly fond of music. She eats it.	T.C.	No, you go away.
	D.	Go away?
	T.C.	Yes, go back to your soup-well.
	D.	But I like notes for dinner.
	T.C.	I don't care, you aren't having these.
	D.	Oh how disappointing. I rather fancied eating them, they look rather nice.
	T.C.	Small! Small! help me stop this monster.
	S.C.	All right, I'm coming...you rotten soup-dragon, you aren't having our notes. No No you dont push push (they push the soup-dragon)
	Both	push (Slowly the soup-dragon backs off. Then it turns and walks away sadly.)
	S.C.	Well that's one good thing done.
Well, that has got rid of her. Now perhaps they can get on with what they were making.	T.C.	Have you made that wheel yet?
	S.C.	Yes, I was just fixing the last bit over there...there we are, will that do?
	T.C.	Yes, bring it down. (S.C. brings the wheel down to the quarry. They set it down at the end of the line of notes and roll the wheel along the notes which are picked up by the wheel as it rolls)
	T.C.	That's good, but we must fix it somewhere.
	S.C.	That pipe-tree stump.
	T.C.	Yes, that'll do. (They carry the wheel across and lift it up onto the stump)
	T.C.	O.K?
	S.C.	O.K. I'm ready.

(T.C. stands and conducts the notes as S.C. gives the wheel a spin. The wheel spins faster as she increases tempo

Aha, it rises!
And it flies!

until it suddenly lifts clean off the stump and sails up in the air. It sideslips and starts running amok through the inside of the planet. The wheel ultimately comes to rest in a tree.)

S.C. There it is. Come on
(S.C. climbs the tree, reaches the wheel and the tree collapses. Other Clangers are standing watching silently)

S.C. Come on T.C. help me carry it.
(In silence they carry the wheel to the boat. They take off the original spiral. They fit the wheel in its place)

T.C. Right?

S.C. O.K.
(S.C. spins the wheel once slowly as T.C. conducts the music.)

All Look at that! Oh I say! Well fancy! What an extraordinary thing.

T.C. Quiet please!
May we please have hush?
(The Clangers are silent as S.C. climbs into the boat.)

T.C. Right?

S.C. Right!
(He turns the wheel. The music starts. The boat rises

Now, that's good!
That really flies.

as T.C. conducts. The boat flies round the house set (and over the soup-dragon set) before rising into the open and heaving to in the sky some distance above the planet. There it stops and hovers.)

S.C. Good, now we will fish.
(He stands up, takes out a magnet on a rod and line and listens. We hear a whistling noise. He casts and the

he's caught something

magnet clinks hold of something.
He reels in and takes something off the magnet.)

It's like a little fish.

S.C. Ooh good. Let's show them.
(He spins the wheel the other way and the boat goes down. It lands amongst the Clangers)

T.C. Have you caught anything?

S.C. Yes, look at this.
(He shows a tiny fish like flying saucer.)

T.C. Ooh isn't it pretty.

It's very small.

Mj.C. No, too small

Mrs.C. No, too small

S.C. Yes perhaps, too small.

Mj.C. Yes, too small

F.C (Beep beep)

S.C. All right then, back you go.

Yes, quite right, that's the best thing to do...Throw it back...

(He runs and throws the flying saucer back into the sky. It hums and beeps away.)

Perhaps it will grow!

Captions.

Episode 8

The Top-Hat

Leonardo da Vinci's iconic painting of the *Mona Lisa* has beguiled onlookers throughout the centuries. The expression of the sitter's lips, tinted with hazy sfumato, defy definitive interpretation. Even the most acutely perceptive card shark would wonder: does the lady have a full house or merely a pair of twos?

And the smile of the Froglet, albeit simple and cartoonish, has the same enigmatic quality. In fact, the species as a whole is shrouded in mystery. Where are they from? What do they want? Where are they going? Such questions hang in the mind but remain unanswered, and it is very likely that this is the intention. After all, the arrival of these teardrop monopeds is by way of a top hat, an object synonymous with the mischievous tricks of stage magicians the world over – surely a sign that explanations are not on the menu.

The Froglets tease Mother Clanger with a game of peek-a-boo. Perhaps their painted smiles signify that they are fun-loving. Soon after, however, they are found comatose, exhausted through lack of sustenance. But still the smiles persist. They can't return whence they came, via the top hat, so it would seem they are not in charge of their destiny and are vulnerable to the flotsam and jetsam of circumstance. Perhaps the smile is a brave grimace.

Resolution comes at a place deep within the planet, nestled in an obscure rocky labyrinth unknown even to the Clangers. Here, beyond the rules of gravity, Small Clanger discovers a sort of muddy pool on its side, and another Froglet within. The top-hat Froglets join their friend, tumbling into the caramel water. Are they happy about this? Have they finally found their true home, or is this pond simply another eccentric gateway in some infernal journey? As with the shaded expression of Leo's muse, we can never really be sure.

Episode 8. The Top-Hat

Commentary track		Music and Effects track
Narrator		
This is the planet Earth, our home, the place where we live. We can stand on our earth and look out at the vast empty sky and see millions of stars shining like bright dots...and in between the stars...just empty space...but is it empty? We can imagine strange stars in the sky. Perhaps we can also imagine other things too. Unknown objects, too small to see from here, hurtling about in the space between the stars. What would they be like? Who knows? but perhaps some enterprising fisherman could sail his boat across this vast endless sea and cast his rod and line to catch some very unusual fish.		Introductory music
		Introductory music ends
	S.C.	There's one. (He casts his magnet rod and misses.)
	S.C.	Missed it. (He reels in his rod)
	S.C.	There's another. (He casts his magnet rod and it clinks on to something. He hauls in a top-hat.)
Small Clanger has caught something. Very odd.	S.C.	What's this? Very odd. (He looks at it, decides to take it down. He spins the wheel and descends.)
	Mj.C.	What have you caught?
	S.C.	This thing.
	Mj.C.	How extraordinary!
There's something in it!		(They stand the hat on end and look it up and down. As they do so a pair of eyes looks out over the top of the hat. The eyes blink at Mj. Clanger. They blink at us. They blink at Small Clanger.)
	S.C.	Hallo little object. (The object descends again.)
	S.C.	Don't go away, come out. (The object rises and blinks)
	S.C.	Come out
	F.	Craak
	S.C.	Come out, we won't hurt you.
	F.	Craak bonk craak bonk craak bonk (Three froglets in quick succession jump out of the hat.)
Look, three of them!	Mj.C.	Ooh, three of them.
	S.C.	How do you do. Pleased to meet you.
They are sort of froglets aren't they. How extraordinary!		(The froglets do not shake hands with S.C. They have no hands. They dance off follow-my-leader fashion around the Clangers, along the edge of the door and vanish down one of the holes.)

S.C. How extraordinary!
(They look in the hat. It is empty.)

Mj.C. How remarkable!
(They go indoors. Mrs.C. is hanging out a bedcover. She lowers it and reveals the three froglets.)

Mrs.C. Eek!
(The three froglets croak and croak away into Mrs.C.'s housedoor.)

Mrs.C. Hi! Where do you think you lot are going?

They are going into the bed-caves. Mother Clanger won't be pleased about that.

(She runs to look in the door but the Froglets appear from another door above and look down at her.)

Mrs.C. I can see you...I know you are in there..Now come on out at once...I know you're hiding.
(The froglets blink at her from above. They blink at each other. They blink at us.)

F. Craak? Craak?
(Mrs.C. steps back and sees them.)

Mrs.C. There you are you articles!

You know, those froglets are just making fun of Mother Clanger.

(The frogs march along the side of the cave and vanish into another hole. Mrs. Clanger watches them angrily.)

Mrs.C. You know you aren't supposed to go in there. That's our house. That's Tiny Clanger's room. Come out of there at once! At once I say! I shall go and fetch Mj. Clanger. I shall!
(She turns and sees the three froglets standing in a row behind her.)

Mrs.C. Eeek!
(The froglets laugh and hop away across the set to the place beside the door. Major Clanger and Small Clanger enter.)

Mj.C. Hi Mum! We found three froglets. Have you seen them?

Mrs.C. Yes I have, up there.
(The Clangers turn and see the froglets standing behind them)

Mj.C. Oh there you are. I want a word with you.
(The frogs laugh and then they hop away upside-down over the doorway and down to the trees)

Poor Mother Clanger! She's quite put out by all this disturbance.

Mrs.C. They went in and out of the house and suddenly turned up just next to me.

Mj.C. How extraordinary!

Mrs.C. Be a dear and fetch me some soup, Small Clanger.

Oh soup. Yes of course, time to fetch soup from the soup-wells.

S.C. Yes, all right.

Here comes Tiny Clanger

(Tiny Clanger appears across the path.)

off T.C. Hi, there are some extra-ordinary things here.

Tiny Clanger seems very worried about something.

Mj.C. I know, froglets.

T.C. But they aren't at all well. Come and look. Come and look, Small Clanger!

S.C. All right, I'm coming.
(He poles away on the soup-trolley, Tiny Clanger jumps aboard as he passes and they go to the soup-wells. On the way they stop because the apparently lifeless froglets are lying on the path.)

S.C. Ooh dear.

T.C. Ooh dear.

Oh dear, they are not at all well.

Are they alive?

S.C. I don't know. What shall we do with them?

T.C. Put them on here and take them to the soup-wells.

S.C. All right.

That's right, put them on the trolley and take them to the soup-wells. The soup-dragon will know what to do about them.

(They take off the jugs, put the froglets on the trolley and wheel it down to the soup-wells. Small Clanger goes to the soup-dragon's well and unscrews it.)

S.C. Excuse us Dragon, do you know what is wrong with these beasts?

D. Eh..what? What's that?

S.C. Our visitors are not well.

D. Oh, oh yes, they are hungry I expect. I'll give them some soup. Pass me the jug.

Yes, perhaps some hot soup would do them good.

(S.C. passes the small jug to the Dragon who pours out soup and gives it back.)

S.C. Here you are Froglets. Hold it up Tiny Clanger.
(S.C. administers soup to the froglets in turn. They revive, but not much.)

F. (Faint croak) on voice track.
(Mj. C. appears on the path.)

Mj.C. What happened?

S.C. They are not well.
(Mj.C. turns and runs out.)

T.C. Where has he gone?

S.C. I don't know.
(Mj.C. collects the top-hat and runs in with it.)

T.C. They are falling over again.

They are still not at all well.

S.C. Oh dear, I hope they aren't too ill.

They must think of something.

Mj.C. Here you are, put them back in their hat.

Put them back in the hat?

(Mj. C. puts down the hat. He lifts one froglet and puts it in the hat. He lifts another and puts it in but of course there isn't room. The two froglets make a pile. Mj. Clanger puts the third one on top.

They won't go in, No.

S.C. No

T.C. No

Mj.C. They won't go in, no.
(The Clangers shake their heads. The Soup-Dragon looks out.)

Narration		Dialogue
	D.	Hi, try this soup for them. It's rather special. I haven't got much of it.
Ah yes, some rather special soup, blue and white pudding soup; very nourishing.		(Dragon hands out a can of blue soup. They administer it to the froglets who wake up at once and dance around the dragon croaking for more.)
Yes, that seems to have done the trick, and they want some more.		
	S.C.	Here is the can.
	D.	There isn't any more. If you want more you must fetch it.
There isn't any more. If they want more, somebody will have to fetch it from the pudding-soup wells. Small Clanger will fetch some if the soup-dragon will tell him how to find the way.	S.C.	Where from?
	D.	You go below through that hole.
	S.C.	This one?
	D.	Yes, that one. Then you go along and down and along this way and up and you come to a lake on the side. That's a soup-lake.
	S.C.	Oh all right. (S.C. goes below. The others watch him go.)
	T.C.	Is it all right?
	Mj.C.	Oh yes, perfectly safe. (S.C. goes through various tunnels.)
	S.C.	Oh which way now? Up here I think...yes...that's right... now then, down here... Right then What's this place? Funny-looking well that. (S.C. comes to the sideways lake.)
	S.C.	Very odd. (He picks up a stone and throws it up at the wall. It falls into the soup with a small splash.)
	S.C.	Ooh-er! (A froglet breaks surface and looks out.)
	F.	Craak!
It's another froglet!	S.C.	Oh! Are you a froglet? (The froglet hops on to the bank.)
	S.C.	Oh how marvellous. There are some of your friends upstairs. Will you come up with me?
	F.	Craak!
	S.C.	Come on then. (They dash upstairs.)
	S.C.	Look! they have friends! (The froglets hop in a ring croaking with delight. They hop in line to the hole and hop into it. T.C. and S.C. follow. The frogs hop through the caves. They hop to the lake. One by one they hop into the water. The Clangers watch. The four froglets look
Goodbye Froglets...or whatever you are!		out at them and croak once. They submerge.)
		Captions

Episode 9

The Egg

The Soup Dragon is in a foul mood. She's sullen, short-tempered, distracted and uncharitable. The chances of the Clangers getting soup any time soon are slim, and this is truly alarming. Apart from the occasional bowl of blue-string pudding, soup is the Clangers' only form of sustenance. The lesson is clear: if you live on a small rock lost in the vastness of space, don't base your only means of survival on the whims of a grumpy dragon.

However, the main topic at hand is the miracle of birth, and there is certainly nothing more miraculous than the circumstances leading up to the birth of a brand-new soup dragon. Anyone looking for the 'logical' in 'biological' should look away. The ingredients for making a dragon, apparently, are random objects gathered together from around the planet, then heated up in the metal egg the music notes arrived in.

Ultimately, it is often wise not to pick over minor details, no matter how spurious they may be, but instead turn to look to the final result. The Soup Dragon, on discovering that she is now a mother, is quickly lifted from her ennui. And what's more, her charming little offspring is immediately ready and willing to get stuck into helping out in the family business. Good news all round!

The Clangers C9/1

Episode 9. The Egg

Commentary track		Music and Effects track
Narrator		usic A
This is the planet Earth. The home of the human race, our home. Here, on the surface of this cloudy planet, you and I, our families, our friends, are working, playing, living, dying. Eating, drinking, getting married, being born, laughing, dancing, singing, worrying and, sometimes, weeping, all on the outside of one small star. We can turn our eyes away from the earth and look out at the myriad other stars in the sky. We can wonder about the lives of other creatures on other planets.. Are their lives sad? Are they lonely? Are they perhaps always happy, calm and free from worries, going about their daily lives gaily and cheerfully without ever the slightest sign of peevishness or bad temper?		Fanfare
		(The soup-dragon is prowling about on the outside.)
Ah now, the soup-dragon.	D.	Well I don't know, I really dont. This place is getting me down.
	C.1.	Good morning dragon.
	D.	Pah! Good morning nothing, it's a rotten morning, you're all rotten.
Oh dear, she doesn't seem very friendly today.		(She goes down through a hole. Other clangers come out of another hole.)
	Mj.C.	Have you seen the soup-dragon?
Yes, he has seen the soup-dragon all right.	C.1.	Yes, she went down there.
	Mj.C.	Oh she's in a right paddy this morning.
Major Clanger will go and have a word with her. See if he can find out why she is upset. Well, you know how it is, day in, day out, slaving over a hot volcano. A dragon gets fed up now and then.		(The Clangers go over to the hole where she w ent down.)
	Mj.C.	Hallo old dragon, are you down there? Are you all right? We are coming down to see you and have a chat. (He climbs down. As he does the dragon climbs out of another hole and sniffs about)
	D.	I don't know, I really don't. It's a right bind this soup-stirring all the time. Day in, day out slaving over a hot volcano and it isn't as if anybody ever.. and.. you know.. (Mis to interior. See the Clangers with jugs queueing up beside the soup-well.)
Soup, soup, soup.	All	Soup...soup...soup...please.

	D.	Oh rubbish, oh fiddledidee, fiddledidee. The soppy old soup-shop is shut solid, I'm not serving soup.
Soup? soup.	All	Soup? soup? soup?
	D.	Oh go jump in the firmament, the lot of you..
What is she doing? She's picking the macaroni!		(The dragon starts picking macaroni tree branches.)
	Mrs.C.	Ooh, isn't she odd?
Now what can they do to help her?	T.C.	What shall we do?
They'll all pick macaroni for the dragon.	Mrs.C.	I don't know, we could help her. (They watch the dragon take a big armful of macaroni tree branches and carry them off)
	T.C.	All right then, we'll help her. (The Clangers collect macaroni tree branches.
There, a big heap of macaroni branches.		The dragon goes outside with her branches, dumps them on the ground and grumbles away. She sits in a hole and looks the other way. Clangers follow her and drop their macaroni branches on the pile. T.C. approaches her very cautiously.)
	T.C.	We put some twigs on your pile. Is that all right?
Now Tiny Clanger should leave her alone. The dragon knows she brought out some macaroni.		(The dragon doesn't answer)
	T.C.	Er dragon... we put twigs on your pile.
	D.	Oh yes, yes thankyou very much or something. (she goes back to her sulk)
Oh dear.	T.C.	Ooh dear.
Yes, go indoors and leave her.	Mrs.C.	Well, we'd better go indoors and leave her. (All the Clangers go in except T.C. who stands looking at the sad dragon.)
Music!	T.C.	Music. (She goes to the music trees and speaks to them)
Yes, perhaps a merry tune will cheer her up...shall we?	T.C.	The dragon's sad. Shall we play music for it?
	M.T.	(certainly certainly)
Yes, good.	T.C.	Right then...one two
Very pretty, but I wonder if she really likes music.		(She conducts. The trees play music. The cloud joins in. The dragon takes no notice. Then she lifts her head wearily, turns round.
	D.	Oh blow! The cloud moves over her and sprinkles some drop-notes on her. She is furious.
	D.	Ugh you 'orrible thing. Go away! Go away. Go away and leave me in peace!
Ah now Tiny Clanger is taking advice.		(T.C. presses the button on her radio hat to call the chicken. She looks up and presses it again.

		We track in on the chicken's star, see the chicken's box buzzing. The chicken presses the lever and answers.)
She is consulting her friend the iron chicken. The iron chicken will know what to do.	Ch.	Hallo Tiny Clanger. How are you?
off	T.C.	Very well thankyou. I wonder if you can help me.
	Ch.	Why certainly.
Yes, it's the dragon, she seems to have gone all broody. She sits and grumbles.	T.C.	Well, it's our dragon, you see, she seems to have gone broody. She sits and grumbles.
	Ch.	Ooh!
and they cant get any soup.	T.C.	Yes and we can't get any soup.
	Ch.	Oooh! well well well.
And she has carried out masses of macaroni branches and laid them in a heap.	T.C.	But she has carried out a lot of bits of macaroni branches and laid them outside here in a heap.
	Ch.	Oh well that's easy. Oh yes, that's nothing. That's clear enough to anybody. O.K. Now I'll tell you what to do. Are you listening?
Ah yes you see, the iron chicken knows what that means. She will tell Tiny Clanger exactly what to do.	T.C.	Yes.
	Ch.	Ohe, fetch the egg, the iron egg.
One, fetch the egg.	T.C.	Yes.
	Ch.	Two..find a jewel just like this one you gave me. Can you do that?
Two, fetch one jewel-berry.	T.C.	Yes, I think so.
	Ch.	Put it in the egg with three notes of music, some copper leaves and four drops of water. Do you understand?
Three, put them all in the egg with three notes of music, copper leaves, four drops of water and give it a good shake.	T.C.	Yes.
What a complicated list of things to do.	Ch.	Good. Then put the egg on the next and go indoors; keep out of the way. O.K.?
	T.C.	O.K. Over and out. (Then the Clangers bring her the things she ordered.)
Here they are. They've fetched the things already.	G.C.	Here you are.
The egg	T.C.	Thankyou. (She opens the egg)
	C.1.	Will these do?
The jewel	T.C.	Yes, put them in here. (She holds out half the egg)
The copper leaves	C.2	This is the biggest I could find
Now where is the music	T.C.	Pop it in (She holds out half the egg)
	S.C.	Here are four good notes.
	T.C.	They will do nicely, pop them in. (S.C. Pops the notes in)
There it is.	T.C.	Now what?...oh yes, four drops. (She walks across to the cloud)
Ah yes, four drops of water Perhaps the cloud will be kind enough.	T.C.	Please may we have four drops? (The cloud obliges)
Yes, good.	T.C.	Thankyou.. now put on the lid.. That's right
Now a good shake.		Shake well (She shakes it)
And put it on the nest		and place it on the nest.. so... there. (T.C. puts on her helmet again and calls up the chicken)

	Ch	I'm here, hallo.
	T.C.	All done and correct.
All done and ready. Now everybody keep out of the way while she fixes up the machine.	Ch.	Right... now all of you keep out of the way while I rig this gubbins up.
That's right, everybody below, everybody below please.	T.C.	Right-ho. Now everybody below please.
away		Come on underground now. (T.C. ushers them away down holes. She climbs in last, buzzes the chicken)
	T.C.	All down now.
All down now.		(She closes the lid)
	Ch.	Right ho. Thankyou. I shan't be long.
Now there's an extraordinary-looking machine. Mind you, that is an exceptionally clever chicken and very experienced with electrical devices of all sorts.		(she rigs up a device)
I wonder what it does.		Now then That goes there Yes that's right Now, line it up Yes, yes, that will do. Switch on. (She switches on and the device shines pinkly.
It shines. It shines a greenish light.		We see the glow spread across the sky. The light on the planet has dimmed as the glow shines like a spotlight on the egg in the nest.
Look, it's shining on the egg. The egg is changing.		As we watch it, the egg glows pinkly and is subtly transformed. The soup-dragon rises from her place and comes to look.)
Ah that interests her, an egg, on her nest.	D.	Ooh how delightful. An egg on a nest. Ooh, just what I was looking for. (The light expands as she climbs onto the nest and sits on the egg. The chicken calls up T.C.)
	Ch.	Is she sitting on the egg?
Is she sitting on the egg?		(T.C. looks outside)
	T.C.	Yes, yes she is!
	Ch.	Right then, I'll switch off.
Switch off.		(She switches off, the motors die down, the light fades. The Clangers come out of their holes.)
It's hatched, the egg is hatched.	D.	Hi, I've hatched an egg. It's hatching. Look everybody it's hatched. (She stands up and reveals the broken egg and a tiny soup-dragon.)
	D.	Hallo little dragon.
	L.D.	Hallo mum.
Soup-time! Come on everybody, soup-time. That was all she wanted, a baby soup-dragon.	D.	Come on everybody, soup-time! soup-time, soup-time. (She turns and trots indoors followed by her baby and the Clangers. Tiny Clanger remains behind and calls the Chicken.

Thankyou chicken, goodnight.	T.C.	Goodnight chicken, thankyou.
	Ch.	Goodnight, over and out.
Goodnight Tiny Clanger.		
		(Inside the Clangers' planet the soup-dragon hands out soup to the Clangers.
And it's soup-time at last.		
	S.D.	Soup for you
	C.1.	Thankyou
	S.D.	Soup for you.
	C.2.	Thankyou.
	S.D.	Soup for you.
And now the soup-dragon is no longer the only soup-dragon in the universe. Now there are two soup-dragons, both doing well, working hard and very happy.		(music)

Episode 10

The Hoot

Another episode, another curious catch from a fishing expedition in the music boat. This time it's a tiny trumpet, which, after becoming lost in the caves of the Clangers' planet, quickly grows into a large and loud horn-type thing; or, to give it the official name, a Hoot.

Major Clanger is far from overjoyed with the young Hoot's noisy, needy honking and, rather than enquiring into the Hoot's wants or needs, rudely stuffs a cotton-wool ball in its horn. One would need a heart of stone not to feel sorry for the poor Hoot – born into a world where it's clearly not supposed to be and stifled in its expression as a wind instrument.

Tiny Clanger introduces a foreign agent into the Hoot's biology: music notes from the music trees. The notes, dropped into the Hoot's horn, transform the instrument from a honker into something more tuneful and easier on the ear. Something, in fact, for the Clangers to happily dance to.

Although here on Earth the practice of genetic modification has long been an ethical 'hot potato', on the Clangers' planet such concerns don't exist. That's not to say such interventions don't have consequences, as we shall see in the next episode...

The Clangers

Episode 10. The Hoot

Commentary track		Music and Effects track
Narrator		Music B
If we go out of doors on a clear night and look up at the sky, we can see millions of stars. Bright stars, twinkling stars, dim stars. So many that we couldn't begin to count them, nor know what they would really look like if we could see them close to... but we can let our imagination wander through the universe and wonder to ourselves what shapes these distant stars might have. Would they all be plain spheres like our earth or could they come in many sizes and all manner of strange and marvellous shapes?		Fanfare
		(We pass the hoot-planet and come upon Small Clanger fishing from his boat. He is looking up.)
Now, we know that isn't a star. That is Small Clanger fishing from the music boat.	S.C.	I can see something.
He has heard something. Got it!		Yes, there it is. (He casts his line and catches something. He reels it in.)
What's he got? A little trumpet, A little hoot, I wonder if it plays.	S.C.	Well what's this then? A little trumpet. Isn't it odd? I wonder if it plays. (He blows it, it burps faintly) Ha ha, oh well, we can take it home. Down we go. (He spins the wheel and down they go)
	T.C.	Have you caught something?
Tiny Clanger wants to know if he has caught something. He has, and he will play it for her indoors.	S.C.	Yes, a little hoot. Come indoors, I'll show you. (They run in to the House set by the hole)
	S.C.	There, look, it's a little golden hoot. Listen, it plays. (He blows it)
	T.C.	Ooh that's good, may I try? (She blows it)
What a little hoot		What a little noise!
off	Mrs.C.	Clangers! Clangers! where are you?
Ah now Mother Clanger is calling them. (Music)	T.C. Mrs.C.	We're over here. Would you run down to the wells and fetch me some soup, please.
She wants them to fetch her a jug of soup from the soup-wells. Ah well, a Clanger's work is never done. The hoot, look, it's rolling!	S.C.	All right, come on Tiny. (He runs out. Tiny Clanger leaves the hoot on the ground and follows. The hoot rolls this way and that and falls into the hole. Small Clanger pulls out the trolley. Tiny Clanger fetches the jug. They pole away towards the soup-wells. They dismount and unscrew the soup-well.)
On last note And here they are at the soup-wells.		

	S.C.	Good morning Dragon, may we have soup?
	D.	Good morning Clangers, certainly you may. (She takes the jug, goes below and pours soup)
	D.	Here you are.
	S.C.	Thankyou very much.
	B.D.	Eek Eek Eeek.
That's the baby dragon's voice		(They look down at another smaller hole. The Baby Dragon looks out.)
	B.D.	I say there's a terrible noise down here, a sort of hooting noise... listen.
What a strange noise.		(S.C. & T.C. come to the edge of the hole and listen. There is a faint hooting sound.)
I wonder what that is.	S.C.	I wonder what that is.
Is it from the hoot they brought?	T.C.	Is it from the hoot we brought?
No, that was a very small hoot.	S.C.	I doubt it. That was a very small hoot. (Three froglets jump out of their hole. They stand at the edge of their hole looking down.
Ah, here are the froglets.		Then they look up at S.C. and T.C. and blink. Then they jump up and down
There's that noise again.		croaking. Then stop and look down again.
It's coming from the caves.		S.C. comes over to listen. The hooting is louder from the froglets' hole.)
	S.C.	I'd better go and look. You take the soup home Tiny and see if you can find the hoot.
Small Clanger is going to go below to see if he can find out what it is that is making that noise.	T.C.	All right
	S.C.	I'll get myself a lamp from the tree. (He does so.) Right, I'll go down now. (S.C. descends below. Tiny Clanger pushes the trolley out of shot. Small Clanger makes his way along passages and caves towards the hooting which gets louder and louder. He approaches the sound and it grows louder. Suddenly he turns a corner and sees before him an octagonal cave with a hole in the roof where the light is shining down onto a large golden Hoot. S.C. walks round it and whistles up the hole. Tiny Clanger above hears him whistle. She is beside the hole where the Hoot fell in.)
	T.C.	I can hear you.
(off)	S.C.	Fetch a rope.
	T.C.	O.K. (She runs off, fetches a rope. She ties one end to something or holds it.)
	T.C.	Right-ho. (Small Clanger climbs out)
	S.C.	That Hoot is grown enormous. It is down there making a terrible noise. Come on lets pull it up.

	S.C. & T.C.	Pull pull pull pull pull pull pull pull pull pull pull pull
That must be the same hoot that Small Clanger found, but hasn't it grown enormous?		(The Hoot comes up, momentarily silent. S.C. sets it up and unties the rope. T.C. approaches it. It hoots.)
	T.C.	Eek what a noise. ssh now: don't hoot so much.
	S.C.	Come on Tiny Clanger let's go and tell the others.
They're going to tell the others what they've found.		(They move out of shot. The Hoot doesn't want to be left. It hoots again.)
	T.C.	All right, all right, we'll take you with us.
I don't think that hoot likes to be left alone.		(They carry it to the centre of the square.)
	S.C.	There now little hoot, we shan't be a minute.
Stay there little hoot, they won't be a minute.		(They go away. The hoot is still for a moment, then it hoots and hoots. Clangers appear from all over the place.)
What a din! what a noise, what a loud thing! Major Clanger won't like that noise.	All	What a din! what a noise! I say that's a loud thing. I don't fancy that. (Mj. C. walks up to the Hoot.)
	Mj.C.	Be silent.
Yes, be quiet!		(The Hoot hoots again.)
	Mj.C.	Be silent I say. (The Hoot strangles its hooting)
strangled hoot		
	Mj.C.	That's right. (He walks away. The Hoot starts up again.)
That's better. Hoots. Be silent. Strangled hoot.	Mj.C.	Be silent. (The Hoot strangles its hoot)
	Mj.C.	That's right. Now then! (He walks away.
Well it's certainly trying to quiet anyway.		The Hoot hoots again. Mj. Clanger walks to a cotton-wool tree, plucks a handful, marches up to the Hoot and stuffs it into its horn. Then he walks away.
Well that has stopped it.		The Hoot continues muffled. S.C. & T.C. come and look at it)
Poor hoot.	S.C.	Oh poor hoot.
Poor hoot, that must be uncomfortable. Stop hooting and they'll take out the gag.	T.C.	Oh poor hoot. That must be uncomfortable. Stop hooting and we'll take out the gag. Stop! Stop! That's right. (T.C. takes out the gag)
There you are. Stay quiet and they won't have to gag you.	T.C.	There you are. If you stay quiet we shan't have to gag you. Good Hoot.
Good hoot.	S.C.	Good Hoot.
Good hoot.	T.C.	Catch! (She throws the gag and it lands on S.Clanger's nose and is spiked there.)
Look, it's landed on his nose.		
	T.C.	Hee Hee Hee Hee (This is too funny and the Hoot laughs)
Quick do something, stop it hooting! Quick!	T.C.	Quick! (S.C. runs the gag into the Hoot with his nose).

Tiny Clanger has an idea	T.C.	I've an idea! (She runs outside, collects a handful of notes from the music trees, brings them in.)
	T.C.	Now keep very quiet, Hoot. That's right. (S.C. pulls out the gag and Tiny Clanger throws in a handful of notes. S.C. replaces the gag.)
	T.C.	Right, now a good shake. (They shake the Hoot.)
	T.C.	There, now take out the gag... hoot for us, Hoot.
Very interesting.		
	T.C.	That's better.
	S.C.	That's good, play for us.
Very musical. Definitely an improvement, yes, yes, that seems to have solved that little problem....		(The Clangers come out and dance with each other as the Hoot plays a harp-jig.)
		Captions.

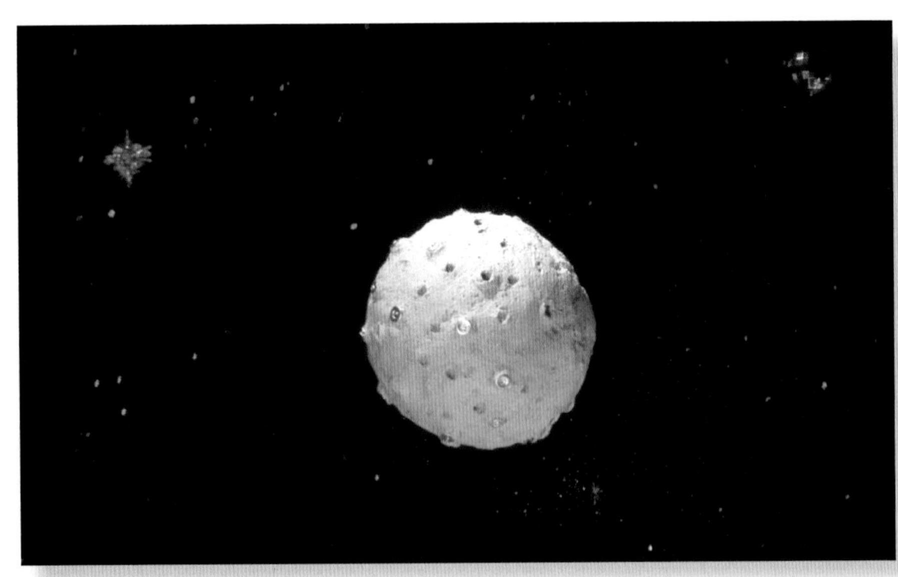

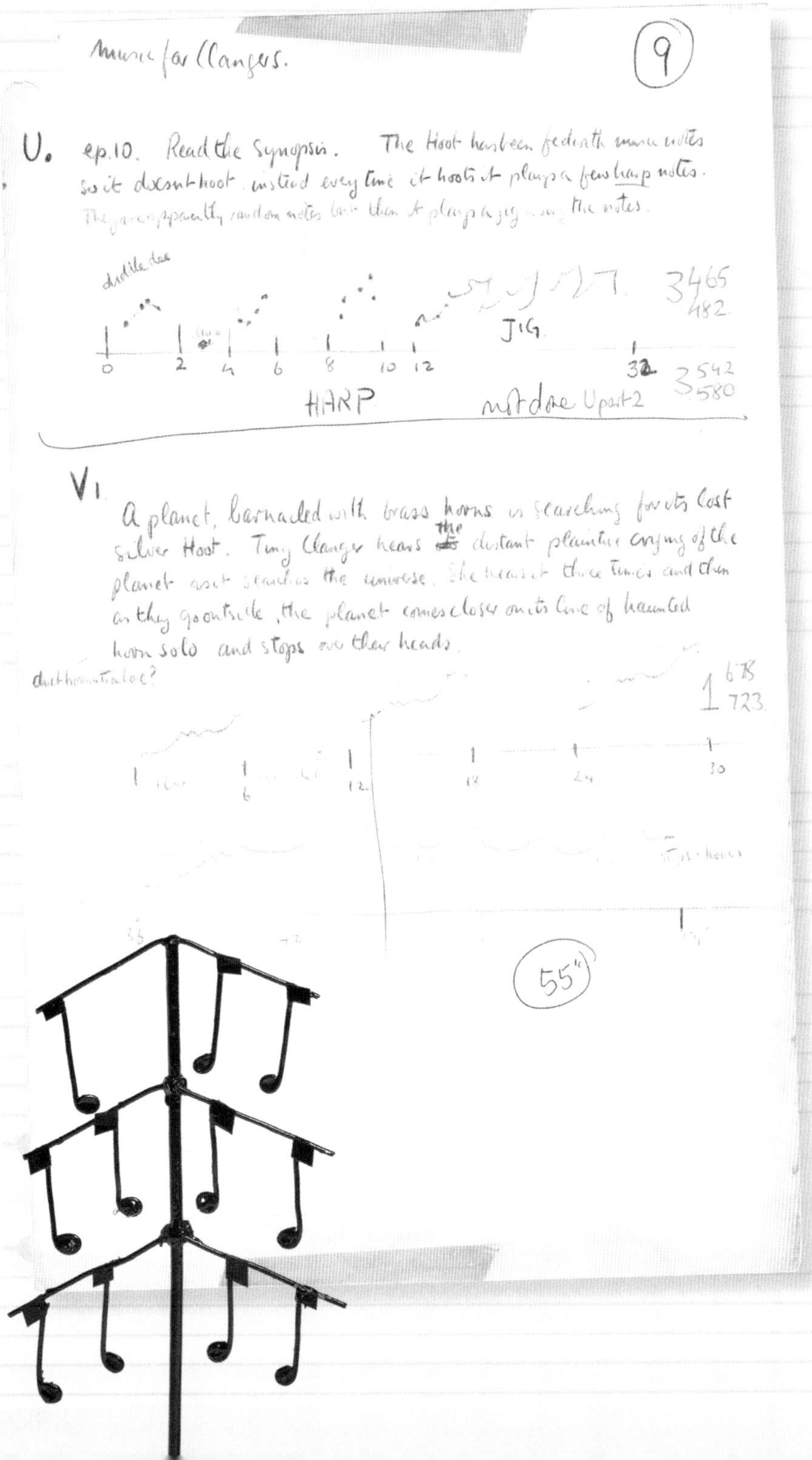

music for Clangers.

(9)

U. ep.10. Read the Synopsis. The Hoot has been fed with music notes so it doesn't hoot. instead every time it hoots it plays a few harp notes. They are apparently random notes but then it plays a jig using the notes.

diddle dee

0 2 4 6 8 10 12 32

JIG

3 465/482

3 542/580

HARP

not done U part 2

V1. A planet, barnacled with brass horns is searching for its lost silver Hoot. Tiny Clanger hears the distant plaintive crying of the planet as it searches the universe. She hears it three times and then as they go outside, the planet comes closer on its line of haunted horn solo and stops over their heads.

1 678/723

6 12 18 24 30

55"

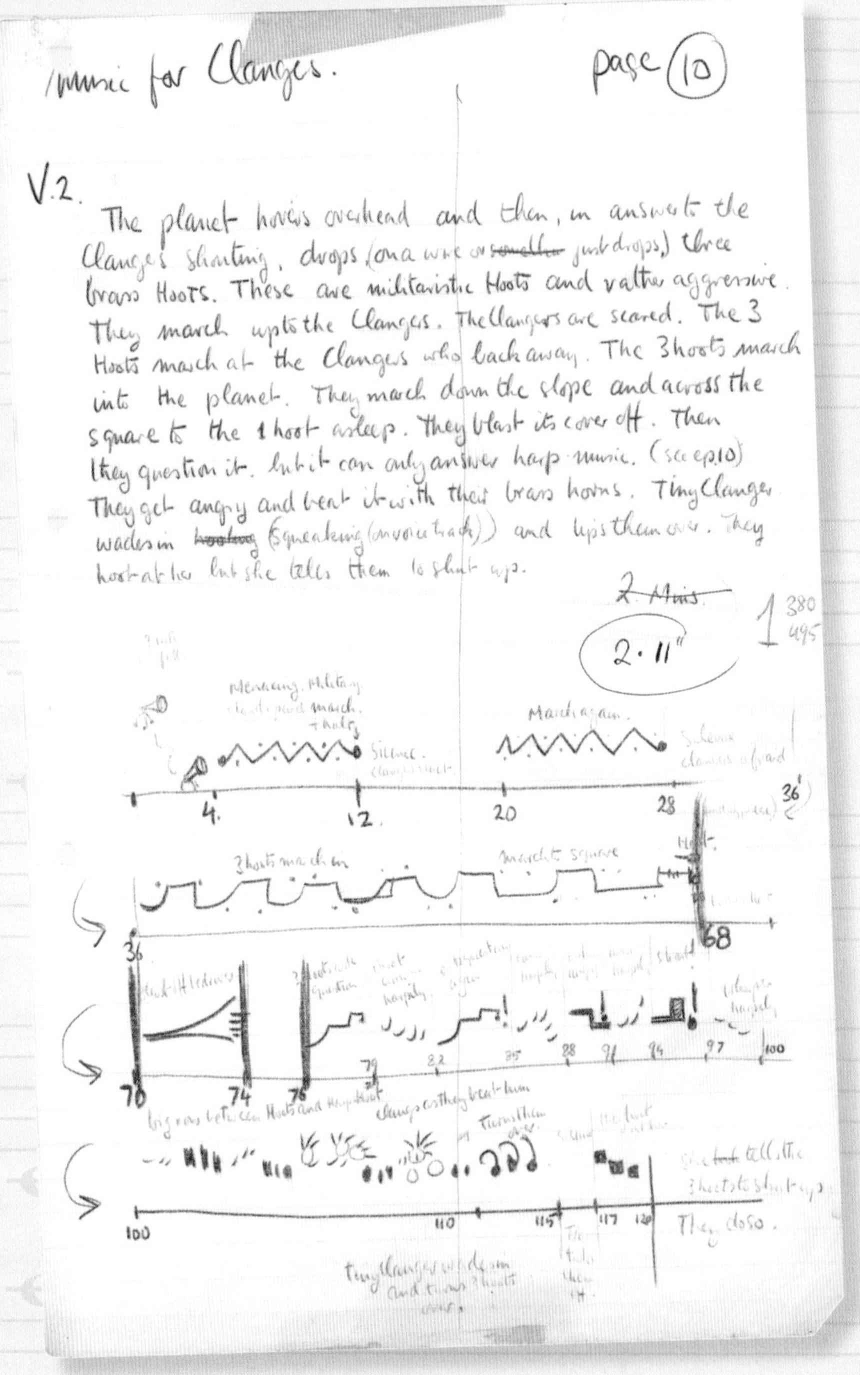

music for Clangers. page (10)

V.2.

The planet hovers overhead and then, in answer to the Clangers shouting, drops (on a wire or ~~smoke~~ just drops) three brass Hoots. These are militaristic Hoots and rather aggressive. They march up to the Clangers. The Clangers are scared. The 3 Hoots march at the Clangers who back away. The 3 hoots march into the planet. They march down the slope and across the square to the 1 hoot asleep. They blast its cover off. Then they question it. but it can only answer harp music. (see ep10) They get angry and beat it with their brass horns. Tiny Clanger wades in ~~hooting~~ (speaking (on voice track)) and tips them over. They hoot at her but she tells them to shut up.

~~2 Mins.~~

(2·11")

1 380 495

Menacing Military march. 3 hoots

Silence.

March again.

Silence

4. 12. 20 28 36'

3 hoots march in

march to square

36 68

70 74 76 79 82 85 88 91 94 97 100

100 110 115 117 120

They close.

Tiny Clanger wades in and turns 3 hoots over.

Music for Clangers. Page 11

(TC has picked up hoot and shaken out the notes. Now she stands

V.3 before it and conducts one huge, beautiful horn-note from it.
The 3 hoots are delighted and hoot "do it again"
The hoot does it again The 3 hoots are delighted again
and all the hoots dance a happy hoot-dance in a ring
with the two clangers. until Mrs Clanger comes out
and says 'do you mind some people want a bit of sleep' 1 495 535

Hoot-dance.

0 5. 10 20 40

48"

V.4. The four hoots have returned to their planet and the planet moves off and away on a lovely nostalgic line of French horn.

1 535 560.

10 20 30.

29"

Episode 11

The Meeting

We find the Clangers as we left them: joyfully dancing to the new voice of the Hoot. The mood is robustly upbeat, but not very far away from these 'sunlit uplands', clouds are gathering. New music is heard – forlorn and operatic. A strange new world creeps from the darkness; its inhabitants herald their arrival with calls of Wagnerian splendor.

Strange, silver visitors drop down from this new world and stiffly goose-step around the planet with singular intention: they seek to find their missing comrade. And when they do find it, they are appalled. It is not like them! It speaks with a foreign tongue, a difference which is simply intolerable! The purity of their kind is tainted and they become violent. A dismal scenario all too familiar down here on Earth.

But rejoice, because this is the Clangers' planet. Tiny and Small Clanger step into the fracas and, emptying the music notes from their Hoot friend, present a new sort of Hoot – a 'hybrid' of music tree and Hoot; a meeting of two kinds.

In a spectacular change of mood, the visitors' brittle philosophy melts away. In fact, they couldn't be more delighted – their culture has been blessed with fresh nuance and will undoubtedly become richer for it.

As Hegel would say: Thesis + Antithesis = Synthesis. And through diversity we move on.

The Clangers C11/1

Episode 11. The Meeting

Commentary track		Music and Effects track
Narrator		Music A
If we look at this little planet, this earth, our world, we can see that one side of it is dark and that one side is lit by the light of the sun. On the dark side of the world it is night-time and on the light side of the world it is daytime. And, as the world goes round, so the time of day changes for the people on the world. That is our day and our night but only for us, only on our world. We can look away from the earth and ask ourselves what time it may be on other planets and other stars. Not all of them go round once in twenty four hours like the earth does. Some may have short days and nights. Some may have no day and no night, just an everlasting twilight and the creatures who live in such a world would have to invent their own days and nights, their own times for sleeping and times for waking, for working and for dancing.		Fanfare
And there are the Clangers, dancing to their friend the hoot. You remember they filled it with notes from the music trees.		(The Clangers are dancing to the singing of their friend the hoot)
	Mrs.C.	Look at the time, my goodness it's late.
Look at the time!		(She points to the clock)
Come on everybody, time for bed. Bed-time Bed-time	Mrs.C.	Come on everybody, time for bed. Bed-time Bed-time Bed-time (The Clangers kiss each other goodnight.)
Goodnight Goodnight Clangers Goodnight, goodnight	Mrs.C.	Goodnight Tiny Clanger Goodnight Small Clanger Come along Mj. Clanger, bed-time
There, and they all settle down for sleep.		(Clangers are seen retiring. Tiny Clanger goes to her room, opens the door, picks up her rug and wraps it round her before curling up in her hole... she sits up suddenly and looks out.)
	T.C.	Oh the poor old Hoot, out there all by itself.
Oh yes, the poor old hoot all by itself.		(We see the Hoot all alone in the square. Tiny Clanger walks in with her bed-cover. She fixes it round the Hoot like a cloak.)
There that's better. Goodnight little hoot, sleep well.	T.C.	There, that's better. Goodnight little Hoot, sleep well.
Oh, I can hear music.		(She goes out, goes back to bed. We hear distant music of the Hoot's planet searching.)

I wonder what that is		(It is repeated)
	T.C.	What's that noise Small?
	S.C.	I don't know.
Yes, it's louder.		(The phrase is repeated)
	S.C.	Come on, let's go and see.
They're going outside to look.		(They run out. Outside we see the surface of the planet and the night sky. We see the Hoot-planet in the distance. T.C. and S.C. come out and wave
It's a star, a planet.		to it. It heaves to above them)
	S.C.	Ahoy there, are you looking for a small silver hoot?... ahoy there. (The planet does not answer)
	T.C.	What shall we do?
I wonder if that's where the hoot came from.	S.C.	I don't know. I don't know what it is there for. Hallo there! (The planet still doesn't answer)
Perhaps they had better go and fetch Major Clanger.	S.C.	Go indoors and fetch Mj. Clanger Quick now.
	T.C.	Right-ho. (She runs indoors, runs to Mj. Clanger's hole, wakes him up.)
	T.C.	There's a big *thing* outside in the sky. We don't know what it is.
Poor Major Clanger, he was asleep.	Mj.C.	All right, I'll come. (Mj. Clanger emerges and goes with T.C.)
	S.C.	There is something going on, look...
	Mj.C.	Oh yes, I think there is.
Things falling out of it. Three hoots. I hope they're ffiendly.		(Three hoots fall from the planet. They approach the Clangers with martial gait).
Well the Clangers are friendly anyway. They are always very polite to visitors.	Mj.C.	Good morning Hoots, have you come to find your friend?
	S.C.	He's downstairs, indoors.
	T.C.	I expect he'll be pleased to see you. (The three Hoots approach again, driving the Clangers in front of them.)
They don't seem to be very friendly do they?	Mj.C.	Here I say! There's no need to be unfriendly. We haven't done you any harm you know.
The other hoot wasn't noisy and pushing and unpleasant, so why should these hoots be like that.	S.C.	Your friend wasn't noisy and unpleasant you know so I don't see why you should be. (The three Hoots push past them and march into the planet.
Perhaps they are looking for something. (after blast) ...and they've found it, but it doesn't hoot any more. It makes music notes, pretty notes from the music trees.		They confront the Hoot in the square, blow off its bedcover and argue with it and it answers with harp-music.
They are angry.		They get angry and beat it with their horns. Tiny Clanger interferes and turns the three hoots over.)
That's right, Tiny Clanger, that's right, make them leave him alone.	T.C.	You're a rotten lot. Leave him alone! (The Hoots hoot at her.)
Yes, you tell them to shut up.	T.C.	Shut up, all of you.

	T.C.	Now then Small, come and help me. (They pick up the Silver Hoot and shake it. Out fall the music notes one by one. They stop.)
	S.C.	Is that all right? (They shake it again. There is one note left. They up-end it and shake out the note.)
That's shaken the music notes out of it. Now we'll see what sort of noise it makes.	S.C.	That's all I think. (They stand up the hoot. Tiny Clanger stands in front of it, raises her baton and
That's better. music V.3 That's marvellous! and they like it.		conducts one huge beautiful horn note. The three Hoots are delighted. They all dance a Hoot-dance together until Mrs. Clanger wakes up and looks out.
	G.C.	Here! Here! Here! This is no time for singing and
Oh yes, Look at the time. Bed-time. Clangers want to sleep. Be quiet! quiet! quiet (whisper)		dancing, look at the clock. It's bed-time, Look! Bed-time. Now you lot be quiet Quiet! Quiet!
listen	T.C.	Listen! (we hear the faint call of the planet.)
Time for hoots to go home.	T.C.	Time to go, come on. (T.C. and S.C. pick up see-saws and lead the Hoots outside. There they set up the see-saws and wallop the four Hoots up to their planet.)
	All	Goodbye.
Goodbye Hoots. and away they sail away to their distant musical constellation somewhere in the sky.		Goodbye Hoots Goodbye. (They watch the hoot-planet sailaway to distant constellations.)
		(Captions)

Episode 12

Treasure

As the advent of the music boat brings the Clangers out of an age of relative isolation and new opportunities present themselves with every fresh catch, we must ask ourselves: is this good? As we here on Earth know all too well, every step into a brave new world brings at least as many problems as advantages.

If Tiny Clanger had not cast her line off into the darkness at the start of this episode, she'd have remained blissfully unaware of the immediate corrupting power of coinage. As soon as she returns with her haul it begins to lead her down a dark path. Shockingly, she attempts to buy the silence of her own grandmother. And as the story unfolds we find her becoming ever more isolated, even turning her back on a good game of cotton ball.

For many, the reality of currency is troubling – if it merely represents wealth, where is this so-called wealth kept and what is it made out of? And there's good reason to be wary; it's all just a kind of modern witchcraft where the witches wear suits and bowler hats and, as we know, the whole thing can collapse around our ears at any moment.

Luckily Tiny's treasure has a solid, tangible value everyone can understand. Peel away the fool's gold and find within a dark pleasure far more enjoyable... Chocolate!

Episode 12. Treasure

Commentary track		Music and Effects track
Narrator This world of ours, this cloudy planet, warmed by the Sun, protected from the dangers of space by a thick overcoat of warm atmosphere is a cosy, pleasant place to live. We know it is because we live there. Millions of us, all together, the human race... But if, in our imaginations we turn away from the earth and think about other planets, other less fortunate stars, we realise that life there might be very different, very bleak and dull. The solitary fisher setting off to catch what she can in the vast empty spaces of the universe may feel very much alone.		Music B Fanfare
There is Tiny Clanger, fishing from the music boat.		(Tiny Clanger stands up and starts to cast about with her rod.
There is something coming. She's caught it!		She casts, clinks as she catches something. She reels in.)
I wonder what it is.	T.C.	Ooh what's this?
A net, full of gold coins!		Oh a net-ful of gold things.
		(She pulls in the net of gold coins, spins the wheel and descends.
What a marvellous thing to have caught, a bag full of treasure and all for Tiny Clanger.		She climbs out, looks furtively to left and right. She lifts out the bag of coins and looks at them miserly.)
And she drags them indoors very secretly, very quietly.	T.C.	Ooh hoo-hoo hoo-hoo
		(She chortles with delight, looks furtively around her and drags the sack of coins furtively indoors. Grannie Clanger comes out of her little hole under the ramp and watches.)
	G.C.	Hallo Tiny Clanger, what have you got?
oooh! She's dropped them.		(T.C. jerks with alarm. The bag drops over the ramp. T.C. tries to catch it and they both fall on Grannie Clanger.)
	G.C.	Here here look out! Look out!
	T.C.	Ssh! sh! sssh be quiet.
Hush! be quiet.	G.C.	Why should I?
	T.C.	I'm creeping in with treasure.
She's creeping in with treasure.		Here, I'll give you one. (She gives G.C. a coin.)
	T.C.	Ssh!
Hussshh!		
	G.C.	Sssh! all right ssssh! (Tiny Clanger creeps away dragging the sack of treasure. Grannie Clanger looks closely at the coin. She shakes her head.)
Grannie Clanger doesn't want that. (calling)	G.C.	I don't want this thing. Here you are! (She throws the coin at T.C. Tiny Clanger trips again.)

	T.C.	Eeek! (The bag breaks and the coins roll down into the square.)
Look, what funny-looking things! Look, round shiny things. Whatever are they for?	C.1.	Look there, what funny looking things. (He picks up a coin.)
	C.2.	Hi, look at these. (He picks a couple of coins.)
	C.1.	Yes they're good.
	Mj.C.) S.C.)	What have you got?
Tiny Clanger brought them in and dropped them.	C.2	Tiny Clanger has brought these in.
They are mine! says Tiny Clanger. They are mine, mine. I found them and they are	S.C.	Oh aren't they pretty.
mine! (off)	T.C.	They're mine. They are mine. I found them. Mine. (She walks in, takes the coins from their hands and piles them on the table.)
	T.C.	They are mine, I found them.
	C.1.	All right.
	C.2.	All right then. (The Clangers carry the coins to the table. They pile them up on the net-sack.)
	S.C.	There you are then.
	T.C.	Thankyou.
and Tiny Clanger drags her treasure away, up to her private cave.		(She wraps the coins in the net and drags them behind her up to room. The baby dragon comes to watch.)
	B.D.	What's going on?
There's the baby dragon.	S.C.	I don't know.
	B.D.	Come on, let's play ball.
Oh! he's come to play ball with the Clangers. They often play ball together, but today Tiny Clanger is busy.		(The baby dragon and S.C. play with a cotton-wool ball but after a few seconds they stop and look at T.C. She is counting the coins onto the shelf beside her.)
	T.C.	Two, three, four, five.
(off)	S.C.	Are you coming down to play ball Tiny Clanger?
No, I think she is too busy	T.C.	Six, seven.
to play ball. (off)	S.C.	Are you coming?
She is counting her treasure.	T.C.	No, I'm busy, can't you see I'm counting my money... eight, nine, ten. (S.C. and the Baby Dragon look at each other.. shrug, and go on playing ball. Mrs. Clanger comes out with the soup-jug.)
Now here is mother clanger.	Mrs.C.	Hi, Tiny Clanger. Please will you fetch some soup.
She needs soup, but I'm afraid Tiny Clanger is too busy polishing her money to fetch soup.	T.C.	But I can't. I must look after my money.
	Mrs.C.	Why?
	T.C.	Because I must.
	Mrs.C.	But we need soup.
	T.C.	Well ask Small to get it. I'm busy. (She points to Small Clanger who is enjoying himself playing ball with the Baby Dragon.)
It's not worth it, she'll go and fetch the soup herself.	Mrs.C.	Oh it's not worth it. I'll go myself. (She puts the jug on the trolley and takes it herself. Mj. Clanger comes out with some cups)

	Mj.C.	Come and help me lay the table please, Tiny Clanger.
Help lay the table? Well as a matter of fact she really thinks she should stay and look after her treasure. Perhaps somebody else would help lay the table.	T.C.	Well, as a matter of fact I don't think I had better. Really I should stay here and look after the money. Could you perhaps ask...
Small Clanger for instance.	Mj.C.	Oh all right. All right. Here you are, Small Clanger, put these things out please. (Small Clanger and the Baby Dragon stop playing and Small Clanger puts out the tea-things. The Baby Dragon sees the pile of money and creeps up on it.)
Look, look out! Baby Dragon's after your money!		
	T.C.	Eeek! Go away! Go away! shooo! shoo! (The Baby Dragon turns and runs away. He and S.C. laugh.)
But it's only a joke, he wouldn't really steal Tiny Clanger's treasure.	S.C.	Hee! hee! hee!
	B.D.	Ta ta!
Bye Bye Baby dragon.	S.C.	Bye bye! (The Baby Dragon leaves. Mj.C. and S.C. sit down to tea. Another two Clangers join them and sit down.)
	Mj.C.	Come and sit down Tiny Clanger.
	T.C.	In a minute. I am just polishing my money. (Mrs.C. comes back with the soup)
Here we are then, here's mother clanger with the soup.	Mrs.C.	Here we are then. Where's Tiny?
Where's Tiny?		
	Mj.C.	Up there.
Tiny should be sitting at the table.		
	Mrs.C.	Now Tiny Clanger, you must come down at once.
	T.C.	No.
	Mrs.C.	Come down I say and have your tea.
	T.C.	No.
	Mrs.C.	You do as you're told young Clanger.
She's dropped it. She's spilt the money and the soup!	T.C.	No, no, no, no, eeek! (She turns and spills the pile of money. It slides down, turns over the trolley... and spills the soup.)
Now she can just wipe it up.	Mrs.C.	Now look what you have done. Come and wipe it up at once! (T.C. climbs down and starts to wipe it up.)
Soup, they want soup.	C.1.	Soup, where's our soup?
They had better ask Tiny Clanger about that.	Mrs.C.	Soup, you'd better ask her about that!
	S.C.	Soup! I want soup.
Soup! Soup!	All	soup soup soup want soup soup! (T.C. picks up a coin and carries it over to the table.)
There you are, what about that?	T.C.	There you are. (Mj. Clanger looks at the coin. He picks it up, sniffs at it, turns it over. T.C. goes back to wiping up.)

Will that do instead of soup? No I don't think it will. They can't eat that!	Mj.C.	Here! Here! This is no good! We can't eat this! (T.C. turns to look at them, she droops.)
Soup! soup! they want soup. Tiny Clanger will just have to fetch some more soup.	All.	Soup! soup! soup! We want soup. (T.C. picks up the soup-jug and puts it on the trolley. S.C. is nosing at the coin.)
What's this? The covering has come off.	S.C.	Here I say, look at this. (He peels the gold off the chocolate penny.)
Brown stuff inside.	S.C.	Look. (He picks up the chocolate penny)
	S.C.	(Sniff) ooh, smells nice. (He bites it.)
Tastes nice. Yes, Small Clanger likes that.	S.C.	(eating) hmm, delicious, hmm. I like that, that's good.
	Mj.C.	Let me taste it.. that's nice.
Delicious, hmm very nice.	T.C.	Here you are. (She runs across with more coins)
Oh well, in that case, Tiny Clanger knows what to do.		Here you are. (She puts coins on the table. They all start to eat. T.C. runs with coins to Grannie Clanger. She runs up to another Clanger in its hole and gives it a coin.
(on chewing) Very nice, very delicious.		Then she takes the jug and trolley and two coins and rolls off to the soup-wells. The Clangers are all eating chocolate.
And here we are at the soup-wells.		T.C. arrives at the soup-wells. She runs up to the dragon.)
	T.C.	Here, taste one of these!
	D.	Chocolate pennies, delightful!
hm chocolate pennies	T.C.	You have one, Baby Dragon.
delicious.	B.D.	Ta very much! (munch munch)
	D.	Soup? D'you want soup?
Soup, ah yes, don't forget the soup.	T.C.	Oh yes please, I'm afraid I spilt the last lot.
	D.	Ah well, not to worry. (pouring)
There we are		Here you are.
	T.C.	Thankyou, bye bye.
	D.	You're welcome, bye bye (munch, munch). Nice aren't they?
	B.D.	Scrumptious. (The Clangers have finished. T.C. brings the trolley to the road by the table and walks down to the table. There are some empty cases but no coins.
Look, all gone, every single piece of chocolate treasure is eaten. Not one left for Tiny Clanger.		T.C. droops. She sits in her place and looks away. S.C. walks up to her.)
	S.C.	Here, you have one too.
Ah no, Small Clanger has saved her one.	T.C.	Thankyou. (She takes the coin and wonders what to do. She takes it upstairs and puts it where the others were. She sits by it
She will have to look after it very carefully.		drooping slightly. The others are clearing away leaving Small Clanger in the square. The Baby Dragon appears with the cotton-wool ball.)

C12/5

S.C. Are you coming to play ball?

T.C. No. (shakes her head)

(S.C. and B.D. play ball.)

No, Tiny Clanger hasn't time to play ball. Tiny Clanger must look after her treasure.

(T.C. watches them. In the end she can bear it no longer.)

T.C. Wait for me, I'm coming!

The treasure?
What about the treasure?

(She jumps to her feet and clambers down out of shot. Then she climbs back into shot, unwraps the chocolate, stuffs it into her mouth as she runs out.)

T.C. Come on then!

Oh, oh well that's that then. Perhaps it's just as well, after all, what would Clangers want with real money? You can't eat it can you? and it isn't nearly as much fun to play with as a cotton-wool ball from the cotton-wool tree.

(The three play ball and chase about.)

(Captions.

Episode 13

Goods

Again, the Clangers attempt to finish their Stonehenge-like construction, and again they are forced to abandon it and take cover as an unexpected object falls from the sky, knocking the building for six.

One is moved to wonder if the Clangers' mysterious building may have some sort of religious significance – are the Clangers drawn to such matters? The question becomes all the more poignant when the building project is abandoned and instead the new object is assembled and utilised. It is a machine that produces endless varieties of plastic objects, and when it is accidentally set to 'automatic' by the Soup Dragon it will not stop.

The Clangers are initially quite taken with some of the products; they might prove useful. But as more and more stuff pours out of the machine, the cave soon becomes so filled with an ever-growing pile of plastic commodities it resembles a landfill site here on Earth, and the Clangers become justifiably alarmed.

Is the rude demolition of the Clangers' 'temple' by a maker of shoddy trinkets a remark on our own 'spiritual' predicament? The ocean of tat which now blights the Clangers' home is certainly a consequence we know all too well, as we continue to amass temples of junk in our efforts to worship the god of consumerism.

For us it's a pickle we've yet to solve. For the Clangers, thanks to their new friends the Froglets, a remedy is quickly found.

If only we on Earth had a magic top hat.

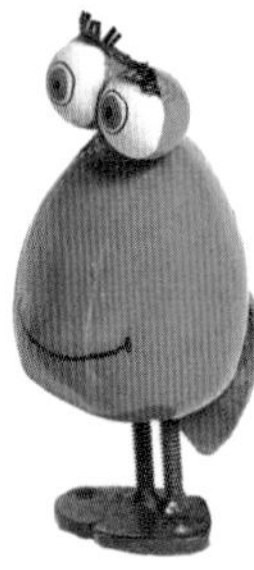

Episode 13. Goods

Commentary track		Music and Effects track
Narrator		Music B
If we look at this earth of ours, this little planet where we live, we would never realise, just from looking at it, how complex and convenient the lives of the people who live there have become. One can see no factories, no roads, cars or railways, no toothbrushes, no plastic mixing bowls, transistor radios or alarm clocks. None of the millions of articles that man manufactures to comfort his short life. By comparison we can imagine how dull and empty must be the lives of beings on other planets which do not enjoy the benefits of a modern industrial civilization. How hard and simple and sometimes dangerous.		Fanfare
		(The Clangers are building a stonehenge.)
	C.1.	Look up there.
There's something coming.		Look! something coming!
Look out!	C.2.	Run!
Look out!	all	Run! Run! Run.
Get below!		(They run below and clang the lids down. They crouch below and listen to debris falling.
wait for it! oooh!		No more falls and they climb out. They inspect the damage.)
	Mj.C.	The whole thing is bashed to bits.
The whole thing is smashed to pieces but look at all that extraordinary stuff.	C.1.	Yes, but look at all this extraordinary stuff.
It looks like part of a machine.	Mj.C.	Yes, but what use is it? I don't know.
Yes, look the pieces join together, that piece will join on to the other piece.	S.C.	The pieces seem to join together. Look, this piece joins on that one in the middle.
	T.C.	And this one is a wheel.
The best thing would be to take all the pieces indoors and try and fit them together.	Mj.C.	Let's take all the pieces indoors and see what we can make of them.
	S.C.	All right, lets do that. (The Clangers carry them in. Tiny Clanger looks around to find any last pieces. Indoors the Clangers are busy assembling the pieces of the extraordinary-looking machine. Small Clanger goes out to look for Tiny Clanger.)
	S.C.	What are you doing?
Now, what has Tiny Clanger found?	T.C.	Looking at this. (S.C. goes across to T.C. and looks at the thing.)
	T.C.	What do you think it is?
That must be part of the machine.	S.C.	I don't know. (The thing is a wheel, marked with slots and symbols like bowler-hats and spoons, teapots, etc.)
	S.C.	It must be part of the machine.

They had better take that indoors.	T.C.	We'd better take it in. Come on. (They take the wheel downstairs. The machine is nearly finished. Mj. Clanger is looking puzzled.)
	T.C.	We found this.
	Mj.C.	Oh good, that will go on here. Give it to me! Thankyou. (He fits the wheel on and skilfully assembles the last part of the machine. A Clanger is filling a hopper on top with granules from a plastic bag, and another is threading in a roll of coloured lavatory paper.
That machine looks more or less complete.	Mj.C.	Are you all set up there?
	C.1.	Yes, that seems right.
	Mj.C.	Good, then we'll try it. Stand clear. (Mj. Clanger winds a handle, pulls a long lever, winds another handle, slides a slider along, pulls a rope and collapses exhausted. The machine goes on by itself and then triumphantly produces a very small teaspoon.)
Oooh	T.C.	Oooh.
Ooh.	Mrs.C.	Oooh
Isn't that lovely.	All	Ooh ooh ooh.
What is it?	S.C.	What is it?
It's a teaspoon of course.	Mrs.C.	It's a teaspoon of course for gardening. (Mj. C. has recovered. He gets up, sets the dial again and works the machine again. This time it produces a tin teapot.)
A teapot, yes, a plastic teapot.	T.C.	Look at this! This is good! It's a trumpet. (She blows it.)
	S.C.	Do something for me please.
Oh poor Major Clanger, he's exhausted. He's tired out. Small Clanger can have a try.	Mj.C.	No I'm exhausted, you try. (Small Clanger works the machine which produces a tiny jelly-mould.)
A hat, a pretty hat.	Mrs.C.	A hat! a pretty hat. (She picks it up and puts it on)
Look dragon, admire her pretty hat.	Mrs.C.	Look, dragon, my pretty hat. (The soup-dragon who has come to see what is happening looks closely at the machine. She sees a piece of wire and a rod sticking out.)
	D.	What's this then?
Ah now, what's this?	Mj.C.	I don't know.
A key.	D.	I think it's a key.
	Mj.C.	Where does it connect?
It fits into that switch and it turns on a motor.	D.	I think it fits in here. (Mj.C. pushes in the flex and rod. There is a whirring sound.)
	D.	There you are it's electric. I must get back to my cooking. (The dragon goes away while Mj. Clanger turns to the machine. He sets the dial, pulls a lever. The machine makes its noise and produces swiftly a small bowler hat. Mj. Clanger puts it on.)

A hat for Major Clanger.	Mj.C.	How do I look?
Very pretty.	All	Oooh oooh very pretty.
	C.l.	May I have one too please?
	S.C.	And me too
	All	And one for me too
And of course, they all want one.		
Major Clanger will make them all hats.	Mj.C.	Certainly. (He walks up to the machine and pulls the lever. The machine whirrs into life, produces six bowler hats in a line.)
	S.C.	Thankyou. (Mj. Clanger nonchalantly switches off the machine but it
Thankyou that will do!		goes on working, instead of bowler-hats it starts
Er, stop it now Major Clanger.		producing top-hats. Mj.Clanger pulls another lever, but the machine only goes
He can't stop it without the key!		faster. He pulls out the plug. The machine goes on. It produces piles of patent tin openers, plastic cups, handy plastic boxes, and fancy goods of all types. Mj. Clanger tries all the levers but only succeeds in changing the type of articles. In the end he runs to the Soup-Dragon and tells her what is happening. The Soup-Dragon comes running and sees the huge pile of consumer goods. She leaps on the machine and does battle with it. In the end it is vanquished and
Oh, stopped at last.		all is still.)
What a lot of things.	Mrs.C.	Oh dear. (The dragon climbs out of the pile of things.)
	D.	That's done for it. It's dead now. (She walks away.)
They don't want all that stuff!		
	Mrs.C.	I don't want all this stuff!
What are they going to do with it all.		What are we going to do with it?
They could drop it into a hole perhaps.	S.C.	Let's put it down this hole. Like this. (He drops a jelly-mould down the hole. There is a croaking sound
Oh perhaps not.		and it shoots out again.)
	S.C.	Oh (A froglet jumps out of the hole)
Ah a froglet. Perhaps the froglets can think of something.	S.C.	Sorry I thought it was empty. We want to get rid of all this rubbish. The froglet calls down the hole to his fellows.
Ah the top-hat.		Up comes the top-hat they arrived in some episodes ago and a handkerchief, followed by two more froglets. The froglets climb under the handkerchief,
They are going to do a conjuring trick.		lift it on to the top-hat.)

A woolly rabbit	F.	(croaks Hey presto) (They pull back the handkerchief and show a woolly rabbit. All the frogs laugh. Mj. Clanger picks it up.)
Yes but that's no good. They want to get rid of things not collect more things!	Mj.C.	That's no good. We want to get rid of things, not collect more.
Tiny Clanger likes it,	T.C.	I'll have it, I like it! I want it.
but no there are too many things already.	Mj.C.	No there is too much stuff here already. (He puts the woolly rabbit back in the hat. It vanishes.)
It's vanished, it's gone.	Mj.C.	It's gone! (The frogs laugh)
Perhaps they could vanish other things.	S.C.	We put the stuff in the hat. (The frogs jump about with amusement. The Clangers pile in the objects including the pieces of machine. In the end there is nothing left but the hat.)
And that's the last thing. (clop) Gone!	Mj.C.	There, that's done.. whew!
Poor Major Clanger he's worn out! Woolly rabbit Woolly rabbit	T.C.	Woolly rabbit, I want woolly rabbit. Woolly rabbit, out of there!
Tiny Clanger wants that woolly rabbit. And there it is.	Mj.C.	Oh, froglets, would you mind? (The frogs laugh as they lay the handkerchief over again and pull it off - there is the woolly rabbit. Mj. Clanger picks it out.)
Say thankyou to the froglets.	Mj.C.	Here you are then, say thankyou to the froglets. (T.C. crosses to the froglets, thanks each in turn.)
	T.C.	Thankyou
	F.	(craak)
	T.C.	Thankyou
	F.	(craak)
	T.C.	Thankyou
	F.	(craak)
	Mj.C.	Thank you froglets. (The froglets laugh and two jump into their hole.)
Don't forget the hat	Mj.C.	Don't forget the hat. (The last froglet jumps into the hat. It vanishes, leaving the froglet standing there.)
	Mj.C.	Goodnight.
	F.	(croak)
Goodnight froglets Goodnight Clangers Yes, the place does look a bit empty without all those plastic things. But you know, I think the Clangers may be better off without them.		(The froglet jumps down the hole. Tiny Clanger takes her father's hand, and with the woolly rabbit under her arm they "walk away into the sunset".)
		(Captions)

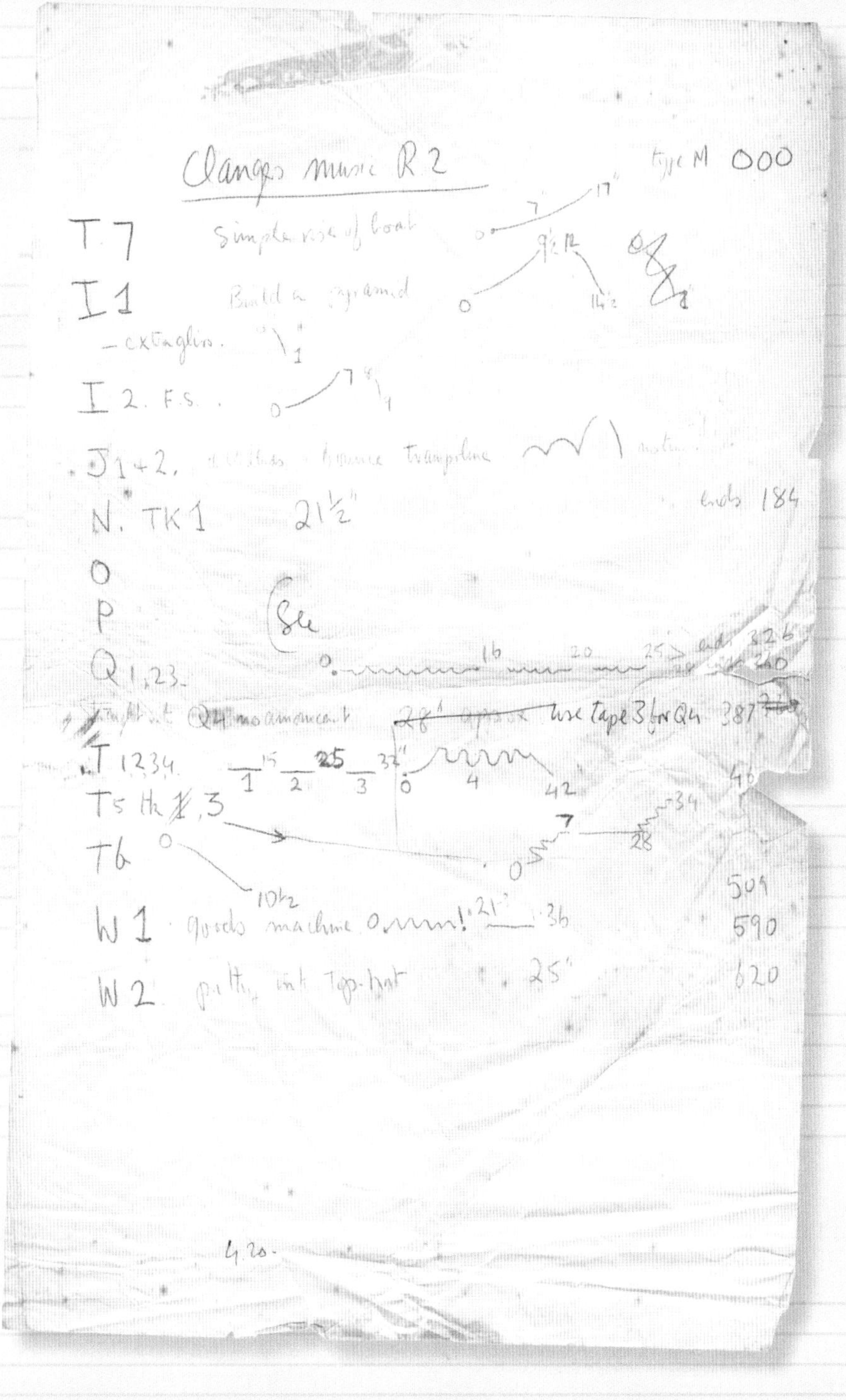

Clangers music R 2 type M 000

T 7 Simple rise of boat 0 7" 17"

I 1 Build a pyramid 0 9½ 12 14½

– extinguish.

I 2. F.S. 0 7 8 9

J 1 + 2. acrobats bounce trampoline

N. TK 1 21½" ends 184

O

P

Q 1, 2, 3. 0 16 20 25 ends 326

~~Q4~~ Q4 no announcement ~~28' approx~~ use tape 3 for Q4 387

T 1, 2, 3, 4. 1 15 2 25 3 32" 0 4 42 46

T5 Hz ~~1~~, 3 7 28 34

T6 0 10½ 0

W 1 goods machine 0 21" 36 504 590

W 2 putting into top-hat 25" 620

4.20.

The Clangers. Music Tape. Reel 1

Tape starts on M. deck. at 000. 0000

A fanfare 5½. creepy. 29, 42, 54. Sonorous. 1.12 > 1.22 0127

B. " 5½. creepy. 24. Sonorous. 51" 0198

C fanfare. 4. Cond. 11 Cond. 18" 0230

No announcement.. D + E and E 1 Xylo glisses 20 ups + 20 downs. = 12" 253

F take 1
flute up. 5. wriggly 14. dancy. 17 > 21 292

G3. flute 3. -6. 10 12½. wavy. 23. dancy breaks. 39. bonk bonk bonk 41" 342

faster. G 3A. 2½ 5 8. 10. wavy 18 . . 31. bonks 32 380

green

V2. TK2 falling 1½ (Retake 6½) falling 4½ 5 march 14 19 march 29½
35 main march! 1.09½ 1.14 question + answer 1.47
battle 2.06 2.08 shout. 2.12 485

straight into V.3. 0 note 4 5 reply 9 11 Note again 23. 24 jig 33 42 48 535

straight into V.4. 0. 10 harp 30 560

K TK1 0 18 34 38 574 600

H 1, 2, 3. (2 false starts at beginning) 0 1 35 0 2 28 0 3 15 26 29 H1 637 H2 657 H3 678

V.1 tk 1 0 5½ 13 21½ 25½ 35 39½ 64 723

G4 + 4A 0 15 0 9½ 745.

G5 tk 1 = fragment. very good + fast only 7" usable.

G6 tk 1 Chat. fluttered last 3 secs. only 8 secs. 781.

G6 Xylo 0 4. 805.

G7. no announcement G7. 0 7 18½ 23. 815

M TK1 0 11 13

J 142

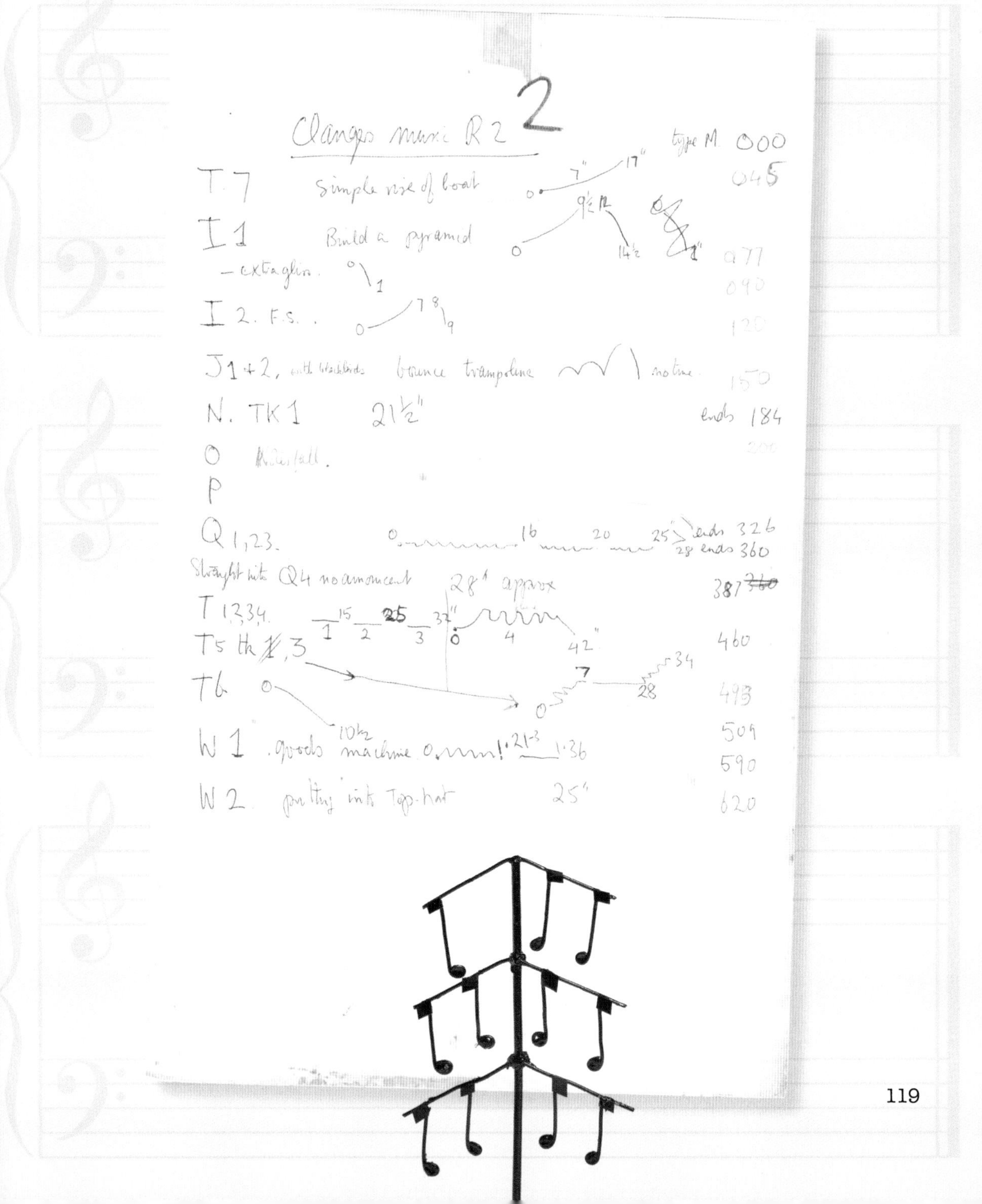

2

Clangers music R 2

type M. 000

T 7 simple rise of boat 0 7" 17" 045

I 1 Build a pyramid 0 9½ 12 14½ 8" 077

– extraglim. 0 1 090

I 2. F.S. 0 7 8 9 120

J 1 + 2, with blackbirds bounce trampoline no time 150

N. TK 1 21½" ends 184

O Waterfall. 200

P

Q 1,2,3. 0 16 20 25" ends 326 28 ends 360

Straight into Q4 no announcement 28" approx 387 ~~360~~

T 1,2,3,4. 1 15 2 25 3 32" 0 4 42" 460

T5 th ~~1~~,3

T6 0 10½ 0 7 28 34 493

W 1 goods machine 0 1.21.3 1.36 509 590

W 2 putting into Top-hat 25" 620

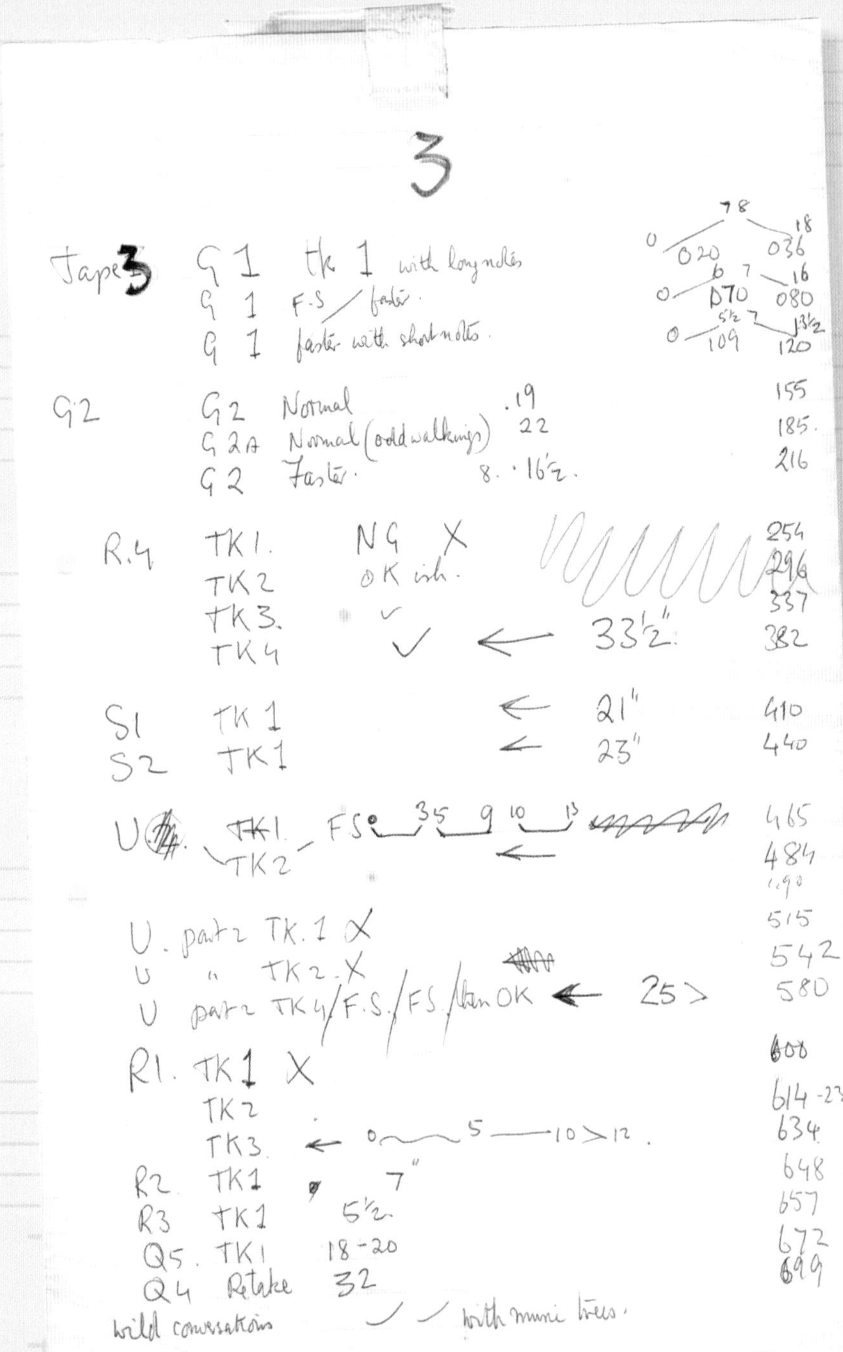

3

Tape 3 G 1 tk 1 with long notes
G 1 F.S / faster.
G 1 faster with short notes.

0 020 036 18
0 070 080 16
0 109 120 13½

G2 G2 Normal .19 155
G 2A Normal (odd walkings) 22 185.
G 2 Faster. 8. · 16½. 216

R.4 TK1. NG X 254
TK2 OK ish. 296
TK3. ✓ 337
TK4 ✓ ← 33½". 382

S1 TK 1 ← 21" 410
S2 TK1 ← 23" 440

U TK1 FS 35 9 10 13 465
TK2 ← 484
490

U. part 2 TK. 1 X 515
U " TK 2. X 542
U part 2 TK 4 / F.S. / FS / then OK ← 25 > 580

R1. TK 1 X 608
TK 2 614-23
TK3 ← 0 5 10 > 12. 634
R2 TK1 7" 648
R3 TK1 5½. 657
Q5. TK1 18-20 672
Q4 Retake 32 699
wild conversations ✓ ✓ with music trees.

Tape 4.

P, group

P1 /°theme 1/5. or repeat 0—6½

P2 0/ theme 1 4½/ gap 1½ 6/ theme 1 9/

P.3. 0/ theme 2. 4/ gap 3 7/ theme 2 /9. 104

11/ theme 1 and theme 2/16

129

P4 0/ theme 3 /6

/ th1 / th2. / th3.. /16

151

P5 0 tune 1 repeat P4

tune 1 9

10½ tune 3 17½

~~tune 3~~

P1 repeat 0 - 6½

da di doo di dady doo doo

dady doo doo 6

8 dady doo doo 11

dady doo do 15

dady doo doo 19

P. 6 allow. 5 secs

3 Seesaw bonks. 4½. all same bar end. bonk.

Clangers II. Music Reel 5

035

2A. TK1 7" ends 048.
069
2B TK2 6"–8" ends 082
090
2C. TK2 14 – 15. ends 114
130
2D. TK1 8. – 12 > 20 ends 157.
chat. 196.
3A TK3. 2.11. ends 327
338.
4B TK.1. 15. — 25. — 29 \ 33" ends 370 short
380
4B TK2. F.S. ends 385.
387
4B TK 3. 7. — 19. — 30 \ 39 ends 423 long
426
4C TK.2 .4 — 14 — 26 waltz. 41. ends 462.
472
8C TK1 — 6, 9. –18 plong 21. ends 491.
499
8E TK1 hooty up 9. 13. viols up. 25 happy down 32
ominous 40 happy. 49 Bassoon pips 58
ominous up. 1.06 droppy. 1.12. down 1.20.
pumping. 1.22. ends 560
567
8E TK2. 1.20. ends 625.
633
11C TK1 - 24" - 41 ends 662 — 668
- 11C TK2 higher clarinet 42 ends 695 — 698
13C TK2. 9. 18. oboe. 26. flute. 36. pizz 44.
pizz 57. viols. 1.02. down. 1.12.
horns. 1.31. oboe bassoon. flute 1.46.
1.55. 2.03. violin coda 2.20 end. 2.32 790

Changes II Music Reel 6

			000
			020
13BD?	Tk 1	solo 18" tutti 43"	ends 082
~~3B~~	~~Tk2~~.		095
3B	Tk2	22"	ends. 122
			152
8A	TK1	(jumps at 17/21, 28/30, 47/50, 61/63) 64"	ends. 224.
			~~238~~ 245.
10D	TK1	(50) 59".	ends 305
			310
10D again, slower.		1.12".	ends 378
			385
8D	TK. 1	15" (Nice slow dropping)	ends 400
			410
13B	TK 3.	5" 17" 34" gap 45" phrases/ 465 xylo/ 478 xylo	ends 485
			489
8B.	TK2.	0 — 9) 11½.	ends 500
			510
12A	TK.4	6" - 29	ends 534
			548
4A	TK.1	raspy, raspy high, (hollowed, (slide out short) 567 short long longer. 580	ends. 580
			586
13A (2nd Part)	TK2.	10"	597
			600
10A	TK2	0-12. 610 14-28 622. 32-43 632 47.-60	642.

Short blank at end

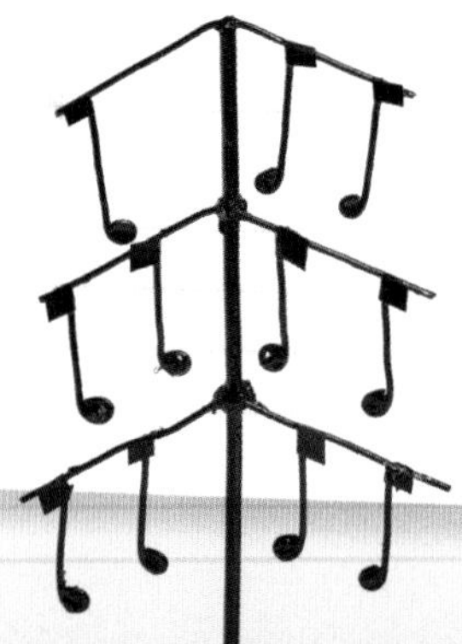

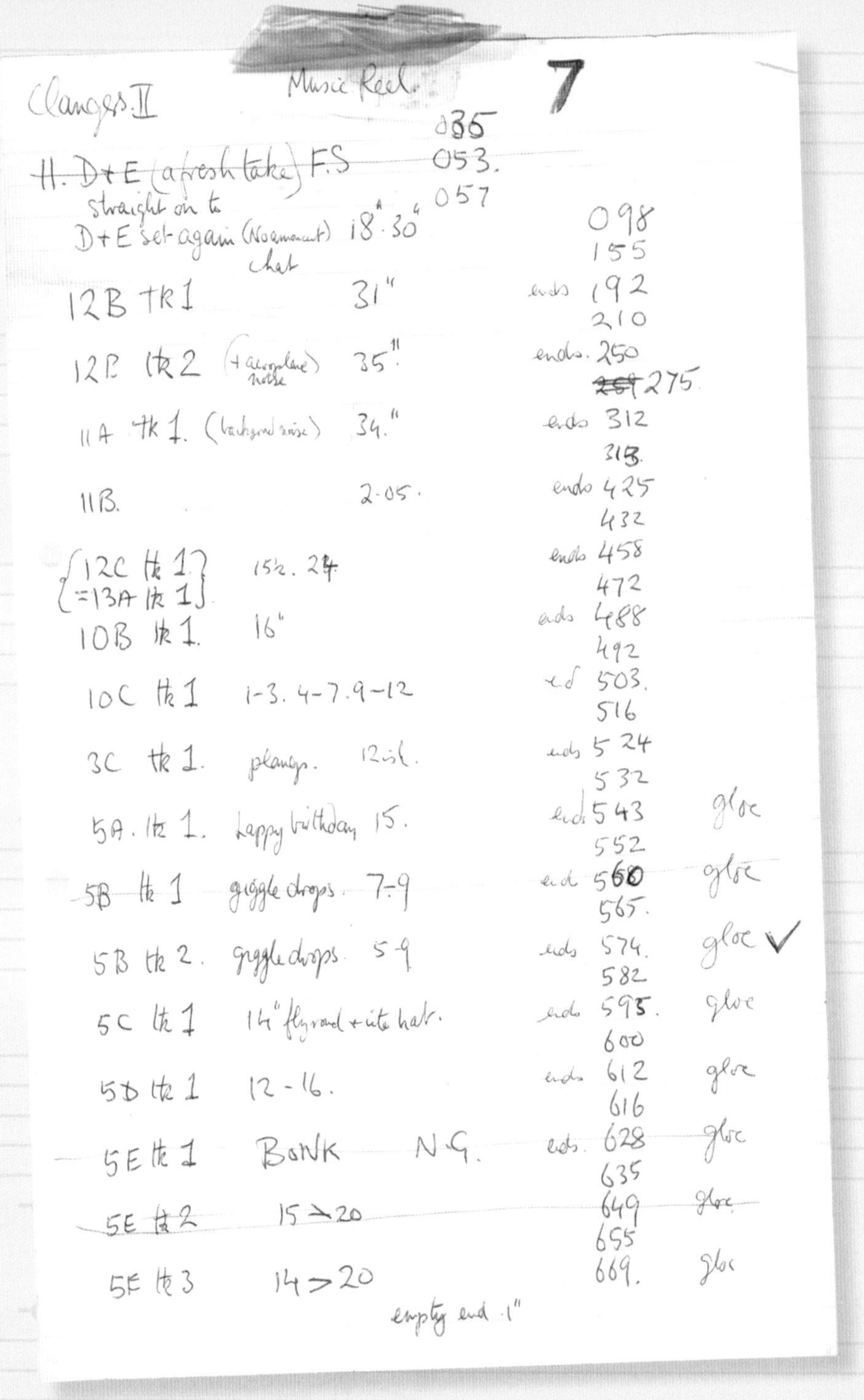

Clangers II Music Reel. 7

035

~~11. D+E (a fresh take) F.S~~ 053.

straight on to 057

D+E set again (Noamanent) 18" · 30" 098

chat 155

12B TK1 31" ends 192

210

12B tk 2 (+ aeroplane noise) 35" ends. 250

~~259~~ 275

11A tk 1. (background noise) 34." ends 312

318.

11B. 2·05. ends 425

432

{12C tk 1 = 13A tk 1} 15½. 24 ends 458

472

10B tk 1. 16" ends 488

492

10C tk 1 1-3. 4-7. 9-12 end 503.

516

3C tk 1. plangs. 12isl. ends 524

532

5A. tk 1. happy birthday 15. ends 543 gloc

552

~~5B tk 1 giggle drops. 7-9~~ end 560 gloc

565.

5B tk 2. giggle drops 5-9 ends 574. gloc ✓

582

5C tk 1 14" fly round + ute hat. ends 595. gloc

600

5D tk 1 12-16. ends 612 gloc

616

~~5E tk 1 BONK N.G.~~ ends. 628 gloc

635

~~5E tk 2 15 → 20~~ 649 ~~gloc.~~

655

5E tk 3 14 → 20 669. gloc

empty end ·1"

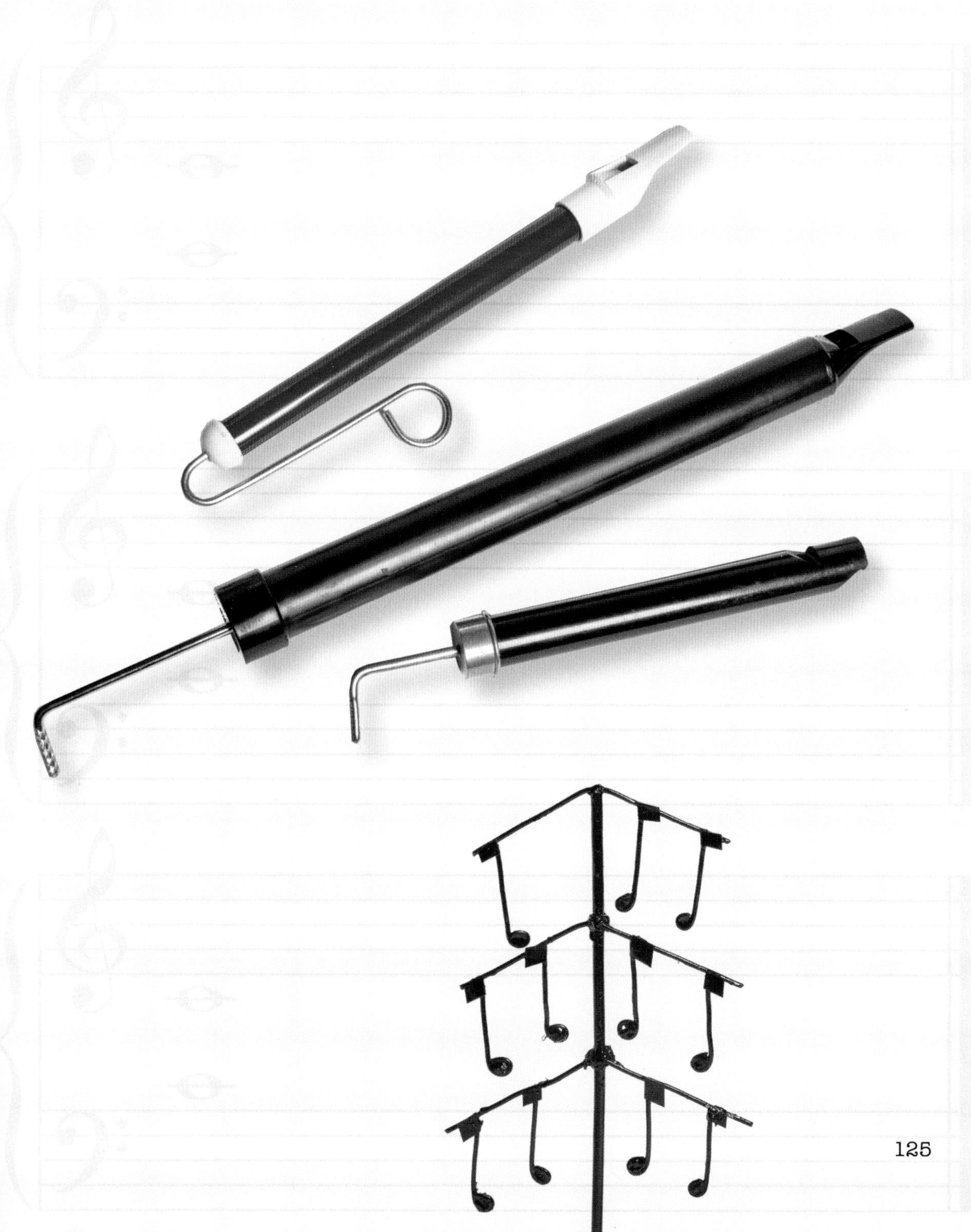

SEASON 2

Episode 1

The Tablecloth

It is 18 April 1971 and *Clangers* is back for a second season. And what a corker of a story this is to kick off with.

The main thrust of the episode is about how to deal with the Froglets, who seem to keel over at the slightest provocation. They suddenly become unbearably cold and need Tiny and Small Clanger's help to get warm again. But in an audacious twist of plot a spaceman from Earth arrives in his rocket. In a flurry of sparkling fire he lands on the planet's surface.

Surely this monumental moment in the history of both species – perhaps the nearest humanity has come to meeting extra-terrestrial life – will lead to something stirring and profound? As it happens… no. It merely plays out as a convenient plot device to bring about a happy conclusion to the mildly irritating event of Mother Clanger's favourite tablecloth being repurposed as shawls for the chilly Froglets.

The Clangers show scant interest in the brisk arrival and departure of their silver visitor, but a great deal of interest in the lovely new tablecloth he has left behind: a flag, optimistically emblazoned with the union of the stars-and-stripes and the hammer-and-sickle.

However, the true drama of the episode went on behind the scenes. The firework special effect used for the rocket's departure accidentally set the planet's surface on fire. Luckily, Peter Firmin was on hand with a bucket of water.

The Clangers CII.1/1

Episode 1. The Tablecloth

Commentary track		Music and Effects track
Narrator		
This is the planet earth. This is the place where we live. The home of the human race. It is a pleasant warm planet. Well, most of it is... most of the year... because the sun shines on it and the cloudy atmosphere keeps the warmth in like a blanket. Very cosy, very convenient, but the earth is really rather an exceptional planet. One would have to look away from the earth and search through the universe to find another planet so pleasant to live on. Even the Clangers' planet is pretty bleak and cold on the outside. The Clangers live inside the planet in their warm caves.		Introductory music
Look Froglets! They should be indoors.	F.	(Rattle Rattle Rattle Rattle.)
Yes, they're cold. They're shivering	F.	(Rattle Rattle Rattle Rattle.)
	T.C.	Look, Small Clanger, the froglets are cold.
	S.C.	Oh dear.
Something must be done about them.	T.C.	Something must be done about them.
	S.C.	Something must be done about them.
	F.	(Rattle Rattle.)
	T.C.	I know! Blue-string pudding!
	S.C.	Yes! Of course. (T.C. runs to a lid and dives in. Mother Clanger is mixing hot blue-string pudding in the big oval dish.)
	T.C.	Please may I have some hot blue-string pudding for the froglets?
	M.C.	For the froglets?
	T.C.	Yes, they're outside and they go Rattle Rattle Rattle.
	M.C.	Oh dear! Poor froglets.
	T.C.	May I take it?
	M.C.	O.K. (T.C. runs out with the pan of blue-string pudding. Small Clanger helps her up with it. They drag it over to the froglets)
	T.C.	Here you are froglets!
Yes of course, hot Blue-string pudding for cold froglets.	F.	(Croak? Croak? Croak?)
	T.C.	Blue-string pudding.
	F.	(Croak?)
	T.C.	Here you are then! Take hold of this.
	F.	(Croak, croak... whizz.) (The froglet takes the end of the blue-string in his mouth but instead of eating it he spins round and round so that the blue-string is wound on to him like a ball of wool).

Hey! That's not right! They're supposed to eat it, not wear it.	S.C.	That isn't right, they're supposed to eat it, not wear it!
	T.C.	Well it doesn't matter. They can wear it if they want to. Here you are next froglet!
Ah yes, I suppose they can wear it if they want to. It'll certainly keep them warm. How extraordinary.	F.	(Croak, croak... whizz.)
	T.C.	And the next froglet please.
	F.	(Croak, croak... whizz.) (Croak, croak, croak... they croak away.)
	S.C.	How extraordinary.
	T.C.	How unusual... come on, we'd better take this dish in.
	S.C.	Right-ho. (They drag the dish in. They meet the soup-dragon.)
Ah the Soup-dragon, she's very fond of blue-string pudding.	S.D.	Ah hallo Clangers. What have you got there? Blue-string pudding? I like blue-string pudding.
	S.C.	No I'm afraid it's empty, look.
Empty... ah too bad, poor old soup-dragon. She was looking forward to some blue-string pudding.	S.D.	Oh dear, oh dear, oh dear, and I just fancied a bit of blue-string pudding. Ah well, ah well, I'll just have to see what else I can find...
	S.D.	Oh yes, hallo Froglets, what elegant handsome overcoats you have. Yes! Very pretty. Oh yes, very pretty, do show me the other side.
	F.	(Croak, croak).
	S.D.	Oh yes, very pretty, very good, what's it made of? Blue-string pudding. Oh yes, blue-string pudding. I like blue-string pudding.
	Fs	(Croak? croak? croak?) (The soup-dragon picks up the loose end of one of the coats and eats it as she talks. The froglets jump about agitatedly.)
	S.D.	Oh yes, very nice, (munch munch). I like that, oh yes, blue-string pudding.
	Fs	(Croak croak croak.)
	S.D.	Here I say! I don't want an over-coat, no, I'm just having a nibble at the blue-string pudding.
	S.D. (off)	Help! Help! I'm being strangled in blue-string pudding! Help!
	T.C.	Listen! It is the soup-dragon's voice, come on! (They run out).
	S.D.	Help, help, I'm all wound up in this blue-string pudding of froglets winding.
	T.C.	All right! All right! I'm coming. (She cuts away the blue-string entanglement and frees the dragon and the froglets.)
Oh dear, what a dreadful experience. What a terrible thing to happen to a soup-dragon.	T.C.	There you are.
	S.D.	Oh pooh. Oh thankyou very much. Oooh, what an experience... thing to happen, oh dear, oh dear, oh dear. Oh dear, oh dear, oh dear.. (She picks up a mouthful of blue-string and mutters as she chews it walking away.)
	Fs	(Rattle Rattle Rattle.)

And the poor froglets. They're cold without their overcoats.	T.C.	Oh dear, the poor froglets.
	S.C.	They're cold without their overcoats.
	Fs	(Rattle rattle rattle.)
	T.C.	Poor old froglets.
They must do something!		(They run indoors, grab the tablecloth off the table while Mother Clanger's back is turned and run out.
That's Mother Clanger's tablecloth.		Tiny Clanger cuts out overcoats for three froglets from the tablecloth. Tiny Clanger fits them on the froglets.)
	T.C.	There you are, yes, that suits you.
	F.	(croak)
Extra line	T.C.	And one for you.
	F	(croak)
	T.C.	And this one is for you. Stand still now.
	F.	(croak)
	T.C.	Yes, those are nice overcoats. Very cosy for froglets, do you like them?
Have you seen my tablecloth? –	Fs	(croak croak croak... croak away)
	M.C.	Hi! Have you seen my tablecloth?
	S.C.	Seen your what?
	M.C.	My tablecloth!
	S.C.	Oh, do you mean this?
		(He holds up the tablecloth with a flourish and reveals the holes.)
	M.C.	Eek oh oh eeek oh oh. It's full of holes. Who made all these holes? Who did it.
// Yes, explanations. I don't think Mother Clanger is going to be very pleased about this.	S.C.	Well as a matter of fact I did. You see the froglets were cold, they went rattle rattle rattle. So I came in.. and.. well... I borrowed it.
Poor Mother Clanger	M.C.	Oh dear oh dear.
Yes, they look very pretty on the froglets.	T.C.	They look very pretty on the froglets, look!
	M.C.	I don't care. You took my tablecloth and spoiled it, oooh ooh.
	Fs	(croak croak croak)
		(They stop and turn and look left)
	Mj.C.	Listen!
	S.C.	Listen!
Listen!		(They listen and hear a distant whistling sound.)
	Mj.C.	Something coming down! Come on!
Something coming		(The Clangers run out, all except Mother Clanger who crouches with her ears over her eyes.
		We see a point of light in the sky over the Clangers' planet.
		The Clangers see it and point up. It comes closer. The Clangers take cover.
		We hear a louder noise. A space-module descends on a flame.
Too long before door opens?		The Clangers watch from under their lids and behind rocks as an astronaut comes out of the space module. His intercom is heard chatting astronauts' chat as he lopes across the planet's surface setting up a piece of equipment like a parking meter. He brings out a large flag and sets it up on a pole. He steps back, salutes the flag. He turns and lumbers off into his space craft. The Clangers watch him climb in. They take cover as it blasts off, then

they come out and watch it go. They look at the flag.

Well, he didn't stay long, did he? Half a dozen more planets to do before teatime I dare say. But look what he left.

T.C. Oh! It's a tablecloth.

S.C. Yes yes, a tablecloth.

Mj.C. Yes of course!

(They carry in the tablecloth.)

M.C. Ooh ooh! ooh it's lovely! Oh thankyou Clangers thankyou. Oh thanky.

Oh don't thank the Clangers.

T.C. Oh we didn't get it. The funny man in a rocket brought it.

(She points up. Major Clanger has put mugs of soup on the table. The Clangers look up and drink the health of the Astronauts.)

Yes, thankyou!
Thankyou whoever you are.
Thankyou for a lovely new tablecloth!

M.C. (Thankyou

T.C. (Thankyou

Mj.C. (Thankyou

S.C. (Thankyou.

(Two drumbeats

(End music and captions.)

CLANGERS II Music.

02.

2A. Astronaut jumps up, runs, trips and vanishes down a hole.

0 4 6 5. 048 069

2B. Astronaut rolls down a slope and stops

5 069 082

0 8

2C. Astronaut jumps up alarmed. He runs away, runs into Soup-dragons arms. They dance round together inadvertently. He breaks away, trips and falls into the Soup-well.

5 090 114

0 5 9 12 14. Splash sound effect added later

2D. Astronaut jumps up and runs away, round planet

5 130 157

0

(fade out) 15"

Episode 2

The Rock Collector

He's back! The rocket man is back. And he has an unusual receptacle with him.

Imagine the scene on the launch pad back on Earth: extensive checks have been carried out by a small army of scientists and technicians and the countdown is about to start, when suddenly a bespectacled minion rushes into the mission control centre and cries, 'WAIT… he's forgotten his *wicker basket*!'

We're all familiar with the term 'close encounters of the third kind', made famous by Steven Spielberg's classic film. On Hynek's scale, from which the title is taken, the encounter in this episode must come pretty high – at least a four or a five – if indeed the scale caters for an event in which aliens swap your rock collection for spaghetti.

Recently, NASA has taken the precaution of enlisting the help of theologians to consider the religious significance and ramifications of possible future contact with alien beings, but back in these early days of space travel it seems such niceties were yet to be considered. In Stanley Kubrick's *2001: A Space Odyssey*, for instance, the astronaut Dave Bowman found himself totally unprepared for the thoroughly esoteric nature of first contact, and such preparations weren't made for the Clangers' visitor either.

However, to be fair, some events are simply beyond prediction. No one can reasonably expect to be confronted by large, knitted, mouse-like creatures or find themselves floundering in a cavern full of hot green soup overseen by a neurotic dragon.

Suffice to say, outer space can be a very strange place.

CII. 2/1

<u>The Clangers</u>

<u>Episode 2. The Rock Collector</u>

Commentary track		Music and Effects track
Narrator		
This is the earth. Our planet, our home. It sails serenely through the vast emptiness of space; through the silent nothingness between the stars. How silent is it? Silent to our ears perhaps, but if we had ears that could hear the sounds of radio waves, then the space between the stars would be far from silent for all the radio messages in all the worlds are buzzing about in space, waiting to be picked up by the right sort of equipment.		Introductory music
There's that...er... thing the rocket man left on the Clangers' planet.		
And what a noise it's making.		
	T.C.	What is it? How extraordinary.. HI everybody! Come and look at this! (Many Clangers emerge from holes and gather round the equipment.)
	C.1	((How extraordinary! What an (unusual object!
	C.2	(How peculiar! I've never seen anything like that before!.. ad lib.
	Mj.C.	Listen! (They listen. We hear something approaching.)
Listen!		
	Mj.C.	Look.
Look! Something coming		(They look up and see a point of light in the sky.
	S.C.	It's coming down here. This thing is calling it.
That thing's calling it!	Mj.C.	Come on everybody, get below!.. Come on, below! (The Clangers dive into their holes and clang shut the lids. The space module, homing on to its radio beacon, descends on a flame and lands. The hatch unscrews and an astronaut climbs out. He moves in slow lumbering leaps to the radio beacon and turns a key (puts a coin) in it. The Clangers watch him covertly as he fetches a basket from inside his craft and lopes about collecting rocks and putting them into his basket. One particular rock is hard to get away. He puts the basket down by one of the lids and turns to go and fetch a pick from his spacecraft. The lid lifts and Small Clanger looks at the basket. Small Clanger sees the astronaut is not looking so he whips the basket in under the lid and takes it below.)
What is he doing? Collecting rocks. What dull things to collect.		(The Astronaut fetches the pick and starts to loosen the rock.) (Small Clanger shows the basket to

the other Clangers and tips it out.)

M.C. What odd things to collect!

Mj.C. We could give him much more interesting things to take home.

S.C. Yes, but what?

They could give him something better than rocks.

T.C. I know, blue-string pudding!
(She runs out and comes back with a big dish of blue-string pudding)

Ah yes, blue-string pudding!

Mj.C. Yes, that's good. Tip it in.
(The astronaut lifts the rock and turns to put it in the basket. He looks at where the basket was and is puzzled. He turns to look the other way and while he does so the lid lifts and Small Clanger puts out the basket and retires. The astronaut turns again, sees the basket and is even more puzzled. He picks up the basket and heads for the spacecraft.)

No basket! How odd, it was there just now.

Oh there it is!

Well, he is going. He has taken the basket with him. I hope he likes blue-string pudding.

S.C. I hope he likes blue-string pudding.

M.C. Oh yes, everybody likes blue-string pudding!

Yes, everybody likes blue-string pudding.

(The astronaut climbs back into the spacecraft. The radio beacon is silent for a moment and then squawks and beeps wildly. The hatch bursts open and out comes a shower of blue-string pudding followed by the basket and a furious astronaut.

He didn't like it!

S.C. He didn't like it.

Mj.C. He didn't like it. No.

S.C. (No
T.C. (No (They shake their heads).

(The astronaut looks around. He comes to a lid and looks at it closely. He hauls at it and it opens with a clang revealing Tiny Clanger.)

He seems a bit puzzled

Ah there's Tiny Clanger.

T.C. Good morning! How do you do?
(The astronaut does not shake her hand. He runs away. He trips and falls into a hole. The astronaut rolls down a slope inside the planet. He rolls to the froglets. He sits up and looks around.

He's running away!
How extraordinary.

Fs (croak! croak! croak!)
(Three froglets greet him. He leaps up again and runs. He runs through the copper-leaf trees and into the arms of the soup-dragon.)

He's running away again!

S.D. Ah how d'ye do, how d'ye do? Do you come here often?
(They dance together inadvertently for a moment but the astronaut pulls himself away and runs.)

S.D. Oh what a rude person!
(The astronaut stumbles away and trips into the soupwell with a splash.

He's fallen in the soup!

S.D. Hi, you've fallen into the soup-well! Come out! Come out! Oh dear, perhaps he'll drown.

		(She looks up and calls the Clangers.) Fetch a rope or something, rope! It's fallen in the soup, the soup! (The Clangers lower a rope through a crater hole above the soup-well.)
	S.D.	That's right, I'll tie it to his leg. There we are. Right-ho! Haul away.
	Cs	Pull, pull, pull, pull, pull, pull, pull, pull, pull, pull.
Oh dear he's very soupy!		
	M.C.	Oh dear, oh dear. The poor chap is covered with soup.
	S.C.	We must wash him! Tiny Clanger, you call the cloud, I'll fetch the brooms.
	T.C.	All right! (She runs to the top of a hill and whistles.)
	T.C.	Can you please come over here and rain on this bloke?
That's better		
	S.C.	There, that's better.
	Mj.C.	I wonder if he is all right. I will speak to him... Hallo, are you all right?
Oh there he goes, he keeps running away. He'd better not run too fast!		(The astronaut squawks again and runs. This time he runs so fast he disappears over the horizon.)
	Mj.C.	What an extraordinary chap, he keeps running away.
Oh dear!	M.C.	Look! Mind out!
Yes, I thought he would, he has run into orbit.	Mj.C.	Mind out! (The Clangers throw themselves flat as the astronaut sails past overhead.)
	M.C.	We ought to try and catch him. (The astronaut flies past on another orbit. Small Clanger brings out the fishing rod with a magnet on the end. The astronaut astronaut passes again and Small Clanger casts the rod. It catches the astronaut with a clink and Small Clanger reels it in.)
	Mj.C.	Put him in his carriage.
Yes, put him in his carriage.		(The Clangers unceremoniously bundle the confused astronaut into his spacecraft.)
	T.C.	Hi! don't forget this!
Oh yes, don't forget that noisy thing.		(She picks up the radio beacon and shoves it into the spacecraft.They slam the hatch and retire.)
I wonder if he is all right. Yes, there he is, look!	M.C.	I wonder if he will be all right. (The astronaut's face appears briefly at the window.)
Goodbye. Come back soon, they shout. No, I don't think he'll be back soon. I don't think he really liked it here.	Clangers	Goodbye, good luck. (The space-craft makes preparative noises, counts itself down and blasts off.
	T.C.	Goodbye! Come back soon! Come back soon.

Captions

Vernon

Page 2

Music for Clangers' Actions

we spoke of a flute as this would be looser and more musical than the clanger's voices which are to be distorted Swannee whistles. ?

~~Ep 1~~

D pulling a rope out of a hole. 2 secs

these together

E pulling it back into the hole. 2 secs

E1 faster & faster 10 secs. 1 230–253.

F wild capering piece as of chasing about on rough ground or a flap-winged flying machine trying to take off. 21"

Mad capering 1 253–299

G (group) Clangers walk. This is a basic accompaniment to their odd flap-footed walk.

G1 fairly slow walk 3 000 120

Not done

G2 faster walk Same only played faster (Shorter time OK) 3 120 216

I 1292 – G3. running along 40½" Could be same only much faster, extend to make up to 40"

1 342 – G3A. 33"

1 723 { G4. Slow walk down 14"
G4A. shorter 9½"
and sit, very dejected

1745 G5 7" jump up and run gaily upstairs

1787 G6 4½" run away and hide very frightened

1787 G7 23 Short, very gay, Clangers dance in a ring, about 20"

Oliver did his editing by eye, scissors and tape.

Episode 3

Glow-Honey

This episode follows a classic story structure as old as the hills and, if those scriptwriting books are anything to go by, the blueprint for nearly all stories.

The hero leaves the comfort of the familiar homeland and travels to a strange new place where much mettle is vigorously and rigorously tested. Eventually, in triumph, the hero returns home a better and wiser soul. The 'hero' in this case, Small Clanger, finds himself on an adventure rather by mistake, and returns only with the lesson that he won't do *that* again in a hurry.

Such reluctant protagonists are a Smallfilms staple. Mr Pogle hated magic and all it entailed; Noggin the Nog favoured staying at home if at all possible; and Bagpuss could barely stay awake.

On his travels, Small Clanger discovers caves full of sentient flowers. The idea of a dark underworld populated with intelligent, well-mannered flowers who don't suffer fools gladly is rather melancholy. But in a good way, like the sweet sadness one feels when visiting a coastal town in winter.

When Small Clanger is confronted with demands on his character, he chooses to engage an enviable talent available to all Clangers: the ability to cover one's eyes with one's ears and wait for it all to go away.

Luckily the resourceful glow-buzzers are on hand to help out.

The Clangers CII.3/1

Episode 3. Glow-Honey

Commentary track		Music and Effects track
Narrator		
If you look up into the sky at night, it seems quite dark. There seems to be no light there, but this isn't quite true because there is really plenty of light shining in all directions in space.but of course you don't see it until it shines on something. See, the outside of the Clangers' planet is brightly lit by the sun, but of course we know the Clangers live inside their planet in the caves under those lids, but their caves aren't dark. They must have some form of lighting. Look there they are! Glow-buzzers. They buzz around the caves filling those little hives on the wall with glow-honey and they shine out like lamps.		Introductory music.
Ah yes, there's something else you ought to know about glow-honey. Glow-honey is nice! It's very delicious.... but the glow-buzzers don't like Clangers taking it without asking.	S.C.	Look! Look up there! That's glow-honey. Glow-honey is nice! I'm going up to get some. (He prepares to climb.)
	T.C.	Oh no, you mustn't! You mustn't, that's not allowed. (She holds him back.)
	S.C.	Oh yes it is. (He climbs up. He steals a lump of glow-honey.)
	G.B.	Buzz Buzz
	S.C.	Glow-honey is nice!
Yes, give it back.	G.B.	Buzz Buzz Buzz (They buzz around him angrily.)
	S.C.	All right! All right!
	G.B.	Buzz Buzz.
	S.C.	All right! You can have it back, here you are! (He gives back the lump of glow-honey and the glow-buzzers carry it away.)
Oh no, Tiny Clanger wouldn't steal glow-honey!	T.C.	(to glow-buzzer.) There, isn't he silly? I wouldn't steal your glow-honey. No. (The glow-buzzer flies up and fetches her a little lump of glow-honey.)
	T.C.	Ooh! ooh! Thankyou, thankyou very much. (Munch munch).
	S.C.	What are you eating? Glow-honey?
	T.C.	Yes, the glow-buzzer gave it to me!
	S.C.	Oh the rotten things!.. where are they? (The glow-buzzers are going down into a cave near where Grannie Clanger is sitting knitting. Small Clanger comes over and looks.)
	S.C.	Oh they are going down this hole. I wonder where that leads to. (Small Clanger climbs into the hole. He makes his way down a

Narration		Action / Dialogue
Small Clanger is following them. Perhaps he'll find out where the glow-honey comes from. There are plenty of caves that even the Clangers don't know about.		dark passage. Glow-buzzers buzz past him. He sees light. He comes out into a cave he has never seen before... It is full of tall handsome flowers.)
Look at that, look at all those flowers.	S.C.	Well! Look at that. Look at all those flowers. (We look at all the flowers.)
Ah there's a glow-buzzer, perhaps that's where they get glow-honey from, inside the flowers! Yes, I wonder. Er oh (ooh!)		(A glow-buzzer flies into a trumpet-shaped flower and flies out again.) (Small Clanger pokes his long nose into the flower. The flower draws away at this indignity and swipes him round the ear'ole with a heavy leaf.)
Yes, I think one must be very polite to these flowers.	S.C.	Eeek, ow, owch, ooh that hurt! (He rubs his ear, bows to the flower.)
	S.C.	I beg your pardon. (The flower bows back.)
	S.C.	I didn't mean any harm. (He bows again, the flower bows back. Bowing to each other he backs away.)
	S.C.	I hold you in very great esteem.. your servant! (He turns to look for the way out.)
Yes now, where did Small Clanger come in? That's rather a difficult question. He has been wandering about everywhere through these caves of flowers.	S.C.	Now, where did I come in? (He looks around to find the way out but he can't find it. He wanders through the caves of flowers. He sees some small flowers. He addresses them.)
He is going to have a job to find the way out.	S.C.	Excuse me, I seem to be lost, can you please tell me the way out? (The flowers wave their heads.)
	S.C.	The way out?
I don't expect the flowers know the way out!	S.C.	Oh all right then... thankyou... (He wanders away feeling very sad.)
I don't expect they have ever been outside their caves. Poor Small Clanger. He is lost.	S.C.	Oh dear. Shall I ever get out of here? Oh dear! (He wanders around completely lost. He sees two glow-buzzers.)
Hallo! glow-buzzers!	S.C.	Oh I say...I say...I say, I'm lost, can you please help me find the way out?
	G.B.	Buzz buzz buzz. (They buzz round his head twice and then buzz off through the cave.)
No, they've gone. Oh dear. Poor Small Clanger	S.C.	Oh dear, they've gone away! Oh dear. Oh dear! (He sits down, wraps his ears over his eyes and mopes.
Look, even the flowers are worried about him. How is he going to get out of those caves?		
Ah! look! Major Clanger and Mother Clanger! If somebody could get a message to them.	M.C.	Look at that..Major Clanger, come and look at that!
Yes. The glow-buzzers. Look, they have made an arrow.	Mj.C.	Oh yes! That's very pretty isn't it. You are clever buzzers, yes you are, yes.
Now if one of them just follows the arrow. The glow-buzzers will take them to Small Clanger. Oh dear, she's not taking any notice. Well, yes, if she won't come on her own, they will have to drag her.	M.C.	Yes, clever, yes! (Major Clanger turns and goes away. Mother Clanger picks up the tablecloth. The exasperated glow-buzzers buzz down and grab the end of the tablecloth and pull at it.)

CII.3/3

No, that's not going to work.	M.C.	Hi! What are you doing? HI! that's mine... No I don't want to be pulled along... No, come back! that's mine!.. Help Major, help... (Major Clanger runs to help. Together they pull the tablecloth slowly away from the glow-buzzers who in the end give up and let go so Major and Mother Clanger fall over backwards.)
	Mj.C.	(Eek owch oops!
	M.C.	(Oops eeek owch!
	Mj.C.	What extraordinary buzzers.
	M.C.	Yes, and I bumped my bottom.
	Mj.C.	You poor old thing. (He helps her up.) (The glow-buzzers go back to the hive, confer, then two of them buzz away.
There's Grannie Clanger. No use talking to her. She's fallen asleep over her knitting as usual.		They see Grannie Clanger with her knitting. They buzz around her but she does not respond because she is asleep. The glow-buzzers confer for a moment, then they fly down and pull out the needles of
They are taking her wool. Look at that! They're flying away with it! Through the caves, and they are giving the end of it to Small Clanger.		Grannie Clanger's knitting. They pick up the end of the wool and fly away with it as it unravels in her lap. They carry the end of the wool to Small Clanger in the cave.)
What about that then?	S.C.	Hey? what? what's that? Thankyou! That's the end of Grannie Clanger's wool. That way must be the way out.
They are very clever little	G.B.	Buzz-buzz-buzz.
glow-buzzers. That was a very good idea.	S.C.	Thankyou... yes, I'll follow it. Yes, here is the cave.
Thank you Glow-buzzers.	(off)	Thankyou glow-buzzers, goodbye!
There you see, that will	G.B.	Buzz buzz.
show him the way out. There it is. He can pick up the wool as he goes along and it will lead him right through all the caves to the end of the wool.... and Grannie Clanger.		(Small Clanger makes his way out through the caves, looping the wool as he goes. He comes to the Clanger's cave and face to face with Grannie Clanger.)
	S.C.	Ooer... Oh er I expect you're wondering about this?
Oh dear. I'm afraid she is not very pleased.		(He holds out the tangle of wool to Grannie Clanger. She looks at it, then snatches it.)
I don't think she is really interested in all this talk about flower caves and glow-buzzers. All she cares about is her knitting. Somebody pulled the needles out.	S.C.	Well, the glow-buzzers borrowed it you see, they brought the end of it into me because I was lost in there and couldn't find my way out and the flowers wouldn't tell me the way out so I asked the glow-buzzers and they didn't answer, they buzzed straight up and out here and in the end they fetched me the knitting... and
	G.C.	But they pulled the needles out!
	S.C.	Er yes... yes... I'm sorry!
	G.C.	Oh it doesn't matter! (She turns away and sits down to start knitting again. The glow-buzzers bring her a little flower.)
Ah, the glow-buzzers have brought her a little flower.	G.C.	Oh, a little flower...how nice, thankyou, thankyou. (G.C. settles down to knit.)
(Sniff) How nice		

CII.3/4

Now is it worth doing some more knitting.
No, a little nap. Yes!

Well, if she's gone to sleep again there's no point in a flower standing about.
Might as well go home.
Goodbye.

S.C. Bye-bye.
G.C. Bye-bye, Goodbye.
(S.C. goes away.)
(Grannie Clanger sleeps. The flower looks at her, turns round and walks away.

Captions.

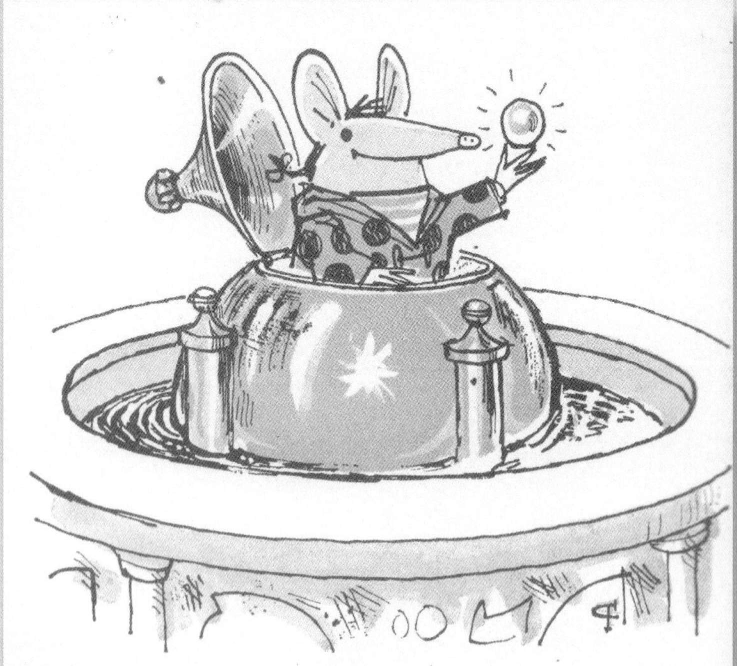

The moon mouse climbed into the ball.
It took out a bright stone
and gave it to Nooka.
It was a jewel, a moon-stone.

The moon mouse from Noggin and the Moon Mouse, *published in 1967.*

Music P.2.

CLANGERS. II

Episode 3.

~~3A~~. Very general background music to set the atmosphere of the cave of flowers where the glow-buzzers collect their honey. (avoid impression of buzzing glow-buzzers perhaps because the glow-buzzers will need a sound effect and this may confuse)
— about 2 mins, choppable if poss 5 196 327

~~3B~~ Glow-buzzers pick up the knitting and fly away with it. 6 095 122"

0 10 18

~~3C~~ 3C. vibe notes for singing plants.

6 548 580

Episode 4.

~~4A~~ some (about 4) highish rough brass notes as T.C blows the teapot 2-3 secs. each

~~4B~~. Background theme as teapots rise in a cloud, fly away and descend again 5 338 423

theyfall faster.

the landing teapots can be all or partly sound effects.

0 they rise 10 they fly. 20 25.

~~4C~~ Luring away the teapots with helicopter.

5 425 462

Music becomes orchestral over the captions

0 5 15 140ish

Episode 4

The Teapot

Inspiration for stories can emerge from anywhere – an unexpected passing thought; a domestic scene glimpsed through a window; a muttered exchange overheard on a bus to the shops… or something found lying around at home. The outbuildings at the Firmins' farm which served as the Smallfilms studios were a treasure trove of bric-a-brac. Sometimes the creation of an elaborate visitor made entirely from scratch wasn't necessary or practical, and instead an object that was simply knocking around the place would do just as well – something like a teapot from a child's playset for instance.

When the cogs of the imagination start to turn, questions arise. Is a teapot really a teapot? Is a teapot's reality defined by its function within a larger network of meaning? And if so, surely it doesn't have to remain that way. After all, if you chop down a tree, you are left with a stump, but if you put chairs around that stump, it becomes a table.

The teapot has disciples, quite literally followers who come when it calls, so there's clearly more to this object than the mere conveyance of a hot beverage. Perhaps, over time, the Clangers could get to know these mysterious tea things and learn more about their ways. But not, alas, on this particular occasion. The 'teapot' and its friends are simply too irritating to tolerate, and so they are sent on their way.

Episode 4. The Teapot.

Commentary track		Music and Effects track
Narrator		
If you could stand on the planet where the Clangers live and you looked up you would see the stars in the sky. If you looked around you would see some very peculiar stars but in between these stars you would see... emptiness. Well, not quite emptiness, there are things whizzing about. Rocks, bits of machinery, various odds and ends, sometimes singly, sometimes in groups. These are the sort of things that Small Clanger is fishing for in the music boat.		Introductory music
	S.C.	There is something...Something over there!.. here it comes! (He casts and misses.)
Missed!	S.C.	Missed it!.. here comes something else... yes! (He casts, his magnet clinks on to something.)
There's something! Got it.	S.C.	Got it! (He hauls it in. It is a teapot.)
	S.C.	What a funny-looking thing... I wonder what it is. (He spins the wheel and the boat goes down. Tiny Clanger is waiting.)
That looks to me like a teapot, but the Clangers may never have seen a teapot!	T.C.	What have you caught?
	S.C.	I don't know... a thing. This is it.
	T.C.	Oooh, isn't it funny. Let's take it in. (They take it indoors.)
	M.C.	What have you caught?
	S.C.	This thing.
	M.C.	What a long nose it has! Just like mine. What is it?
Yes, it has got a long nose just like Mother Clanger's.	S.C.	I don't know.
A hat! No I don't think it is a hat. No, definitely not a hat!	T.C.	Perhaps it is a hat. (She tries to put it on.)
	T.C.	(Muffled, echoey) Yes, it's a helmet! The trouble is, I can't see... help... help. Help... help.
	S.C.	All right, I've got you. (The Clangers pull her feet and she comes out like a bottle from a work.)
	T.C.	Eeek! I got stuck! (They look at the teapot.)
A soup-jug. Yes, well that's not a bad idea.	S.C.	I know what it is. It's a soup-jug! I shall fetch soup. (He puts the teapot on the trolley and poles away to the soup-wells.
	S.D.	Well, how do you do Small Clanger, What can I do for you this merry morning.
	S.C.	Soup, do you think I could have some soup?
It's a bit big for a soup-jug. That'll take rather a lot of soup.	S.D.	Soup? In that thing. But that's enormous! That will take gallons and gallons and gallons of soup!
	S.C.	Yes please.

S.D. ... Oh all right then.

S.C. Here's the jug.

S.D. Oh,yes, it'll take quite a few of these to fill it.
(She fills the jug).
(Here you are.

S.C. Thankyou.
(He pours it into the teapot and hands it back to the dragon.)

S.D. I don't know, I really don't. I mean it's not as if... and anyway! There's soup and soup and soup in jugs, not huge pots and there's only seven hundred and fifteen million cubic miles in this planet and if they go on like this it won't be long before... or behind for that matter.
(She grumbles away as she fills and passes three jugs of soup.)
There, that's your lot.

S.C. Thankyou dragon, thankyou very much.

S.D. Oh you're welcome, you're welcome. ... I suppose.

(Small Clanger arrives home with his teapot of soup on the trolley)

Here he comes. Small Clanger and his soup kitchen. Everybody must line up and he'll serve the soup.

S.C. Here you are then everybody, line up now, I'm serving soup.
(The Clangers gueue up, holding their mugs.)

Mj.C. I'm first, here's my mug... oh thankyou.

C2. Thankyou,

C3. Thankyou.

G.C. Ooh thankyou!

T.C. Thankyou very much!

Now it's Mother Clanger's turn.

M.C. Now my turn... there's nothing in it!

Nothing in it.

S.C. Nothing?

Empty. No soup.

M.C. Nothing, look, it's empty.

S.C. Try again... there, now is there anything in it?

There's plenty of soup in the pot.

M.C. No, not a drop, look...
(She holds it upside-down.)

S.C. Oh dear... there's plenty of soup in here. The spout must be bunged up. I'll blow through it....

Ah yes, blow through it? Ah well, I suppose it is the only thing to do. What a noise!

(He tries to blow through it. At last with a gurgling roar the soup sprays out of the top of the teapot in great bubbly splashes. The Clangers are showered with splodges of green soup... but the sound is marvellous.)

G.C., Mj.C.,M.C., T.C., Eek! ow! ugh! ooh.

S.C. Wasn't that a lovely noise! Listen, I'll do it again!

He's going to do it again!

M.C. No. No you don't.

S.C. No?

M.C. No, certainly not! You've covered us all with soup. Take that thing outside at once!

Quite right! Take it outside. It's a noisy messy thing!

S.C. Outside?
Oh, all right then.
(He takes the teapot outside and blows it. It makes a fine sound which is oddly echoed by a distant similar sound, very faint. S.C. runs to a hole.)

Sounds more like a trumpet than a teapot.

Hi listen.

S.C. Tiny Clanger, Tiny! Tiny! Come out and hear this.

T.C. Hear what?

CII.4/3

	S.C.	This. (He blows again, the echo is repeated nearer.)
Is that an echo or an answer?	T.C.	Oh! Isn't that odd... Let me try. (She blows the teapot. The echo is louder still.)
	S.C.	Now my turn. (He blows. This time the echo is very loud.)
Hey look. Things in the sky! They're coming down. Look out! Get below.		(They dive for holes just as a cloud of assorted hollowware, teapots, coffee pots, milk cans and jugs, cafes filtres, percolators, infuses, measuring beakers and mugs falls around them.)
How extraordinary.	S.C.	How extraordinary.
They must go below and tell the others what happened.	T.C.	How peculiar... We must tell the others! (They take the teapot indoors.)
	S.C.	Hi! everybody, I blew through this teapot and a shower of teapots and things came flying down and down on top of us.
	Mj.C.	What? When you just blew it?
	S.C.	That's right, I just blew it and they came sailing down.
	Mj.C.	Like this?
He's going to blow through it.		(He blows the teapot.)
	T.C.	No, no don't!
That was a silly thing to do. Here they come!		(The echo is heard.) (The cans fall around him before he can reach his bed-cave. Most of the Clangers dive into their bed-caves and slam the doors but Tiny Clanger jumps on the trolley and poles it away through a shower of hollowware.)
Here comes Tiny Clanger to fetch more soup. The soup-dragon's going to wonder what happened to all that soup!	S.D.	Hallo, what do you want in such a hurry?... what? More soup already? You can't have drunk all that in five minutes.
Tiny can tell her what happened but I don't think the dragon will believe her.	T.C.	No, no, Small Clanger blew through it and the pots came raining down out of the sky.
	S.D.	What do you mean, he just blew through it.
	T.C.	Yes.
	S.D.	What, blew through it, like this?
No No not again.	T.C.	No no, don't do it. (She is too late. The soup-dragon blows the teapot. The echo is heard.)
	S.D.	Oh yes, what a funny noise.
Oh dear.	T.C.	Oh dear, oh dear, oh dear. (She runs for cover.)
Here they come Mind out you silly dragon.	S.D.	What's up with you then? Why are you running away, there's nothing to be frightened of...oh... oh... what's that? Things! Things! Oh I'm getting out of here. (She dives into her well and slams shut the hill. The teapots land around the trolley and the teapot in a shower. Tiny Clanger comes back and looks at the heap. Major Clanger and Small Clanger appear. Major Clanger knocks on the top of the soup-well.)
	S.D.	(Muffled) Go away! Go away!
Yes.	Mj.C.	It's all right you can come out.
She's not coming out from there until they get rid of all those nasty bangy things.	S.D.	I'm not coming out! I won't come out until you get rid of them. Take them away!

CII.4/4

	S.C.	Right?
	T.C.	Right!
Small and Tiny Clanger seem to have thought of something.		(She hauls out a ring from the ring-tree and goes to the music tree.)
	T.C.	May I please have four notes.
Notes from the music trees!	M.Trees	(4 notes)
	T.C.	Thankyou very much.
		(She fits them together and pins then to the top of the ring.
Now what are they up to?		Small Clanger brings over the teapot.)
	S.C.	Here you are.
	T.C.	Thankyou.
		(Small Clanger fits the teapot into the ring.)
	S.C.	Right.
	T.C.	Right!
Ah yes, a sort of helicopter. Very good.		(Small Clanger blows the teapot. Tiny spins the wheel.
Up goes the teapot and up go the teapot's friends. There it goes. I suppose it was a teapot. Well, we shall never know.		The music rises and lifts the ring and teapot. It sails away followed by its fellows.)
		Captions.

Episode 5

The Cloud

The yawning void of space can be a lonely place at the best of times, and a single cloud drifting through the sky is no cocktail party either. Put the two together – a cloud far out in space – and you have a double whammy of sheer isolation.

Let's face it: this lonely cloud from the Clangers' planet has little hope of stumbling across a host of golden daffodils (although if it were to squeeze into the recesses of the planet's inner world, there are many unusual yellow flowers to be found, strolling about the place).

But of course, being alone doesn't always mean being lonely. How the cloud feels about its solitude is not entirely clear. However, it seems content to be led into a new experience by Tiny Clanger and the Froglets. And what an experience it is! Suddenly transported from one top hat to another by methods totally beyond our understanding.

Robert Louis Stevenson once said, 'To travel hopefully is a better thing than to arrive.' And if the cloud has any chance, in its brief moment of transit, to feel a glimmer of hope, I should guess this insight would hold true. The arrival at a dank soup well cave with a troublesome dragon as your hostess is unlikely to be at the top of many people's lists when it comes to dream destinations.

The Clangers CII.5/1

Episode 5. The Cloud

Commentary track		Music and effects track
Narrator		
If you could stand somewhere in space, on some unknown star and look around you, you would see thousands of stars... but you would see nothing to tell you whether there was anything alive on any of them. Even this one. This cloudy planet is the earth, our home. We know it is crowded with people and life and things going on. But what must it be like on these other lonelier planets. Most of them have no life on them at all, no towns, no fields and trees, no rivers, no roads, no people... only rock, just rock. Some of these stars and planets must be the loneliest places in the universe. Even the Clangers' planet when the Clangers are indoors in their warm caves is a bleak, lonely place, and the cloud that wanders lonely over it must know what it is like to be alone.		Introductory music.
Ah, there's Tiny Clanger come to speak to it.	T.C.	Good morning cloud. It must be cold out here. Would you care to come inside with us? We are having a party.
	C.	(tinkles)
	T.C.	Right-ho.
A party! The Clangers are having a party!		(She turns and ushers the cloud in.)
	T.C.	Do please come inside.
And the cloud is coming to the party.		(tinkle) (The cloud floats in and T.C. follows. The Clangers are having a party. They raise their mugs in greeting.)
	Mj.C.	(Welcome cloud.
	M.C.	(Hallo cloud, how nice to see you.
	S.C.	(Yes, do come in. (Major Clanger holds up a mug of soup.)
	Mj.C.	Do have a mug of soup.
	C.	(Shakes and tinkles.) (Mother Clanger forks up some blue-string pudding.)
	S.C.	Have some blue-string pudding then.
	C.	(Shakes and tinkles.)
It's Mother Clanger's birthday. Look at her present.	M.C.	It's my birthday. Look I've got a bracelet.
	C	(plays Happy Birthday to You.)
	Clangers	(laugh all together)
Ah there's Small Clanger with the Froglet's Top-hat. Now what's he going to do with that? A conjuring trick!	S.C.	Look at this everybody. (He drags in the top-hat. It is empty.)
	S.C.	See it is empty. I am going to do a conjuring trick. (He lays the handkerchief over the top-hat.)
	S.C.	Abracadabracadabra! Hey presto! (He spins round and pulls away the handkerchief.)

Froglets!	Fs	(Croak, croak, croak.) (Three froglets hop out of the hat.)
	Clangers	(laugh together.)
That's made them laugh look.	C	(laugh, mad giggle, it rains on them.)
Oh no!	Mj.C.	Hey hey ooh I'm wet!
It's raining. Hi! Stop, you're making them all wet.	M.C.	Hi stop, stop that... you rotten thing you've rained on us all.
Oh, he's sent the cloud away.	Mj.C.	You made us all wet! Go away. (The cloud does not answer. Major Clanger glares as it slowly moves out of picture. It goes outside and hovers. Major Clanger goes to the doors and looks out at it. He shuts the big doors.)
It didn't mean any harm. It was only laughing.	T.C.	It didn't mean any harm. It was only laughing.
	Mj.C.	I don't care, it rained all over us.
Oh dear, now Tiny Clanger is upset. She thinks they are all horrid and she's going outside - - with a step-ladder! Of course	T.C.	Well it can't help it! Poor cloud.. poor cloud. I think you are all horrid. I'm going outside...I am.. I'm going outside with my friend the cloud. (Nobody answers her so she turns and flounces away. A lid lifts and a high chair or step-ladder or something is pushed out. Tiny Clanger follows.)
	T.C.	Hallo cloud.
	C.	(tinkles)
She has come out to sit with her friend the cloud.	T.C.	I have come outside to sit with you.
	C.	(tinkles) (Tiny Clanger sets up the step-ladder and climbs up it. She sits by the cloud and puts her arm round it....)
	C.	(tinkle) (They sit there looking embarrassed for a while. A froglet jumps out of a hole and looks at them.)
	F.	(Croak)
Hallo Froglet	T.C.	Hallo froglet.
	F	(Croak... croak-croak.) (It turns and croaks down the hole. The top-hat is thrown up.)
and the top-hat.	T.C.	That's the top-hat.
	F	(Croak... wheep-croak.) (The froglet jumps into the hat and vanishes.)
	T.C.	It's vanished!... Look, Cloud, it has vanished!
	C	(tinkle)
And now two more froglets. What are they up to?	Fs	(Croak! croak!) (Two froglets jump out of the hat and address the cloud.
I wonder.	Fs	(Croak croak croak.)
I think they want the cloud to go into the hat.	T.C.	I think they want you to come into the hat.
	C	(tinkle) (It approaches)
	T.C.	Is that right? Do you want it to go into the hat?
	Fs	(Nodding) (Croak, croak, croak.)
	T.C.	All right then, come on Cloud, in you go.
It's going into the hat, but where is it going?	C	(tinkles and extends itself pseudopodiously into the hat.)
	T.C.	It has vanished.
	Fs	(Nodding) (Croak-croak)
	T.C.	But where is it?

	Fs	(Laugh-croak)
Where has it gone.	T.C.	Yes, but where is it? It may not be all right.
	Fs	(croak away.)
Well, they're off somewhere. I wonder where they are going. There they are in the soup-dragon's cave. And look, there is a hat just like the other one,		(They hop down a hole. T.C. follows. She walks through the Clangers' cave with her nose in the air. The froglets lead her down to the soup-well cave. There they see another, identical top-hat.)
but no sign of the cloud.	T.C.	There's the hat, but where is the cloud?... the hat is empty. (The froglets croak and dance around the hat. Slowly the cloud steams out of the hat and reassembles itself in the sky.)
There it is! There's the cloud quite safe and warm	T.C.	There you are! There you are Cloud.
indoors in the soup-dragon's cave.	C.	(Tinkles) (The soup-dragon has walked over to them.)
And here's the soup-dragon. Tiny will have to explain this,	S.D.	Hallo, hallo, hallo, what is going on here? The Cloud is indoors. Well, how unusual. Good morning cloud.
if she can explain it!	C.	(Tinkles)
	S.D.	Well, fancy that. I suppose you froglets have had something to do with it. Is it to do with this top-hat?
Yes they jump into the top-hat	T.C.	Yes, they jump into it and vanish.
and vanish. Then they come	S.D.	They do?
out of another top-hat, or is it the same top-hat somewhere else.	T.C.	Yes, they just jump in and vanish and come out in another hat upstairs.
She doesn't believe it.	S.D.	I don't believe it! No, No, I don't believe it.
	T.C.	Oh yes they do.
It's all a trick! It just isn't true.	S.D.	No No No No, No no I don't believe it, it's alla trick. It isn't true.
	T.C.	It is true, isn't it froglet?
	F	(croak, croak.. wheep-croak) (It jumps into the hat and vanishes.)
There you are see! It's vanished, completely empty.	S.D.	Well, fancy that, fancy that, it's empty. Look at that it's completely empty. (She shows the hat round.) Completely empty, nothing in it. (She turns it over and shakes it.) There,you see, completely empty. (She puts it down, open end downwards.)
	F	(muffled) (croak croak croak.) (Tiny Clanger runs forward and lifts the hat revealing the froglet head downwards.)
	S.D.	Oh, so sorry, I didn't think of that!
Hmm, the froglets are not too	F	(croak! croak! croak-croak!)
pleased about that.	S.D.	Oh, oh, oh! Well if that's the way you feel about it, I'll just go away.
	F	(croak! croak! croak-croak!)
	S.D.	Well I didn't mean any harm. I mean it isn't as if - and there's no doubt it never rains but what it pours, but there's no gain-saying. (She walks away muttering.)
	Fs	(croak laughs).

Hallo, the cloud is moving.	C	(tinkle)
It is going back into the hat. There it goes, a magic cloud into a magic hat, and there go the froglets. They are magic too I suppose.	Fs	(croak walk.) (The cloud chases round the cave until it turns and dives into the hat.)
	Fs	(laugh-croak and jump into the hat.)
There, they have all gone their magic ways and left Tiny Clanger all alone. Ah well, we can't all be magic.		(T.C. is alone. She looks into the hat.)
	T.C.	Goodbye. (She turns sadly and walks away. A froglet jumps out of the hat.)
A froglet! Has it come to fetch her?	F	(croak-croak) (T.C. returns.)
Yes, it wants her to go into the hat.	F	(croak-croak)
Ooh what a way to travel! Look, she's outside again!	T.C.	Oh all right then. In I go! (She looks at the hat nervously. She looks at us. Then she gingerly climbs into it head-first. She jumps out of the hat which is outside.)
	T.C.	Here I am!
	Fs	(laugh-croak) (T.C. whistles with delight and dances over to the music trees.)
There she is! She is a magic clanger.	T.C.	I'm a magic clanger.
This calls for a celebration!	M.T.	(pling plang)
	T.C.	Let's play a tune. (They play a tune. The froglets dance. At the end a lid lifts and Mother Clanger looks out.)
Time for bed,	M.C.	Come in now Tiny Clanger. Time for bed.
Tiny Clanger, say goodnight first.	T.C.	All right! I'm coming. Goodnight trees.
	M.T.	(pling plang)
	T.C.	Goodnight my friend the cloud.
	C	(tinkles)
	T.C.	Goodnight froglets.
Goodnight Froglets. Goodnight Tiny Clanger Goodnight Cloud.	Fs	(croak-croak) (Tiny Clanger picks up the step-ladder and goes indoors.)
Don't stay out in the cold too long.	Fs	(croak croak croak) (They jump into the hat and vanish. T.C. closes the lid. The cloud is left alone again. It floats around for a while, then it goes in through the top-hat.)
		Captions.

CLANGERS II. Music page 3.

Episode 5. (Cloud themes are all Gloc. (droplets of rain))

~~5A~~. Cloud plays "Happy Birthday to you" once. about 10" 7 532 543

~~5B~~. Sudden wild giggle. (random notes prestississimo, [illegible]) 5 secs

~~5C~~ The cloud slowly extends itself and enters the top-hat. 7 565 574 7 585 595

about 12 secs.

~~5D~~. The cloud slowly steams out of the hat and reassembles itself in the air. (Same as 5C only in reverse-like) about 12 secs. 7 600 612

~~5E~~. The cloud flies once round the cave and then dives into the hat. (Start slow, get faster) 7 655 659

about 10 secs

Episode 6 & 8. Theme for growing flowers, becomes ominous as forest thickens

~~8A~~.

Thistledown seed floats down from the sky. Small clanger tries to catch it but it blows away each time. In the end he waits for it to settle and then pounces. 6 152 224

0 15 25 35 42 45 60 1:04

~~8.B~~. The ~~fl~~ seed grows an inch or two and wilts 6 489 500

0 12.

Episode 6

The Egg

This egg-based episode bears a strong resemblance to the other, earlier egg-based episode, which is also entitled 'The Egg'.

These days, one might think such a similarity could cause questions to echo around the BBC's halls of power: Is the barrel being scraped? Has Postgate run out of steam? But back in the seventies, the executives – of whom many would have seen action during the dark days of the Second World War – were made of stern stuff, and were content to let Postgate and Firmin press ahead. Indeed, the memory of the time when eggs were in short supply could still be playing on their minds. So, the more eggs the merrier.

The arrival of the Iron Chicken's chick is as unusual as the birth of the Soup Dragon's son, if not quite so convoluted. With an abrupt warning from the Chicken, an egg falls from the sky. Luckily, the Clangers have just enough time to catch it in their tablecloth.

Where the egg actually came from, or how it was fertilised, is a mystery. Could an Iron Rooster be perching somewhere out there, with a harem of metal fowls dotted around the Solar System?

In the end, though, such information is not vital. What's important is that the Chick is fit and well and has an abundant supply of its favourite food to make it grow big and strong. Surprisingly, the new mother has no clear idea what her youngster may want to eat. But it's reasonable to expect that it's a diet high in iron.

The Clangers CII.6/1

Episode 6. The Egg.

Commentary track		Music and Effects track
Narrator You know, if you stood somewhere in space and looked around you, you would see some very peculiar stars. This one for instance. This is the earth, where we live. You can see the patchy blanket of cloud and air, but under that the outside of it is teeming with people and animals and trees and plants. There are other stars, and planets, even more peculiar. Some we have seen and know quite well, like the place where the Clangers live. That is covered with dustbin lids but even that is an ordinary sort of planet compared with the iron chicken's nest. There it is. A mass of assorted bits of old iron and scrap floating about in space.		Introductory music.
Ah! There she is, the iron chicken.	Ch.	Oh dear, oh dear, oh dear, where can it have gone to. It was here this morning, oh my goodness, oh dear, oh dear. Oh what shall I
She sounds very agitated. She's worried		do, what shall I do. (She scans the sky with her telescope.)
She has seen something.		There it is! There it is! Oh dear, oh dear. (She runs to the intercom-box.)
She's calling Tiny Clanger on her radio hat.	Box	(Beep-Beep, Beep,Beep.) (Beep-Beep, Beep-Beep.) (Tiny Clanger comes out of her bed-hole and puts on the hat.)
	T.C.	Hallo, yes?
	Ch.	(muffled) I dropped my egg and it fell off the nest.
Oh dear, something dreadful has happened.	T.C.	Oh dear.
	Ch.	(muffled) And it's falling towards you.
	T.C.	Towards us?
	Ch.	(muffled) Yes, if you run out with a cloth or something you can catch it.
	T.C.	Yes, right-ho, come on everybody. Come on! Everybody out.
Now what are they doing?	Mj.C.	Eh what's that?
	T.C.	Come out and catch the egg.
	Mj.C.	Did you call dear?
They are going to catch something.	T.C.	Yes, come on outside, we must catch the egg. (The Clangers rouse themselves and run outside carrying the table-cloth. They hold it out among
Yes! What is it?		them like firemen and manoeuvre into position. Something falls from the sky. They catch it.
An egg, an iron chick.		It is an iron egg.)
	Mj.C.	There it is! The iron chicken's egg.
Wrap it up warm. It mustn't get cold.	M.C.	Wrap it up well in the cloth. It mustn't get cold!
	Hat	(Beep-Beep, Beep, Beep.)
	Box	(Beep-Beep, Beep-Beep.)
	Ch.	Yes? Yes? Yes?

	T.C.	We've caught it!
	Ch.	Oh good! Oh marvellous, oh wonderful. I'll be right down. I'll be with you in two flaps. Oh marvellous! marvellous. (She dives off the iron nest.)
	M.C.	That's right, wrap it up carefully.
No need to take it indoors. The chicken will be down in a minute.	Mj.C.	Should we take it indoors?
	T.C.	No, the chicken is coming down in a moment. (They look up.)
	T.C.	Look! Here she comes. (The iron chicken lands.)
	Ch.	Oh dear, oh dear, oh dear! My poor egg! My poor egg! Is it cracked?
	M.C.	Here it is, look. It's quite unhurt. (She unwraps the egg.)
Thankyou very much.	Ch.	Oh it's marvellous! marvellous. Oh thankyou Clangers... thankyou Clangers... oh thankyou! (She bows to the Clangers.)
But what will they do with it?	Mj.C.	What shall we do with it?
Ah yes, find a warm nest, somewhere for it to hatch. Yes, that will do.	Ch.	Ah I must find a nest, and sit on it. It is nearly due to hatch... Now... Where is there a solid place... no... yes. Yes! In here will do. Would you mind awfully?
	Mj.C.	Right-ho. (He carries the egg over to a crater and puts it in. The chicken settles on it.)
Ah, that's better.	Ch.	Ah yes, yes, that's better, yes... aah!..
I wonder how long it will take to hatch.	T.C.	Will it take long to hatch?
	Ch.	Oh no, no, not at all, a couple of weeks or so, who knows? (crack)
Listen	Ch.	Ooh, what's that? (grind crunch.)
	Ch.	Oh dear! (crunch boingg!)
	M.C.	Are you all right dear?
What's that noise.	Ch.	I don't know, we'd better have a look.
It has fallen through!		(The chicken rises from the nest. The egg has not hatched, it has fallen through.)
	Ch.	Oh dear! Oh dear! It has fallen through! My egg has fallen through. (muffled) Where are you? (The egg is rolling down a slope inside the caves. It bangs into the soup-dragon and tips her into the soup-well.)
	S.D.	Here! What the devil is that? Some joker is joking and bashing me about. Well I mean it isn't as if? (The egg rolls away and falls down a deep crevasse. The Clangers come rushing down the slope towards the soup-wells.)
	Mj.C.	The egg! The egg! Did you see where the egg went?
	S.D.	Yes, it pushed me into the well, and I nearly fell on my nose.
	Mj.C.	Yes, but where is the egg?
Oh the egg, oh that fell over the cliff.	S.D.	Oh the egg? the egg? Oh, that went that way. It fell over the cliff.

	Ch.	Fell over the cliff? Oh my goodness, oh my goodness! Oh my poor egg! Oh my poor egg! Oh what will become of it?
	M.C	Now don't take on so, we will find it for you. (Small Clanger arrives with the fishing rod and magnet.)
	S.C.	Now mind out everybody while I do some fishing. (Small Clanger lowers the fishing rod and dips about with it in the deep crevasse. The magnet meets metal with a clang.)
Got it !	S.C.	That's it! (He hauls up a large broken piece of egg.)
It's broken! Oh her poor egg! Oh dear!	Ch.	It's broken! It's broken! Oh my poor egg, oh my poor egg. (They gaze disconsolately into the crevasse. Three froglets jump out of their hole.)
	Fs	(croak! croak! croak! croak-croak croak croak!) (They turn to the rock and look at it. With a light crumbling sound a baby iron chick walks out of the rock.)
What was that?	Ch.	It's hatched! my baby! my baby! my baby. (She runs over to the chick but before she can reach it it walks into the rock wall again and vanishes. The chicken sticks her head into the hole and calls.)
	Ch.	(muffled) Come back! come back! come back. (With a light crumbling sound the chick walks out of the wall again somewhere else.)
There it is look!	M.C.	Here it is, look!
	Ch.	There you are, you bad little chick.
	Chick	(Mother!) (It crumples exhausted to the ground.)
It's collapsed.	Ch.	Oh the poor thing is hungry! It needs nourishment!
The poor thing is hungry. Now what do iron chicks eat? Green soup.	Mj.C.	Quick Tiny! Quick Small! Fetch food for the baby chick. (Small and Tiny run to fetch food. Small brings a mug of soup.)
	S.C.	Here you are baby chick, have some soup. (The baby chick will not eat soup)
No, not green soup. Blue-string pudding?	T.C.	Here you are baby chick, try some blue-string pudding! (They put a piece of blue-string pudding in its mouth.)
	Ch.	Go on dear, eat it!
No, not blue-string pudding.	Chick	(Mother) (It drops the blue-string pudding)
Ah, Small Clanger has an idea.	S.C.	I know! (He runs away and starts chopping away at a particular piece of quarry wall. The rock is crumbly with assorted nuts and bolts in it.)
Where's this, some sort of quarry?	S.C.	Here, try some of these! (The chicken comes over and pecks up a nut and bolt and eats it.)
Nuts and bolts and washers. Oh?	Ch.	Delicious oh yes! Very good.

CII.6/4

Yes, yes! delicious.		(Major Clanger has carried over the baby chick. The iron chicken feeds it with nuts and bolts. It revives and cheeps and starts scratching and helping itself. The iron chicken watches proudly and pecks up a few bolts for herself.)
Bedtime, yes of course bedtime. Look, Mother Clanger has made them a lovely nest.	M.C.	Look at the time! Bed-time, bed-time, bed-time. Here chickens, I've made you a nice nest of ma macaronis.
Time for bed everybody.	Ch.	Oh thankyou! Thankyou Mother Clanger. Say goodnight to Mother Clanger, chick.
	Chick	(Goodnight Mother Clanger.)
	M.C.	Goodnight my dear. Sleep well.
Goodnight Clangers.	Mj.C.	Goodnight chicks.
Goodnight Chickens.	Ch.	Goodnight Clangers.
Goodnight Mother Clanger,	S.C.	Goodnight Goodnight all.
sleep well.	Clangers all	Goodnight Goodnight Goodnight. (They cover the chickens with the tablecloth and retire to their beds.)

Captions.

SMALLFILMS

Clangers II   MUSIC CUE SHEET   Episodes 1 to 6

Episode 1. The Tablecloth

3'41" Instrumental Background. The Clangers Suite by V. Elliott.

Episode 2. The Rock Collector

2'30" Instrumental Background. The Clangers Suite by V. Elliott.

Episode 3. Glow-Honey

5'05" Instrumental Background. The Clangers Suite by V. Elliott.

Episode 4. The Teapot

3'14" Instrumental Background. The Clangers Suite by V. Elliott.

Episode 5. The Cloud

2'19" Instrumental Background. The Clangers Suite by V. Elliott.

1'55" "Visual" Instrumental. The Singing Cloud by Vernon Elliott.

Episode 6. The Egg

1'29" Instrumental Background. The Clangers Suite by V. Elliott.

N.B. The Clangers Suite and The Singing Cloud were specially composed by Vernon Elliott, arranged by Vernon Elliott and played by the Vernon Elliott ensemble.
They are not at present published.

SMALLFILMS

Clangers II MUSIC CUE SHEET Episodes 7 to 13

Episode 7. The Noise Machine

2'32" Instrumental Background. The Clangers Suite by V. Elliott.

Episode 8. The Seed.

4'30" Instrumental Background. The Clangers Suite by V. Elliott.

Episode 9. Pride

2'21" Instrumental Background. The Clangers Suite by V. Elliott.

Episode 10. The Bags.

3'07" Instrumental Background. The Clangers Suite by V. Elliott.

Episode 11. The Blow-fruit.

4'46" Instrumental Background. The Clangers Suite by V. Elliott.

Episode 12. The Pipe Organ.

2'50" Instrumental Background. The Clangers Suite by V. Elliott.

Episode 13. The Music of the Spheres.

5'40" Instrumental Background. The Clangers Suite by V. Elliott.

N.B. The Clangers Suite was especially composed by Vernon Elliott, arranged by Vernon Elliott and played by the Vernon Elliott Ensemble. They are not at present published.

Episode 7

The Noise Machine

We arrive at the Clangers' planet at a delightful domestic moment, with the Iron Chick's first tentative steps into this strange new world. The Iron Chicken is introducing her youngster to every bird's birthright: the gift of flight. And the Chick takes to it like a fish to water.

However, the meat of the story is about the discovery and use of a device similar to an early phonograph. Whereas the traditional phonograph would inscribe and store utterances onto a waxed disc or cylinder, this contraption encases the sound within a bubble, and when the bubble inevitably bursts, the sound is released. As such, the sound isn't captured for posterity; its demise is merely delayed.

The machine is not particularly useful, but when has that ever mattered? For the likes of the Clangers, it is novel and amusing, and that is enough. Little do they realise that the machine also brings with it a level of peril rarely seen in the season so far.

The creation of the bubbles by the Smallfilms special-effects department involved the repurposing of a gift regularly found in the Postgate children's Christmas stockings (along with a tangerine and something from the joke shop): a tube of balloon-making goo. One massaged a lump of the goo onto the end of a plastic straw and gently blew. It came in a variety of colours and smelled delicious.

The Clangers CII. 7/1

Episode 7. The Noise Machine

Commentary track		Music and Effects track
Narrator		
This planet Earth, where we live, is a pleasant, self-contained sort of place. It has around it a blanket of air and clouds and this protects it from the many strange objects that are whizzing swiftly about in space. Other creatures on less well-protected planets are not so lucky and they have to watch out for these objects and keep out of their way. Except of course some creatures like the Clangers and the iron chicken who actually spend their time collecting them. The Iron Chicken particularly is a great collector. She is always out combing through space like a celestial old-iron bird. Well, no, today she is teaching her newly-hatched chick to fly.		
	Ch.	Come on now, like this, with a run and a jump and a hop-skip-flap!
	Chick	With a run and a jump and a hop-skip-flap.
That's right!	Ch.	That's right! That's right.
	Mj.C.	That's right! It can fly.
Very good, very good for a first try.	C.2	It can fly. It can fly. (The baby chick does a quick circuit and a three-point landing.)
And down it comes. Ooh! Well of course it's made of iron.	Ch.	Very good! Very good! She'll soon be ready to go out collecting with me.
	S.C.	Listen! I can hear something.
Small Clanger has heard something, something in the sky.		(They listen, they hear a faint whistling sound.)
They must send an expedition. Tiny Clanger must fetch the telescope. The other Clangers must fetch the music boat.	Mj.C.	Tiny Clanger, fetch your telescope! Small Clanger. You and the uncles go and fetch the music boat and the fishing gear.
There it is, now what is it, too small to see. Ah but they'll be able to see it through the telescope.		(Tiny Clanger runs for her telescope. Small and the uncles for the boat. Tiny returns with the telescope. Major Clanger holds it for her and she looks through it, scanning the sky.)
	T.C.	Yes! I can see something... chicken, come and look.
Yes, that is something to collect, perhaps more than one thing. The Iron Chicken is in charge of the expedition. Clangers will sweep to the left, chickens will sweep to the right.	Ch.	Yes! yes! oh yes! yes. There is a thing! We must collect that, yes! Come on everybody! Clangers! You take the boat and go round that way! Chick, you fly over that way and sweep to the left. I'll go round from the right. Come on everybody up! up, up, and away! (The two chickens take off, closely followed by Small Clanger in the music boat.)
She can see it.	T.C.	They've seen it! There they go.
Yes, let Major Clanger have a look.	Mj.C.	Let me have a look!

		(Tiny Clanger stands on a hill to hold the telescope for Major Clanger.)
There's one piece of it and here comes the baby chick.	Mj.C.	Oh yes! They have caught it! Here they come.
She's got it and down she goes.	T.C.	Here comes Small. (The music-boat comes down, carrying a sort of horn.)
And down comes Small Clanger with a quite enormous piece of,er, whatever it is.	S.C.	Here you are Tiny!
What an extraordinary-looking thing.	T.C.	Thankyou! (She runs to the machine and fits the horn to it.)
Yes, it fits on to the rest of it. There it is, beautiful.	Ch.	There it is! That's it!
	S.C.	Beautiful isn't it?
	C.2	Beautiful, beautiful!
Yes, beautiful, but what's it fot?	Mj.C.	Beautiful! (They admire it.)
	T.C.	What is it for, Chicken?
Well, she doesn't know.	Ch.	What's it for? I don't know!
There's a handle there at the back.	S.C.	There is a handle here, shall I wind it?
	Mj.C.	All right!
Look at that!	S.C.	One, two, three, four, five, six. (Small Clanger winds the handle. A bubble comes out of the horn and floats away. The Clangers and the chickens watch it.)
Coo!	Mj.C.	Cooo!
That seems to be a sort of recording machine. The noise is recorded in the bubble and comes out when it is popped.	Ch.	I'll pop it! (She reaches up and pecks the bubble, it pops.)
	Bb.	(One, two, three, four, five, six in Small Clanger's voice.)
	Ch.	Cooo!
	S.C.	Coo!...
	T.C.	Coo! It's a sort of recording machine.
	Mj.C.	Let me try it!
Now it's Major Clanger's turn.		(Major Clanger speaks into the small horn.) (Mj.C. recites the first verse of "IF".) (The bubble flies. Major Clanger picks up a macaroni twig and throws it at the bubble.)
There it goes, pop it.	Bb	(recites the first verse of "IF" in Major Clanger's voice.)
	S.C.	Laughs
	T.C.	Laughs (The soup-dragon appears.)
Ah yes, here comes the soup-dragon.	S.C.	Look there's the soup-dragon!
	T.C.	(to microphone.) Hallo soup-dragon.
	S.D.	Hallo hallo hallo, what's going on? (The Clangers and the chickens do not answer.
	S.D.	What's happening, why don't you speak to me? Speak to me!
What's going on, nobody speaks to her.		(The Clangers do not answer.)
	S.D.	Hallo, what's this thing? (She reaches up and takes the bubble. It pops.)
Hallo Soup-dragon, says the bubble.	Bb.	(Hallo soup-dragon.)
	S.D.	Oh I say!
	Clangers	Laugh (Mother Clanger looks out.)

	M.C.	Come on you lot, soup-time! Soup-time!
Come on everybody, soup-time.	Mj.C.	Come on everybody, soup-time.
Now what's Tiny Clanger doing?	T.C.	No, wait a minute, let's do a trick... Music trees, please play for us. (The music trees play a short piece which the Clangers record. Tiny Clanger ties a loop of tinsel wool round the ensuing bubble.)
Ah yes, a bubble of music for Mother Clanger.	T.C.	Right ho. (They go indoors. The chick stays outside.)
	M.C.	Come on, soup-time...Oh I say! what is that?
	T.C.	That is for you. It's a song.
	M.C.	Oooh (She reaches out for the bubble. It pops and plays the tune for her. She dances to it.)
What a nice present, but now it's soup-time.	M.C.	Oh thankyou Clangers. What a nice present. Come and have your soup now. (She takes a mug to the Iron Chicken.)
Soup for the iron chicken? No, it's her favourite, assorted nuts and bolts. Delicious.	M.C.	Here is your favourite... nuts and bolts. (She pours them on the floor.) Your chick likes them too... where is your chick? (The chicken looks at her.)
	M.C.	Where is your chick?
Her chick, yes, where's the chick? the chick.	Ch.	My chick? Where's my chick? Chick! Chick! Chick! Chick! Where are you? Has anybody seen my chick?
The chick, where is it.	T.C.	I think she is still outside.
Yes, it was outside!	Ch.	Oh I must find her.
They must find it!	Mj.C.	Let's all find her. Come on.
	Ch.	Chick! Chick! Chick! (Small Clanger sees a bubble. He pops it.)
That's its voice. It must be in the machine.	Bb.	(Cheep cheep cheep cheep! in baby chick's voice.
	S.C.	It's in the machine.
	Ch.	Oh my goodness, oh dear, oh dear.
There it is in one of the bubbles!	Mj.C.	Mind out. (He takes a deep breath and blows into the microphone. A cloud of bubbles emerges including one containing the chick.)
And down it comes, the bad little chick. I hope it is all right.	Ch.	There she is! There she is! (The chicken flies up and pops the bubble. The chick falls.)
	Chick	Cheep! cheep! cheep!
Yes, it's all right but very naughty ... straight home to bed!	Ch.	You're a bad naughty chick and you deserve everything you got!
	Mj.C.	Is she allright?
	Ch.	Yes, she's all right. She's going straight home to bed! Go on, off you go!
Goodbye chickens, safe journey home!	Mj.C.	Right then, goodbye chickens, goodbye.
	Ch.	Goodbye, goodbye Clangers. (The chickens fly away.)

Episode 8

The Seed

Every sensible person enjoys greenery. Whether it's an amble through the park or tending to leafy vegetables on an allotment, we think of the flora which surrounds us as a good, friendly thing.

But vegetation is at best indifferent to us, with a strong possibility that it is actually decidedly resentful. After all, this world was once its domain. It has been said that before the advent of farming, a squirrel could scamper from tree to tree from Britain's Land's End to John o' Groats without ever touching the ground, if it felt so inclined. Greenery seems benign simply because it grows so slowly and can be pruned and generally gardened before it can mount any serious threat.

The darker side to foliage has often been given full voice through the genre of science fiction. Such classic tales as H. G. Wells' *The War of the Worlds* and Jack Finney's *The Body Snatchers* speak of the sort of terrible events that could befall us if plants and flowers were a bit more savvy and could get more of a move on. Long after reading John Wyndham's *The Day of the Triffids*, I couldn't pass by a hollyhock without flinching.

So it is no wonder the Clangers are alarmed by the speed and enthusiasm with which their latest visitor takes to the once barren surface of the planet they call home.

The day they get out of this predicament is the day pigs will fly... or is that cows?

Episode 8. The Seed

Commentary track		Music and Effects track
Narrator That is the planet earth, where we live. Under the blanket of cloudy atmosphere that covers it there are forests of green trees and meadows of lush grass and gardens of flowers. We are lucky to live there. One could search through the universe and probably find no other planet so pleasant. Even the Clangers' planet which is warm and comfortable inside is a cold barren place on the outside outside. Though I suppose something might be able to grow there... if it was looked after properly.		
	S.C.	Now, that's interesting...I'll catch it! (Small Clanger chases the seed but does not catch it until it settles. Then he dives for it and puts a stone on it to hold it down.)
Got it!	S.C.	Got it! I've caught it. Now I wonder what it is. I must go and tell Tiny Clanger. (He runs indoors.)
	S.C.	Tiny! Tiny! Come and look at this! (They run outside.)
	S.C.	Look! It has begun to grow! (They watch it grow a leaf or two and then wilt.)
Oh it doesn't seem well.	S.C.	Ooh it doesn't seem well.
Of course it needs watering.	T.C.	It needs watering. (She runs to a hill and whistles.)
	T.C.	Cloud! Cloud! (The Cloud answers her.)
	C.	(Tinkle)
Tiny Clanger's friend the Cloud will rain on it.	T.C.	Will you please rain on this seed for us. (The Cloud moves over and rains on the seed.)
There! That's better. Look, there's flowers!	T.C.	That's better. (The shoot revives, grows and flowers.)
Thankyou Cloud, thankyou.	T.C.	Oh that's lovely! That's lovely. Thank you Cloud! (She picks some of the flowers and sticks them on the cloud.)
There what a pretty flowery Cloud. Must call the others to look at this.	S.C.	There, you are a pretty flowery Cloud.
	T.C.	We must show the others!
	T.C.	HI everybody! Come up and see this.
	S.C.	Come up and see this flower-cloud.
	T.C.	Come up and see.
	Mj.C.	What is happening?
	M.C.	What goes on?
	T.C.	Look!
Mother Clanger doesn't like it!	Mj.C.	Whew!
The whole planet is covered with green stuff. She is frightened.	M.C.	I'm frightened! I don't like it. We're trapped.
	Mj.C.	Now it's all right dear, we'll think of something. (Tiny Clanger goes to her bed-cave and takes out her radio-hat).

Ah, Tiny Clanger is going to radio the Iron Chicken. She will tell her what has happened.	Hat	(Buzz-buzz, Buzz-buzz. Buzz-buzz, Buzz-buzz.)
	Iron Chicken	Yes? Hallo Tiny Clanger.
	T.C.	Hallo Chicken, can you help us? Our planet is all covered with green stuff.
	Ch.	Green-stuff?
	T.C.	Yes, it's all over the outside and we can't get out.
Yes, look at that then!	Ch.	Ooh? How extraordinary. I must have a look. (The chicken goes to her telescope and scans the sky. She sees the Clangers' planet all covered with green.)
That's a funny-looking place.	Ch.	Coo! Well fancy that now. Now I wonder what I can do.. (She scans the sky. She sees a cauliflower-shaped planet.)
	Ch.	Ah! yes! sky-moos! That will do. (She runs back to the radio box.)
	Box	(Beep-Beep, Beep-Beep.)
	T.C.	Yes?
Now then, listen what to do. They must fetch something. It looks like a rocket.	Ch.	Right then, set off a rocket, the sky-moos will see it with luck and they will soon clear it up.
	T.C.	O.K. over and out.
	Mj.C.	Come on Small! (They run and fetch a smallish green and white spotted rocket. They set it up under one of the lids. They set off the rocket which bursts in the sky.
	Hat	Buzz-buzz, Buzz-buzz.
	T.C.	Rockets away!
	Ch.	Yes I saw it, very good. (She goes to the telescope and looks at the sky moos's planet.)
They've seen it, they're coming! They're coming!	Ch.	Yes, they have seen it! yes! they are coming. (She runs to the box.)
	Box	Beep-beep!
	Ch.	They are coming! They are coming! The sky-moos are coming!
	T.C.	They are coming!
	Mj.C.	They are coming.
	Clangers	They are coming! The sky-moos are coming.
I can hear them. I can hear them landing. Listen.		(The Clangers sit and look up.) (We hear the sky-moos fly down and land.)
	Mj.C.	Listen! (We hear a succulent champing and crunching.)
They are eating!	M.C.	They are eating!
	T.C.	They are eating!
	Clangers	They are eating! they are eating! The sky-moos are eating!
	T.C.	Let's see?
	Mj.C.	No, not yet. Leave them to eat. We must give them soup. They will be thirsty.
No, Tiny Clanger can't go outside yet. They must eat. That's a good idea. Get soup ready for them. They'll be thirsty.	M.C.	Here is soup. (They lift the big soup-pan onto the trolley.)
Look!	Mj.C.	All right, you can look now. (Small and Tiny Clanger run off. They lift a lid.)
Sky-moos!	T.C.	Look! Sky-moos.

CII.8/3

	S.C.	Oooh. (We see the sky-moos eating the greenery, champing it up in their great mouths. Much of it has gone. The big doors whirr open. The Clangers push out the trolley with the soup-pan on it. The sky-moos champ away! The Clangers unload the pan.)
They are eating well.	Mj.C.	Here is soup for you sky-moos. Soup if you are thirsty. (One of the sky-moos comes over and takes a big draught of soup. It moos appreciatively and goes back to eating. Another moo comes over for a drink. It moos appreciatively.)
You're welcome.	Mj.C.	You're welcome! (The last sky-moo eats the last bit of green. It looks for more. We scan the planet for more but it is clear. It walks to the soup can and has a good drink. It swallows. The sky-moos line up and bow to the Clangers who bow back.
Thankyou sky-moos.	Mj.C.	Thankyou sky-moos. (The sky-moos moo and fly away.)
	Clangers	Goodbye sky-moos, goodbye! Thankyou! Goodbye!
And home they go. I think they enjoyed their dinner.		

CLANGERS II. Music page. 4.

Episode 8. continued.

~~8C~~. The seed grows again and flourishes, it flowers.

5 472 / 491

0 20"

~~8D~~ The flowers stuck in the cloud float down as seeds.

6 385 / 400

0 12

~~8E~~. The new seeds sprout they grow and flower, blow seeds which sprout and grow and flower. then the mood becomes ominous as the flowers grow across the ground like ivy completely obliterating the surface and driving the Clangers to the underside where they dive in and Clang shut the lid.

5 499 / 5 - 625 (2)

sprout and flower. seeds blow new sprout and flower.

0 20 25

CLANG.

40 more and more sprout. become thick advancing forest 60 Clangers run dive in hole. 80 Clang shut the lid. (Sound effect or music)

Oliver, Peter and the Clangers hard at work in the big barn.

Episode 9

Pride

Without doubt a psychoanalyst would have a field day with this one.

While digging at the quarry, Small Clanger discovers a mirror. A seemingly innocuous object which turns out to be anything but. The young Clanger becomes bewitched by his own reflection and wants this new object of desire to remain exclusive to him, much to his sister's chagrin. She and the other Clangers choose to ignore Small. To them, he is now, ironically, invisible.

Like Narcissus gazing into his beloved pool, Small risks the seduction of what is both himself and not himself. This uncanny experience is described by the French psychiatrist Jacques Lacan as the 'mirror phase', where the fledgling Ego lays down its roots through the recognition of an external self-image. However, the story of Narcissus is but a myth and the sweet embrace of self-love is disrupted by the demands of the 'Other' – the pesky outside world. There arises a need to negotiate with this world in order to establish the uneasy equilibrium which is the gateway to adulthood.

In this particular case, the role of the 'Other' is played to great comic effect by the Soup Dragon, who barters for entry into Small's sacred world for the price of a mug of soup. Potentially, this is a painful moment for Small – must his glorious oasis be tarnished by the give and take of the marketplace?

Fortunately, the whole sorry business comes to a smashing resolution and everyone comes away happy and free. This is the Clangers' planet, after all.

The Clangers CII.9/1

Episode 9. Pride.

Commentary track.		Music and Effects track.
Narrator There is the planet earth. On the surface of that cloudy ball you and I and our friends and neighbours are living our lives and doing the things that people do. Sometimes we are friendly and generous. Sometimes we are greedy and unfriendly, keeping things for ourselves when we could be sharing them with our friends. That's the sort of thing people sometimes do and they always will but I wonder if all the creatures on all the planets in the universe are as silly and selfish as people are. Take the Clangers for instance. Their life is very simple on their simple small planet. They have so few things to quarrel about they must be very peaceful and happy. Look at Small Clanger working away at the quarry.	S.C.	(Whistles a happy song as he works.)
Hallo, what has he found.	S.C.	Hallo, what's this? (He has uncovered a mirror surface.)
	S.C.	Oh. (He digs away the surrounding gravel.)
You never know what you'll find in the Clanger's rock.	S.C.	Oh I can see something. (He looks at his reflection.)
Something shiny a great big piece of glass like a mirror.	S.C.	Ooh, that's a Clanger!..That is ME!..What shall I do with it?.. Tiny! Tiny! Come and look at this. (Tiny does not answer so he comes back and digs out the mirror and carries it away. Tiny Clanger is outside polishing the notes of the music tree.)
It shows a reflection, a reflection of Small Clanger.	S.C.	Tiny! Tiny! Look at this! Look, this is ME!
Yes, that is him!	T.C.	Let me see...oh yes! so it is. (She turns the mirror and looks at herself.)
Tiny Clanger must come and see this.	T.C.	Yes, look that is ME!
Now it shows a beautiful reflection of Tiny Clanger.	S.C.	No, it is to reflect ME! (He nudges her out of the way.)
	T.C.	No, I want to look in it.
Oh! er This is only meant to show beautiful reflections of Small Clanger. Yes, Small Clanger himself and nobody else.	S.C.	No, it is mine. It is meant for ME. (He turns the mirror and looks at himself.)
	S.C.	Beautiful! Quite beautiful! (He sets the mirror on a chosen place and goes to fetch some building blocks. Tiny Clanger comes and looks at herself in the mirror.)
	S.C.	HI. Shoo! shoo! shoo! (He shoos her away and fetches more building blocks. Tiny looks in the mirror some more while he is busy making himself an ornamental pavilion.)

	S.C.	HI, shoo! I said that's my mirror for showing ME. (He edges her away and looks at himself. Tiny walks away. She meets Mj. Clanger.)
	Mj.C.	Hallo Tiny, what's wrong?
	T.C.	Small Clanger... he won't let me look in his mirror.
	Mj.C.	The rotten thing!
The rotten thing! He's mean.	T.C.	He's mean... you're mean!
That's right, go indoors and	Mj.C.	Let's go in and leave him.
leave him outside. What is Tiny Clanger doing? Collecting copper leaves. Hmm! she's made a crown! Very pretty, now she needs to look in a mirror.	T.C.	O.K. (They walk away proudly. Small Clanger takes no notice. Tiny Clanger goes to the copper-trees and makes herself a crown of copper-leaves. She puts it on her head. She needs a mirror. She goes out to Small Clanger, looks over his fence.)
	T.C.	I want to look in your mirror. I've made a crown!
	S.C.	Made a crown? Let me see. (T.C. puts it on.)
Yes, it suits her. What's it made of?	S.C.	Oh yes! very pretty, yes it suits you. What's it made of? (He holds out a hand and she passes it to him.)
Copper leaves, how neat. A very beautiful crown.	S.C.	Copper leaves, how neat! (He puts it on his head and looks in the mirror.)
	S.C.	Oh yes! very pretty.
Hey, yes, that's Tiny Clanger's crown.	T.C.	HI give it back, it's mine! (He poses in front of the mirror.)
	S.C.	How exquisitely handsome!
	T.C.	HI. That's my crown!
Yes, marvellous, but it belongs to Tiny Clanger.	S.C.	Now that really suits me. (He sits in his pavilion and admires himself in the crown.)
	S.C.	Marvellous! regal! imperial. (He takes no notice of them. Mother Clanger looks out.)
Ah well, now it's soup-time, time to go indoors.	M.C.	Soup-time, soup-time everybody!
	Mj.C.	Soup-time, come in everybody. (They turn and go in except Tiny Clanger.)
	T.C.	Soup-time, Small Clanger. Are you coming in?
	S.C.	No.
He's not going in! Ah, yes he is!	T.C.	Oh bother! (She stamps her foot and runs in. Small Clanger remains outside admiring himself.)
Small Clanger likes his soup! Here is a froglet.	S.C.	....soup? Ah yes, soup. (He gets up and puts the crown down in the pavilion. He goes towards a lid. He is about to go down when he hears a froglet approaching.)
Now what's he doing? Small Clanger!	S.C.	Good morning Froglet. (The froglet does not answer. It hops into the compound and looks at itself in the mirror.)
He's looking in the mirror!	S.C.	HI what do you think you're doing? HI that's my mirror! (He pushes the froglet out of the way.)
Very elegant.	F.	(croak!) (It pushes back.)
	S.C.	Shoo
	F.	(croak.)

	S.C.	Shoo
	F.	(Croak)
That's right, shut the gate.		(Small Clanger lifts the froglet bodily, dumps it over the wall and shuts the 'gate'.)
	F.	(croak croak)
There's the soup-dragon.		(Small Clanger walks away and goes down a hole. The Soup-dragon sticks her head out of a hole. The Froglet tells her about the mirror.)
Very interesting, hmm.	F.	(croak-croak, croak-croak).
	S.D.	Oh indeed! How extraordinary! How very peculiar!
Now, what about that soup		(Small Clanger goes to the Clangers home cave).
	S.C.	Here I am then, where's my soup?
Hmm, they don't seem to want		(Nobody speaks to him.)
to speak to him.	S.C.	All right then, I'll get it for myself. (He takes the jug to pour himself some soup.)
None left. No soup left.	S.C.	It is empty. HI the soup-jug is empty... There's no soup left... (The Clangers turn their backs on him and walk away.)
That's the only thing to do. He'll have to get some for himself.	S.C.	Oh well, I had better go and get some more for myself. (Small Clanger takes a mug and goes to the soup-wells. The other Clangers watch him go. Small Clanger arrives at the soup-well and looks in.)
Here are the soup wells	S.C.	Hallo Soup-dragon, please may I have some soup?
Where is the soup-dragon?		Hallo! Anybody at home. (The Baby Dragon rises from the next hole.)
Ah there's the baby dragon.	B.D.	(Oh Mum's not at home. She's gone out somewhere.)
	S.C.	Oh yes, do you know where?
	B.D.	Oh yes, outside somewhere.. you know!
The soup-dragon is outside somewhere... oh I wonder what she is doing.	S.C.	I know! (He runs to the outside and sees the soup-dragon sitting in the pavilion wearing the crown.)
	S.C.	What are you doing?
	S.D.	Very pretty don't you think? Suits me doesn't it?
	S.C.	But that's *mine*. That mirror is *mine*! (He gets behind the dragon and pushes her out.)
	S.C.	Out!
	S.D.	But I'm just sitting looking at myself.
Poor Soup-dragon, she was only looking in the mirror.	S.C.	Out!
	S.D.	Oh but I don't want out!
	S.C.	Out! Out! Out!
	S.D.	Oh all right then, all right then! (She goes out of the compound.)
Now he is asking her for some soup.	S.C.	Oh dragon! Could I have some soup please?
	S.D.	Soup? for you?
	S.C.	Yes please.
Yes and the Soup-dragon won't give him any soup. I don't blame her.	S.D.	Oh! You know what you can do to get soup! You needn't think I'm going to fetch you soup. You can get your own soup for all I care. (She walks away muttering.)

	S.C.	Ah well. (He looks at his empty soup-mug.)
Ah well, no soup. No soup for Small Clanger	S.C.	Ah well. No soup. (He sits on his throne and looks at himself despondently. The soup-dragon reappears with a mug of soup.)
Soup-time!	S.D.	Soup-time, soup-time.
	S.C.	Soup?
There, the kind dragon has brought him some soup.	S.D.	Yes, I've brought you a mug of soup.
	S.C.	Oh thankyou, thankyou. (He holds out his hand for the soup.)
Ah, now wait a minute.	S.D.	Oh no no no no! Just a minute.
	S.C.	Soup, I want soup.
	S.D.	I want a look in your mirror.
	S.C.	In my mirror... all right then. (He turns the mirror round so it faces outwards.)
He can have the soup in return for a look in the mirror.	S.C.	Here you are then, give me the soup.
All right, there we are. Hey, that wasn't much of a look.		(The soup-dragon puts the mug of soup on the wall and Small Clanger turns the mirror round again. He reaches for the soup but the dragon reaches it first.)
	S.C.	Give me the soup.
	S.D.	No! you didn't give me a proper go with the mirror.
	S.C.	I did.
	S.D.	You didn't.
	S.C.	Give me the soup.
	S.D.	Turn the mirror round then.
	S.C.	No No No.
Right then, that's what you can do with your mirror and the soup!	S.D.	Right then! (She pours the soup over the mirror and stalks away.)
	S.C.	HI. HI. HI. What have you done? (The soup-dragon goes down a hole)
	S.C.	You can just come and wipe that off. You put soup all over my mirror.
Small Clanger is furious.		(Small Clanger looks down the hole.)
You rotten dragon, you can just come up and wipe the soup off my mirror, he says.	S.C.	You rotten dragon! You've spoiled my mirror. Come on up and wipe it at once. (The soup-dragon rises from another hole with a mug of soup.)
We know you're down there, you can just come straight up again.	S.C.	Come out at once you rotten dragon. I know you're down there.
	S.D.	Yes.
The soup-dragon's down there. She souped his mirror!	S.C.	The soup-dragon's down there! She souped my mirror!
	S.D.	Oh the rotten thing!
	S.C.	No! You're here!
Look out!		(Small Clanger is so surprised he drops the mirror down the hole where it shatters.)
	S.D.	It's broken.
	S.C.	It's broken!
And she's brought him some soup.	S.D.	I brought you some soup.
	S.C.	Thankyou. (Small Clanger drinks the soup.)
Hmm delicious soup, thankyou.	S.C.	Thankyou.
You're welcome.	S.D.	You're welcome.
Oh they're laughing at last.	S.C.	(laughs)
	S.D.	(laughs)

CII.9/5

Mj.C.	(laughs)
all Clangers	(laugh)
I suppose Clangers are just as silly as people really but perhaps with them it doesn't last quite so long.	(Small Clanger takes off his crown, dances over to Tiny Clanger and dumps it on her head. They dance over to the compound and push it to pieces. The other Clangers dance after them and help. Then they go indoors.)

Episode 10

The Bags

Throughout the *Clangers* series there have been many pertinent and recurrent topics on existence, both here and on the little blue planet, including such heady subjects as politics, isolation, consumerism and, of course, the truly dreadful nature of humanity. But one topic has been notably absent: romance.

The arrival of a charismatic outsider brings surprise and wonder to the Clangers' world. His talents are multifarious. His commanding speaking voice produces beautiful shapes and colours that briefly linger in the sky. He has a wickedly mischievous sense of humour – causing Froglets and Clangers to disappear, and making off with the Clangers' blue-string pudding just for a lark. He's able to conjure up delicious and exotic comestibles and he can appear and vanish at will. So, all in all, this mysterious, leathery stranger is quite a character – if a somewhat bizarre one.

As is often the case with more esoteric matters, the Froglets seem to have some knowledge about what's going on. This Gladstone bag is simply too charming to remain alone for long, so the Froglets get on the case, happy to play matchmaker.

With the tug of a silken kerchief, an evening lady bag – glamorously jewelled – is revealed! And, of course, it's love at first sight.

The Clangers CII.10/1

Episode 10. The Bags

Commentary track.		Music and Effects track.
Narrator Well, that is the planet earth, where we live. It is a well-protected place because the covering of atmosphere, of air and clouds keeps out most of the more unwelcome objects that are whizzing about in space. From this distance the sky looks pretty empty except for the stars and planets but of course from this sort of distance you wouldn't expect to see anything unless it was pretty enormous. But things are there just the same and sometimes quite unexpected things turn up in quite unexpected places.		
Now, that for instance. Just what is that and what's it doing there?	T.C.	Now what on earth is that? (She walks round the bag. She goes to a lid.)
It looks like a bag. A Gladstone bag.	T.C.	HI. Small! Come up and see this thing. (Small Clanger emerges. He walks round the bag. He touches it. He goes to another hole and calls down.)
Very peculiar, perhaps the froglets will know what it is.	S.C.	HI Froglets. Come up and see this thing.
	Fs	(croak-bonk, croak-bong.) (Two froglets jump out of the hole)
	S.C.	Look at this thing.
Do they know what it is?	Fs	(croak and hop once round the bag.)
	S.C.	Do you know what it is?
They do.	Fs	(Nod and croak.)
	S.C.	Oh? What is it? (The froglets hop over to the bag.)
	Fs	(Hallo bag) (The bag opens and a word comes out and hovers in phonetic alphabet in the sky for a moment.)
It speaks!	Bag	('alo...)
Say something to it Tiny.	S.C.	Look! it talks! Say something to it Tiny.
	T.C.	How do you do?
How d'you do!	Bag	(How do you do?) (The froglets laugh.)
	Bag	(laughs)
Look they've jumped into it.. and vanished!		(The froglets hop over to the bag and jump in.)
	S.C.	Look! they have vanished. They aren't anywhere inside the bag.
Small Clanger's in the bag. He's inside it.		(Small Clanger climbs into the bag. It clicks shut.)
	T.C.	Hi Small! Small! come out! come out! (The bag slowly vanishes.)
The whole thing has gone! Nothing there. Oh, there it is, with Small Clanger and froglets inside it!	T.C.	Where are you? where are you? what happened? (She turns and sees the gladstone bag behind her.)
Tiny Clanger won't stand for that. What have you done with Small Clanger?	T.C.	There you are! What have you done with Small Clanger? Come on now! (She advances a pace towards the bag and it vanishes and reappears a pace away.)

	T.C.	Where is he? (She advances, the bag retreats.)
What about the froglets?	T.C.	Where is Small Clanger... where are the froglets... what have you done?
Oh now it's gone again.	T.C.	Oh dear, what shall I do? (She turns away and sits, worried.
Oh no, there it is.		The bag appears in front of her.)
I wish it would let them out.	T.C.	I wish you would let them out!
	Bag	(ow) (It opens and the vowel sound appears above it. It vanishes revealing Small Clanger who falls on top of Tiny Clanger.)
There he is!	T.C.	Ow ow, Look out! There you are!
Catch him!	S.C.	Yes
	T.C.	Where are the froglets?
Yes, where are the froglets?	S.C.	I don't know. (Tiny Clanger picks up the net and addresses the bag.)
	T.C.	Where are the froglets?
There they are!	Bag	(Aark, Aark.) (The froglets appear in the sounds and Tiny Clanger catches them in her net.)
Got 'em.		
	T.C.	Are you all right?
	Fs	(nod and croak.)
Ha ha, they look all right.	S.C.	Ha Ha Ha! Ha ha ha!
They rather enjoyed that.	T.C.	Ha Ha Ha! Ha ha ha!
	Bag	(laughs)
Now what's this?	T.C.	I know! Let's play music to it. (She runs to the music trees.)
Will the music trees play some music for the bag?	T.C.	Please music trees, may we play music to the bag?
They will.	Mfs	(pling-plang)
	T.C.	Right-ho. (The music-trees play phrases of music which the bag answers with voice and manifestations. The soup-dragon comes to hear.)
hmm, very interesting.	S.D.	Oh I say that's good. Oh yes, I like that, oh that's good. May I have a try?
The soup-dragon likes that. She would like to have a try.	S.C.	I expect so. (The soup-dragon sings a duet with the Gladstone bag. Tiny Clanger collects the manifestations with her net and instead of vanishing with the echo the manifestations remain solid. Tiny Clanger and Small Clanger make a heap of the black lumpy voice-pieces and sit on the top. At the end of the song they clap.)
What a lot of song. What a great pile of ~~it,~~ Song look at that!	T.C.	That's very good! Look at all this voice!
	S.C.	Marvellous. (Mother Clanger puts her head out of a hole and calls.)
Ah soup-time, yes of course, time to go	(off) M.C.	Small! Tiny! Come in now, soup-time! Soup-time!
indoors. Goodbye dragon goodbye bag. Thankyou. And away goes the song. Away go the Clangers, and away goes the bag. Where to?	T.C.	Oh we must go in now, it's soup-time. Thankyou bag! (The bag shuts with a click and the heap of manifestations vanishes leaving them momentarily in mid-air. They fall, and run indoors. The froglets hop down a hole. The soup-dragon leaves. The bag is left alone. It slowly vanishes and reappears beside the

		Clangers' table inside.)
	Mj.C.	Hallo? What's this?
Hmm, what's this?	T.C.	It's a bag. It makes noises.
It's a bag! It speaks.	Mj.C.	Does it indeed...How d'ye do?
	Bag	(How d'ye do?).
There you are, it speaks.	Mj.C.	So it does!
Better offer it some blue-string pudding.		Well, we had better invite it to have some dinner... Would you care for some blue-string pudding?
Yes, it likes blue-string pudding.		(The bag plays a snaky tune and the blue-string pudding snakes out of the big pot and wriggles into the bag.)
Look it's empty, scoffed the lot.	Mj.C.	It's empty! It's scoffed the lot! Hey bag! Where's our dinner?
Yes, bag, where's their dinner?	Bag	(dinner?)
	Mj.C.	Yes! dinner.
Yes, dinner.	Bag	(makes a noise that manifests cake.)
	Mj.C.	No not that, we want dinner.
	Bag	(makes an ice-cream cornet.)
No, not cream cake No, not ice cream cornets.	Mj.C.	No not that...Blue-string pudding. (The bag makes a bundle of soggy blue-string pudding in the air and it falls all over Major Clanger.)
Blue-string pudding! That's right, blue-string pudding.	Mj.C.	Ahk, eek, ork, yak. What do you think you're doing?
In the pudding pan.	T.C.	(laughs)
	Clangers	(laugh).
Major Clanger is angry. He doesn't like being laughed at.	Mj.C.	That's enough! You can go!..Go on... Go away! Go! Go!.. Go! (The bag mixes itself away to the wall and vanishes.
It must go.	T.C.	Oh the poor bag!
And it's gone. Poor bag. He doesn't care, it was rude.	Mj.C.	I don't care, it was rude. (Major Clanger heaps the blue-string pudding back into the big pot. Tiny Clanger goes outside to speak kindly to the bag.)
Tiny Clanger cares.	T.C.	I'm sorry father turned you out. It was all a mistake.
She thinks the Clangers were rude.	Bag	(All right) (A froglet jumps out of a hole.)
She will apologise.	F.	(croak bonk, croak croak croak!)
There's a froglet and their top-hat. That's conjuring hat.	T.C.	What do you want? (The froglets top-hat is thrown up, followed by their magic cloth and two more froglets.)
Yes, they want her to do a trick.	T.C.	Do you want to do a trick?
	Fs	(nod and croak)
	T.C.	All right then. (Tiny Clanger puts the cloth over the hat.)
	T.C.	Ready?
	Fs	(croak croak croak croak incantation.)
	T.C.	Right?
Ah yes	Fs	(croak)
How romantic, a pretty jewelled evening lady bag. Now all we need is some soft romantic music.		(Tiny Clanger pulls away the cloth revealing a very pretty jewelled lady gladstone bag.)
	T.C.	Oh yes! What a good idea. (She runs to the music trees.)
	T.C.	Please play lovely sweet music for the bags.
Of course, a waltz. Ah. Quiet!		(The music trees play sweet sentimental music. The bags join in, manifesting hearts and flowers.

Clangers II music page 5.

Episode ~~9~~ 10.

main gladstone bag = bassoon. ~~So~~ lady Gladstone bag is a ~~flute~~ oboe?

~~10 A.~~✓ Music trees play short phrases on harp which the Bag repeats as bassoon sound and visible shapes in the sky. 6 600 642

0 harp 5//7 bassoon 12 14. harp 19//21 Bassoon 26 28 harp 33//35 Bassoon 40

40 harp. 45//47 Bassoon 52.

each of these "thoughts" should be ~~[illegible]~~ in a different "mood." A classical phrase, a Schmalzy phrase, a smooth light phrase, a staccato modern, — or what you will — Something which can be amusingly illustrated in the manifestation that appears.

~~B.~~✓ Bag plays a snake-charming tune. high bassoon about 12 secs 7 472 488

~~C.~~✓ Bag makes three noises which appear as.
1 cake. 2 ice cream cornet. 3 a heap of soggy spaghetti 7 492 503

~~D~~✓ The froglets have produced the lady gladstone bag. So Tiny Clanger goes to the music trees and they play some very sentimental hearts and flowers music ~~to~~ to encourage them to get acquainted. After a while the two bags join in and as they 'sing' hearts and flowers entwined manifest themselves in the sky. They fly away together. captions. 6 245 400 (2)

orchestral for end captions

0 hearts + flowers (harp) 10 G bag joins (bassoon) 15 lady bag joins (flute) 20 they fly up together 35. 60.

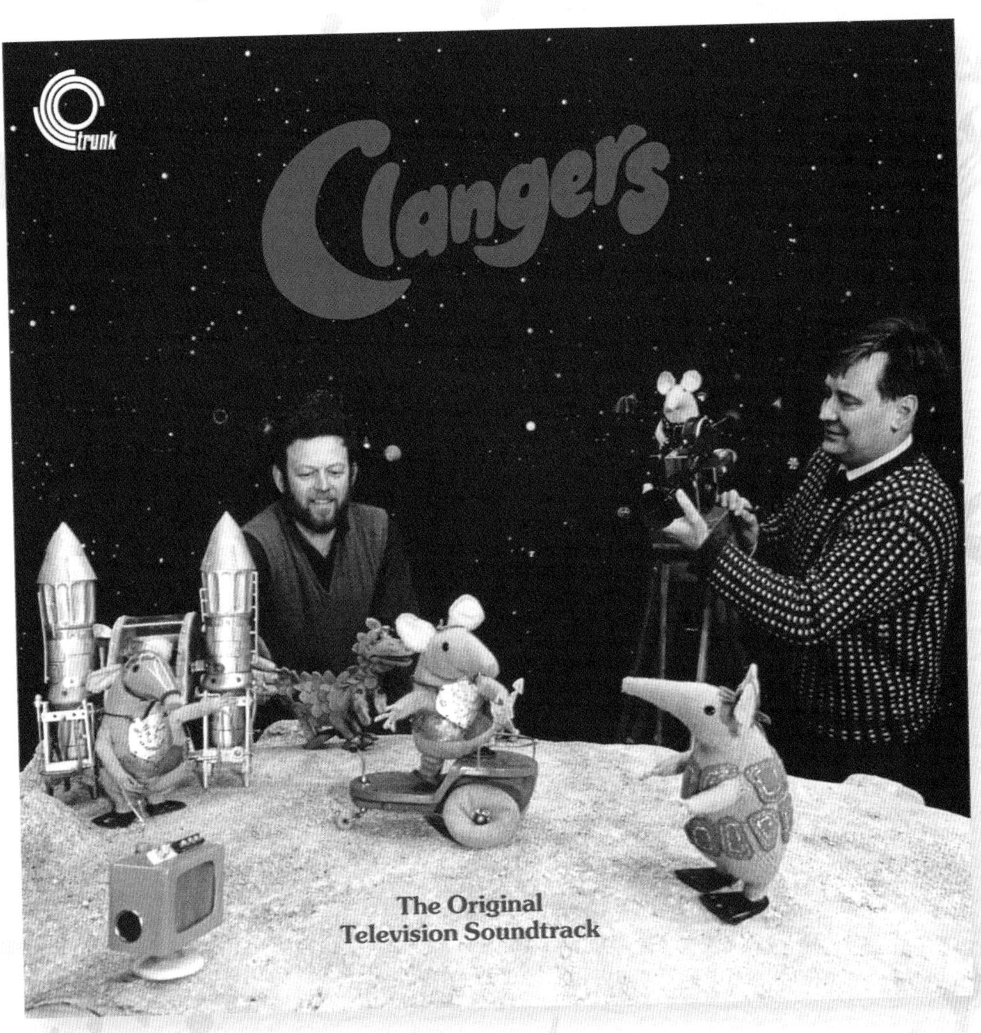

Publicity shot used by Trunk Records for the Clangers music album.

Episode 11

The Blow-Fruit

Each new discovery comes with a question: will it be used for good intent or will it be abused and debased? Certain plants and fungi, for instance, hold extraordinary properties within their chemistry that serve as superb elixirs to ease afflictions when used wisely, but in the wrong hands they can lead us on a path to madness and catastrophe.

When the Clangers find a strange new poppy-like crop flourishing in the deeper caves, their discovery can go either way. And in fact it does. Tiny Clanger fashions its stems into pan pipes to create wonderful music to enjoy with her singing flower-friends, while Baby Soup Dragon – in his first and only substantial role – and Small Clanger repurpose its bulbs for mischief and mayhem.

As is often the case, it is the higher of the two purposes which is driven into exile. Tiny and her friends are forced to leave the very planet itself in order to find artistic sanctuary from those 'barbarians at the gates'.

There is a third way, however. One which is neither purely good nor abysmal. With the new bulbs in harness, Major Clanger's long-held desire to conquer the sky with the contraption he cobbled together in the very first episode finally becomes an actuality.

The Clangers CII.11/1

Episode 11. The Blow-Fruit.

Commentary track		Music and Effects track.
Narrator		
That planet. The planet earth where we live, must be about the noisiest place in the universe with factories and motorcars. Steel-foundries and television sets all thumping and roaring and hooting and quacking away. How peaceful the rest of the solar system seems by comparison. What a marvellous place to be if one just wants to be quiet and peaceful and perhaps make quiet gentle music. The Clangers' planet, for instance. That has music trees growing on it. Tiny Clanger can come out and ask the trees for some notes of music and they will give them to her. There she is.		
Thankyou trees.	T.C.	Thankyou trees, they will do nicely. (Tiny Clanger takes the notes and goes below. She goes to the flower-cave to teach the little flowers to sing.)
Ah, the flowers in the flower	T.C.	Here I am little flowers.
cave.	Fls	(Hallo)
And here's Tiny Clanger	T.C.	Let's do some singing!
come to try out the new	Fls	(Yes please)
music notes.	T.C.	Now sing this note.
There's one...sing that		(ping)
note...yes.	Fls	(ping)
And another...very good.	T.C.	Now this one
What pretty voices the		(pong)
flowers have got.	Fls	(pong)
I'm sure they could learn to	T.C.	Right, and now this one!
sing tunes if Tiny Clanger		(pang)
taught them.	Fls	(pang)
	T.C.	That's good. (The Baby dragon appears in the cave.)
Hallo, somebody calling. Tch! I wonder who it is.	B.D.	Here I say! Tiny Clanger! Here I say! I've found something.
	T.C.	Od dear...I'm sorry!
	Fls	(O.K.)
That's the Baby dragon.	T.C.	Are you calling me?
He's very excited about something. Perhaps he's found a new cave!	B.D.	Yes! Yes! come here! come quickly! We've found something.
	T.C.	Oh all right...excuse me please.
	Fls	(O.K.)
Come on! come on!	B.D.	Come on! come on! come on!.
	T.C.	All right, I'm coming, I'm coming. (Tiny Clanger and the Baby dragon come out of the glow-buzzers hole and see Small Clanger.)
Come on everybody, come and see what the Baby dragon has found.	B.D.	Hi, Small Clanger, Small Clanger, come here! come here!
Come on Small Clanger!		(Small Clanger runs to them.)
	S.C.	What is it?
	B.D.	Come and see this...over here! (They all run. They run to a new cave that nobody has seen before. They squeeze into the cave. It has trees in it like glass tubes with metallic pineapple-type fruit.)
Look at that. A copper pipe tree!	T.C.	Ooh! pipes! (She picks some broken tube-

You can play the pipes! listen.

Those are the fruit, don't eat them, they may be poisonous.

What an extraordinary-looking tree it is!

I suppose they can play catch with the fruit if they want to.

Whee! look at that!
They must be full of compressed air or something!
Mind out!

Yes quite a bit less noise please. Tiny Clanger is trying to tune a set of pipes.

Oh.
He's setting off another blow-fruit.
Whee, there it goes.
Mind out Tiny!

That's the best idea Tiny.
Try and find somewhere a bit more peaceful out of the way of these two noise-makers.

Ah there are Tiny Clanger's friends the flowers.
They'll be interested in her new pipes.

Hey! What's that noise?

They're dropping blow-fruit in the soup well!
What a dreadful thing to do!

That's right Tiny, go home, find somewhere quiet.

The soup-dragon's coming!
Now there'll be trouble!

She'll give them such a walloping if she catches them.
Come back! come back!
I don't know, I really don't.

branches from the floor.)

T.C. These are good to play on.
(She blows through them and they play.)

S.C. What about these?
(He breaks off a fruit and looks at it.)

T.C. You mustn't eat it, it might be poisonous.)

S.C. Oh no.

B.D. Oh no.
(Small Clanger looks at the fruit and wonders what to do with it.)

S.C. Here you are! Catch!
(He throws it to the baby dragon who runs outside.)

B.D. Here you are! Catch!
(They throw the fruit to each other. One of them drops it and its stalk breaks off. It cracks and hisses, flying up like a released balloon.)

S.C. Coo!

T.C. Do you mind making less noise. I'm trying to tune these pipes.

S.C. They go Hiss-wiss-hiss.
(The Baby dragon brings out another and throws it. It goes crack-hiss and flies about.)

T.C. Oh! I'm not staying here.
(She picks up her pipes and goes away. Small Clanger and the baby dragon go back into the cave and come out with two fruit each.)

B.D. Let's go and drop them in the soup-well!

S.C. Coo yes!
(They run out. Tiny Clanger sees two flowers looking out of the Glow-buzzer's cave.)

T.C. Hallo, look at these pipes! They are marvellous...Listen.
(She plays a note on them.)

Fls (same note)

T.C. (another note)

Fls. (repeat note)

T.C. Now this one.
(There comes a tremendous bubbling roar.)

T.C. What was that?
(Small Clanger and the Baby dragon are standing over the soup-well. The Baby dragon drops a fruit into the well. It bubbles up roaring in the soup which leaps up in green foam.

T.C. Oh dear isn't there anywhere we can practise in peace?
Come on, let's go home.
(They walk out. Small Clanger and the Baby dragon are about to drop another fruit into the soup well when the soup-dragon arrives.)

S.D. Just what the hell do you think you're doing? You're a ruddy menace you two! Always up to no good. If I catch you I'll give you such a walloping! Come back! Come back I say! Oh the rotten lot. What a mess! What a terrible mess! I don't know, I really don't.

		(Small Clanger and the Baby Dragon have run away. Tiny Clanger is playing notes with the flowers by the Clangers' table. Mother Clanger is listening. Small Clanger and the Baby Dragon come in. Mother Clanger tells them to be quiet.)
	M.C.	Shhh.
	S.C.	Shhh.
	B.D.	Shhh.
Listen! A real tune. And the flowers are singing it beautifully.		(They are quiet. They listen. The Baby Dragon has a fruit in his hand. He looks at it, wonders what to do with it. He pops it into the soup-jug. The soup-jug blows up bubbles.)
Oh no, not again!		
	T.C.	Oh you rotten lot! Why isn't there anywhere we can go.
Poor Tiny, poor flowers, isn't there anywhere on the planet they can find a bit of peace.		(Tiny Clanger marches off with the flowers.)
	M.C.	Oh you bad Clanger! You bad dragon!
He's a bad dragon.	Mj.C.	Small Clanger, show me that. Hmm, interesting. Might be useful, this. Come on, I've an idea.
Major Clanger is interested in those blow-fruit. They could be used for something. That old flying machine for instance, they could use these instead of balloons to make it go. That would be worth trying.		(Small Clanger and Major Clanger go to find the old ornithopter. Tiny Clanger hauls out the music boat. She and the flowers sit in it and fly up. Small Clanger and Major Clanger work on fitting some fruit to the old ornithopter in place of the balloons. Tiny Clanger and the flowers sing a verse. Small Clanger and Major Clanger haul out the ornithopter and try it. It works. Tiny Clanger and her friends sing another verse. Tiny Clanger looks over the side.)
Ah the music boat, well I suppose if there's nowhere _on_ the planet to practice in peace they'll have to find somewhere off the planet. There's the old ornithopter. It didn't work very well with balloons, I wonder if it will work better with blow-fruit.		
Well at least Tiny Clanger and the flowers have found somewhere peaceful at last.	T.C.	Oh no! look at that!
Yes it works. It flies!..very good!		(The ornithopter rises beside them.)
	S.C.	Hallo Tiny Clanger, hallo flowers.
Oh dear, look at that. They have a visitor. Oh no, go away.	T.C.	Go away! Go away! Leave us alone.
It has stopped, it is broken, down it goes! Ouch!		(The ornithopter hisses and blows bubbles. It rocks, it begins to fall. It falls slowly to the ground. Tiny Clanger looks down.)
Ah well, perhaps they'll have some peace at last.		
Yes, pack it away, leave Tiny Clanger and the flowers to play their music in peace.	T.C.	Now perhaps we'll have some peace... Come on flowers! (They sing their piece.)

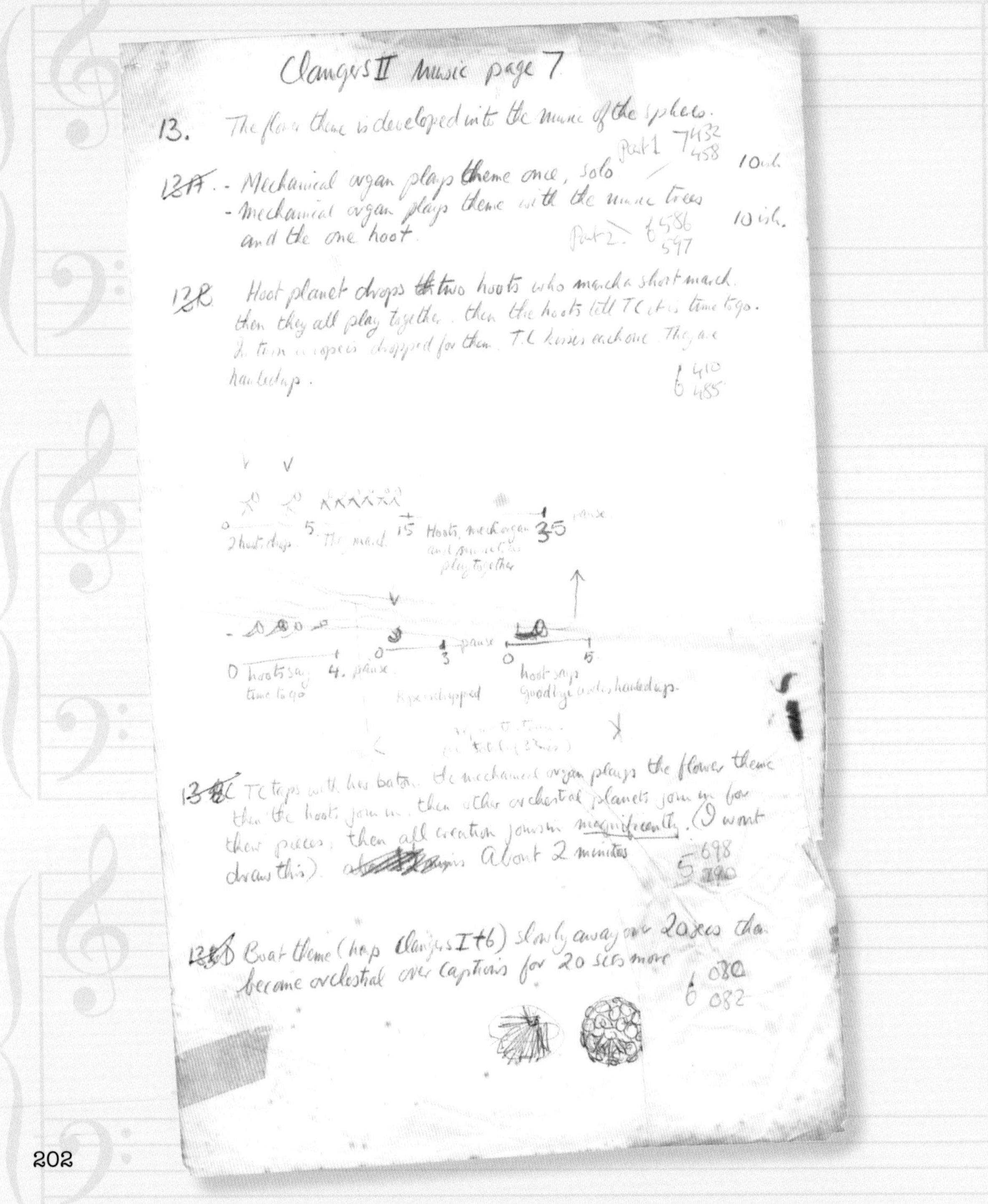

Clangers II music page 7

13. The flower theme is developed into the music of the spheres.

Part 1 7 452 458 10 ish.

13A. - Mechanical organ plays theme once, solo
- mechanical organ plays theme with the music trees and the one hoot.

Part 2. 6 586 597 10 ish.

13B. Hoot planet drops two hoots who march a short march. then they all play together. then the hoots tell TC it is time to go. In turn a rope is dropped for them. T.C kisses each one. They are hauled up.

6 410 485

13C TC taps with her baton. the mechanical organ plays the flower theme then the hoots join in, then other orchestral planets join in for their pieces; then all creation joins in magnificently. (I won't draw this). about 2 minutes

5 698 790

13D Boat theme (hap Clangers I+6) slowly away over 20 secs then become orchestral over captions for 20 secs more

6 080 082

Episode 12

The Pipe Organ

As we know, the Clangers are great believers in recycling, much like their furry cousins down here on Earth: the Wombles. Both species were busily recycling away decades before the human race finally faced the facts and got on with it too.

So it's no surprise to see Major Clanger's flying contraption, which never really lived up to expectations, being reutilised as a pump. Although Major's ingenuity is beyond doubt, exactly how he uses that ingenuity is another matter.

Running a soup-pipeline from the soup wells to the main cave may seem a positive time-and-effort-saving enterprise but, in the larger scheme of things, perhaps a bit of time and effort is something worth holding on to. The more we streamline our lives, the less we find random and unexpected opportunities, and, ultimately, the more humdrum life can become. If Major's pipeline had proved a success, the Soup Dragon, no longer visited for soup, could easily find herself marginalised and isolated from the Clanger community.

Fortunately, the whole project proves to be a disastrous failure. Consequently, the pumping machine is banished from the caves by an enraged Mother Clanger, and traditional soup-delivery is re-established.

Now Tiny Clanger has a turn at a spot of reutilisation. The erstwhile flying-contraption-cum-pumping-machine is converted once again. This time into something marvellously musical: a pipe organ. And, as we shall see, it also serves as a catalyst for the series' spectacular finale.

The Clangers CII.12/1

Episode 12. The Pipe Organ

Commentary track		Music and Effects track
Narrator		
That planet, the earth, is a fairly ordinary and self-contained sort of planet. The people living there don't have much to do with the other planets and stars and heavenly bodies in space. That's a pity really because one can imagine some very odd and interesting planets and stars. The Clangers' planet we know about. Nobody could call that ordinary. Or that one, the Hoot planet. That one is very unusual. Or this one, this is just Tiny Clanger with her friends the flowers in the music boat.		
		(The Hoot-planet is approaching.)
Ah she has seen the Hoot planet.	T.C.	Why! It's the Hoots! Hallo Hoots!
Hallo Hoot planet		Hallo!
and here come three hoots.		(The planet heaves to above them.)
	T.C.	Hallo Hoots!
Now for a really musical greeting.		(Two hoots descend on strings and play a tune with them. Mother Clanger comes out of a hole and calls.)
Ah, soup-time.	(off) M.C.	Tiny Clanger! Tiny Clanger! Come in now. Come in now, soup-time.
Mother Clanger is calling her in.	T.C.	Right-ho! We're coming!
Goodbye Hoots, goodbye,		Goodbye Hoots, we must go in now.
and down they go.		Goodbye.
Down to the Clangers' planet. It's always quiet on the outside of the Clangers' planet, but inside, in the caves		(She takes the music boat down. Small Clanger and Major Clanger are fetching soup from the soup-well on their trolley.)
where Clangers live it is	Mj.C.	Look out the wheel is coming off!
very busy.		(The wheel comes off.)
There's Small Clanger on the	S.C.	We must carry it.
trolley fetching soup from the		(They try to carry it.)
well. Something's wrong. Oh the	Mj.C.)	Pull, pull, pull, pull, pull...
trolley, it's got a wobbly	S.C.)	Pull, pull.
wheel. Look out! Oh, oh dear.	Mj.C.	No, it's too heavy.
That soup-can is heavy. I don't think Major Clanger and Small		(Tiny Clanger appears with her pipes.)
Clanger will drag it far.	T.C.	What are you doing?
Ah there's Tiny.	S.C.	Oh Tiny! Please will you lend me
What is Small doing? He's taken		your pipes?
her pipes.	T.C.	What?what?
The other Clangers are hungry. They want soup.		(Without waiting for her reply, Small Clanger grabs her pipes and runs out. The other Clangers are waiting for their soup.)
	Clangers	Soup! soup! soup!
Ah there's Small Clanger. Now he has gone again!		(Small Clanger collects some blow-fruit from the cave. He rams them into Tiny Clanger's pipes.)
	T.C.	Where has Small gone?
	Mj.C.	I don't know.
		Soup! soup! soup.
Now if there's one thing	M.C.	Haven't they brought that soup yet?
Clangers really care about	C.2	Not a bit of it, and I'm hungry.
it's having their meals at the proper time.	Clangers	Soup! soup! soup!
They want their soup!	S.C.	Right?
Now what has Small Clanger	Mj.C.	Right, all set.
made... a rocket?	T.C.	I don't like it.

CII.12/2

I don't like the look of that. Soup's coming!	S.C.	Fire! (He pulls a string or something and the blow-fruit blow the can away like a rocket.)
Well it has arrived.	Clangers	Soup, eek! (The Clangers dive for their holes as the soup-jug hits the wall and spreads soup in a splodge.)
But Mother Clanger doesn't seem very pleased. Not surprising really. I think Clangers like to have their soup in the proper container.	M.C.	Now just what the blazes do you think you lot are doing? You've made a dreadful awful mess and covered the wall with wasted soup and frightened the life out of everybody and still we haven't any soup. We want soup! Soup in mugs. Mugs like this!
Yes soup in mugs, mugs like that.		(Major Clanger is talking to the soup-dragon.)
Ah now Major Clanger and the soup-dragon are discussing a project. Perhaps they can think of a way to deliver soup. They could invent some sort of engine.	Mj.C.	You see, what we want to do is make it reach all the way there. We can use these pressure things and make it go piff-puff, piff-puff, piff-puff.
	S.D.	Oh yes, what a good idea. We could do that, it would be perfectly reasonable. We could connect it here and let it pump from up there.
Ah a load of copper-tree stalks.	S.C.	Here you are, here is a load of soft-topped macaronis.
They are hollow. Oh I see, they fit together to make a pipe.	Mj.C.	Good, well you make up the piping while the dragon and I fit up the pump... We could use some of the pieces off the old ornithopter I expect, come on, let's have a look.. (Major Clanger and the soup-dragon go off to make the pump. Tiny Clanger views the soup-splodge.)
Soup! They are still waiting for their soup!	M.C.	Soup!
	Clangers	Soup! soup!
Ah yes, two bunches of blow-fruit. They are full of compressed air! Look at that.	Mj.C.	Now then, that bit goes in there and we can fix the beam over like this. Ah, now that's useful...
That's the old flying machine. That is a complicated piece of engineering. Yes, that's a pump. The dragon has brought a bellows.	S.D.	I've brought up both the big concertina pumps. I dare say they'll be suitable to your extravagant purposes...we'll fit it together like this...
	Mj.C.	Ah yes, that's good.
Soup! soup!	(off) (on) Clangers	Soup? soup? soup? soup? soup.... soup? soup...
When are they going to get their soup?	M.C.	Oh I don't know, I'm going to bed.
They are fed up with waiting.	C.2	So am I.
I'm not surprised. What a ridiculous situation.	M.C.	Well what a municipal project! (Major Clanger and Small Clanger and the soup-dragon are working away on the soup pipeline.)
The music trees. Tiny Clanger is making herself some new pipes. The trees are helping her tune them.		(She turns and goes outside. Major Clanger fits in one of the blow-fruits. Tiny Clanger goes outside to the music trees. She starts to tune her new pipes. Small Clanger finishes setting up the pipeline.) (Small Clanger holds the end of the pipe over the big jug.)
Soup time?	S.C.	Soup-time, soup-time.
	M.C.	Soup-time?
Soup-time.	C.2	Soup-time?

Narration	Speaker	Dialogue
	C.3	Soup-time? (The Clangers gather round Small Clanger and the big jug.)
Yes the end of the pipe but where's the soup?	M.C.	Come on then, where's soup?
Ah Major Clanger is fixing it. Look at that machine. It works! It turns! but no soup comes out.	S.C.	Major Clanger is fixing it. (Major Clanger starts the beam engine. It pumps and puffs. Small Clanger holds the pipe. The Clangers watch. No soup comes out.)
	M.C.	No soup comes out.
No soup.	C.2	No soup.
	C.3	No soup.
Oh look! There's soup.	S.C.	Look! (A very small trickle of soup comes out.)
Not very much soup.	S.C.	Look! There's soup. (The trickle stops.)
	M.C.	That's not much soup.
Yes, well perhaps it will come better in a minute.	S.C.	Well wait a minute it'll come. (They wait, the pump pumps faster. It reaches a crescendo.)
The machine is working beautifully. I think. Look out! Look out Small ugh.	C.2	Look out! (They dive for their holes again as the joints of the pipe-line burst and soup spurts everywhere.)
Oh dear, it didn't work very well.	Mj.C.	Oh dear.
	S.D.	It didn't work very well.
No it didn't!	Mj.C.	No, it didn't.
Look out, Mother Clanger is cross. That nasty messy useless thing must go! She doesn't mind what they do with it but it must *go*.	M.C.	Now, that will *do*. That is quite enough of silliness! You will take that nasty thing out of here. Out of this cave. Out of all the caves. You can launch it into space for all I care but it must *go*.
	Mj.C.	Go?
	M.C.	It must *go*! and then you can just clear up this mess. Look! soup everywhere! Soup all over everything! I'm going to bed! (She retires to her hole and slams the door.)
	Mj.C.	Ah well, come on Small! (They push the pump away.)
	Mj.C. & S.C.	Push! push! push! push! push! push!
Yes that'll do, leave it there.	Mj.C.	Oh that'll do, leave it there!
What's that then? Very interesting.	S.C.	O.K. we'd better go indoors and clear up. (They go in, Tiny Clanger comes over to investigate.)
Yes, a Clanger could make something with that.	T.C.	Oh, very interesting, well, I wonder, I think I'll make something with that... yes. (She goes in through the big doors and pulls out the gramophone-box from Episode 7.)
Now what is she fetching up? The horn off the old recording machine. What else does she need? Ah yes, string.	T.C.	Pull! pull! pull! pull! pull! pull! There! That will do. Now, we'll fix the pump on top of it. (She chats to herself as she fits the pump to the gramophone and fixes the pipes on to that.)
Oh look, the soup-dragon has brought Mother Clanger	T.C.	Oh we need some string!
some soup at last.	M.C.	Soup! ah soup! Thankyou Dragon.
You're welcome.	S.D.	You are welcome! (Tiny Clanger runs past with a coil of string.)
Listen...music.	S.D.	Here I say, listen to that! ooh!
I wonder what that is?	M.C.	I wonder what that is.

CII.12/4

That's the pump engine.
She has made an organ, a mighty blow-fruit organ.
Very good!
Yes now that is better.
That is something really useful!

(Tiny Clanger has assembled the pump and the pipes and the Horned gramophone into a mighty Wurlitzer.
She plays a tune on it.
The Clangers clap.
She bows, plays the tune again.)

Knit a Clanger

Wool: 2 ozs. Bright pink. Double Knitting.
Needles: No. 12.

Body

Cast on 12 st.
Work four rows in st. st.
Row 5: Incr. in first and last st.
Row 6: P.
Repeat rows 5 and 6 until there are 44 st. (row 36) ending on P. row.
Now incr. each end of every row until there are 54 st. (Row 41).
Now incr. each end of every K. row until there are 70 st. (Row 57).

Armholes

Row 58: P. 14. Cast off 6. P. 30. Cast off 6. P. 14.
Row 59: Incr. in first st. K. 13. Cast on 6. K. 30. Cast on 6. K. 13. Incr. in last st.
Now incr. at each end of K. rows until there are 78 st. (Row 65).
Continue no incr. for 2½ inches.

Shape for Bottom

1st Row: K. 18. K. 2 tog. K. 8. K. 2 tog. K. 18. K. 2 tog. K. 8. K. 2 tog. K. 18.
2nd Row. P.
3rd Row: K. 18. K. 2 tog. K. 7. K. 2 tog. K. 16. K. 2 tog. K. 7. K. 2 tog. K. 18.
4th Row: P.
5th Row: K. 18. K. 2 tog. K. 6. K. 2 tog. K. 14. K. 2 tog. K. 6. K. 2 tog. K. 18.
6th Row: P.
7th Row: K. 18. K. 2 tog. K. 5. K. 2 tog. K. 12. K. 2 tog. K. 5. K. 2 tog. K. 18.
8th Row: P.
9th Row: Cast off 7. K. 18. Cast off 12. K. to end.
10th Row: Cast off 7.
K. 8 rows of st. st. on each of these sets of stitches.
Cast off.

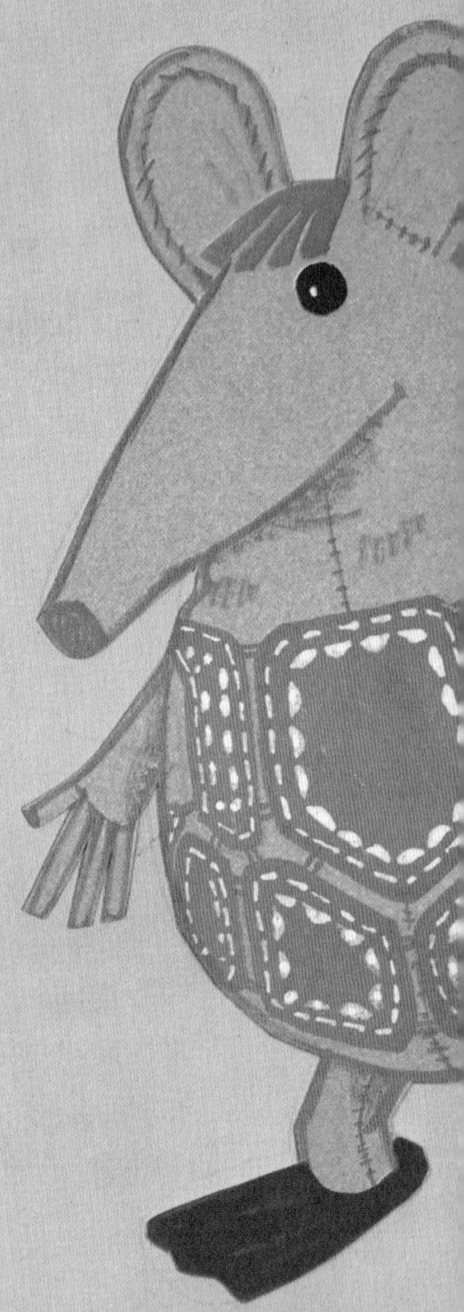

rs
eft ear)
st on 4 st.
w 1: K. 3 incr. in last st.
w 2: P.
ntinue in st. st. Incr. in last st. of every K. v until there are 10 st.
or right ear make incr. in first stitches).
5 rows of st. st.
xt row: K. 2 tog. K. 6. K. 2 tog.
xt row: P.
xt row: K. 2 tog. K. 4. K. 2 tog.
xt row: P.
st off.
ffen each ear with a pipe-cleaner which kes into the head when the ear is sewn into ce. Cut a small piece of pink felt big enough stick to the front of the ear.

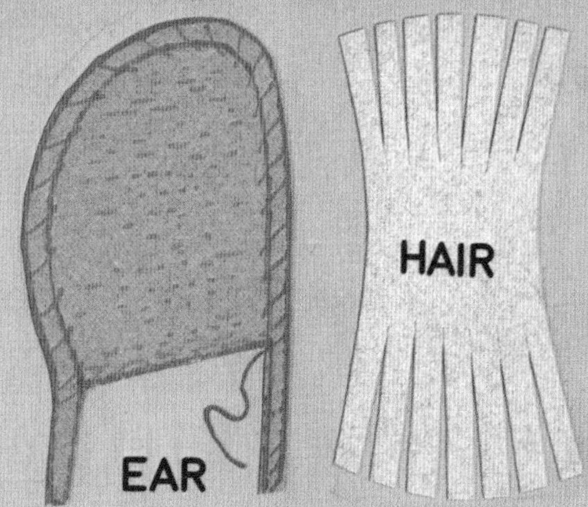

Arms
Cast on 12 stitches.
Row 1: K.
Row 2: P.
Row 3: Incr. in first st. and last st.
Work seven rows st. st.
Row 11: K. Incr. in first and last st.
Work 5 rows in st. st.
Cast off.
Make up the arms and sew into the armholes.
Cut a half-inch circle of brown felt for the nose and sew into place. Sew up the front body seam and stuff well with kapok or old nylons. Then sew up the bottom and legs.
Make the feet, stiffening them with card and sew to the legs, making sure that the legs are well stuffed.
Making sure that the stuffing is tight in the arms, bend two pipe-cleaners in half for each hand and sew into the arm.
Cut out and fix the hair.
Sew on two shiny shoe buttons for eyes.
Sew on the ears.
Stitch under the chin to hold the head down in the right position.
The clothing or armour is made of shapes of felt in any colour decorated with stitching and sewn in place.
If the toy is for a small child or baby the wire could be dangerous. Use wool or felt for the fingers instead.

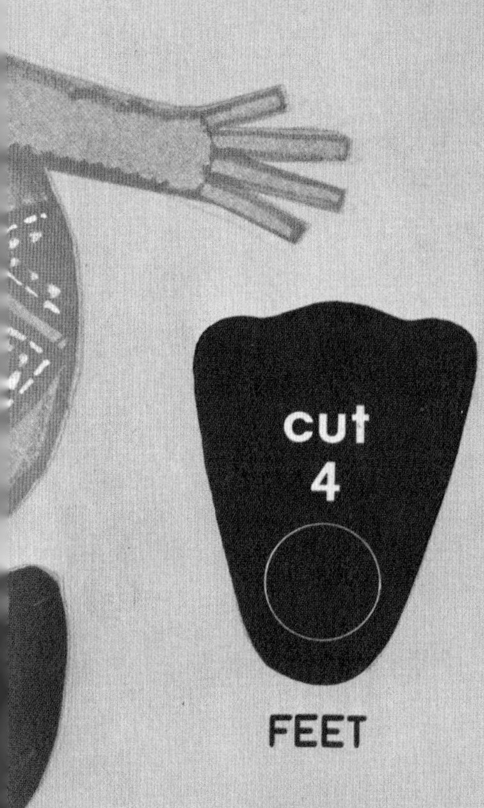

Episode 13

The Music of the Spheres

For the last episode of the *Clangers* series, Oliver Postgate, Peter Firmin and composer Vernon Elliott pull out all the stops with a musical extravaganza. A coda for the series as a whole.

Astonishingly, Tiny Clanger's new pipe organ develops sentience and with it a desire to be with its own kind. The nearest horn-based lifeform similar to itself is of course the Hoots on their Hoot Planet. However, the Hoots are not the only wind instruments to populate the firmament. The sky comes alive with a wide variety of heavenly bodies – hoots and toots and horns of all description, some much stranger than anything we would see on our own world. And it seems they have gathered in the vicinity of the Clangers' planet for an impromptu festival of somewhat haunting horn music, while they gently revolve and cartwheel through the darkness.

Any attempt to understand what is going on is pointless. As we have surely learnt by now from our many visits to the Clangers' world, some beings and some events are simply beyond our grasp, and amen to that.

So, we may as well just sit back, kick off our sandals and soak it all up... happy in the knowledge that this will always be a special place, where all is good, all is kind and all is joyful.

The Clangers CII.13/1

Episode 13. The Music of the Spheres

Commentary track		Music and Effects track
Narrator		
If you look up at the sky at night and see all the stars and planets against the blackness of the sky, they seem silent and still. But of course we are only seeing the very large ones. Maybe the small ones are not all round and not all still and silent. They might be any shape. They might move about and if we had ears like Clangers have to hear the music of the spheres, we might be able to hear each planet and each star singing its own song as it glides forever through space.		
What's that?	S.C.	How odd.
Something fell down one of the Clangers holes.		
Ah Small Clanger and Tiny Clanger have heard it. I wonder what it is.	T.C.	How extraordinary. (The froglets jump out of their hole.)
	Fs	(croak-croak-croak!)
	S.C.	What? (They listen to the noise.)
That's right, it's a Hoot. You remember the Hoots. They come from that planet all covered with trumpets.	T.C.	It's a Hoot! It's a Hoot! You remember the Hoots! I must find it!.. (off) where are you Hoot. (Tiny Clanger runs down to the cave-mouth and runs through the caves until she comes to the Hoot.)
Yes, there it is.		
	T.C.	Hallo Hoot! Hallo! How nice to see you! (She picks up the Hoot and runs out with it. She stops outside the Froglets cave.) (T.C. and S.C. both take hold of the rope and pull up the Hoot.)
Oh what a noise they do make.	S.C. & T.C.	Pull! pull! pull! pull! pull! pull! (They pull up the Hoot and stand it outside beside the music trees.)
Look, music trees, here is a hoot.	T.C.	Look! Music trees, here's a hoot!
	MTs	(plang!)
And this is the pump organ that Tiny made.	S.C.	And look, Hoot, this is the pump-organ thing we made.
	Hoot	(Hallo)
Hi, it speaks.	P.O.	(a sound of greeting.)
It made a noise, all by itself.	T.C.	It makes a noise! by itself!
It's meant for playing music on. It plays music beautifully.	S.C.	Well I never!
	T.C.	Come on then, let's all play a tune. (She works the pump and plays the organ and the music trees join in a short piece of music.)
Small Clanger has seen something.	S.C.	Listen.
Yes, it's the Hoot planet.		(The Hoot-planet is approaching.)
Come to fetch the hoot.	S.C.	(off) HI Hoots! HI Hoots! Your Hoot is here! (The Hoot planet heaves to over-head.)
Here they come. Very ceremonial these hoots. They do everything to music.		(The planet lowers two martial Hoots who march up to the Clangers and do a short ceremonial parade. Then they say it is time to go, and say goodbye.)
Goodbye hoots!	T.C.	Goodbye.

Up you go Hoots. Home you go Clangers. Hi look! The pump organ.		(The Clangers go indoors. The Hoots are winched up. Tiny Clanger is about to go into a hole when the pump organ gives a loud sad cry. Tiny Clanger comes back.)
I want to go with them.	P.O.	(I want to go with them.)
	T.C.	Well of course you can go with them if you want to.
	T.C.	(off) HI Hoots! Will you take this with you? (The Hoot planet drops a rope and hook. Tiny Clanger hooks it onto the pump organ. As she does so the hoot-planet begins to move.)
Hi, wait a minute, give her a chance to fix the rope on.	T.C.	HI wait for me to get off! HI. HI (away) Help! Help!
	S.C.	Tiny Clanger, where are you?
Jump off Tiny, quick!	T.C.	(off) Help! Help! Help!
	S.C.	Oh my goodness!
Oh dear.		(He rushes indoors. He collects some pipe-branches and blow-fruit. He runs outside again, shouting as he passes the home-cave.)
	S.C.	Tiny Clanger! She has been taken up with the Hoot-planet!
	Mj.C.	Tiny Clanger?
	M.C.	Taken up?
	C.2 & C.3	(Oh my goodness! What a dreadful (thing! Oh what shall we do? Let's (run about here and there!
Well don't just run about in circles, you silly Clangers. Do something.	Mj.C.	Well don't stand there hooting. Fetch the boat!
	M.C.	Of course! of course! the boat. Come on! fetch the boat.
Yes - That's right, fetch the music boat.		(They run out. Small Clanger is on a hill. He whistles for the cloud.)
	S.C.	HI Cloud! Cloud!
There's Small Clanger with some blow-fruit. They're full of compressed air, like rockets. He's talking to the cloud. I know, he's going to ride on the cloud. There he goes. And there's the music boat.	Cl.	(Tinkle)
	S.C.	Tiny Clanger has been caught up by the Hoot-planet. We must catch her! (The cloud lowers and Small Clanger jumps on. He releases a blow-fruit rocket and they are blown away. Tiny Clanger is still hanging onto the trailing pump organ. The other Clangers are pushing out the boat.)
Hurry. Oh it's a slow old thing that music boat.	Clangers	(pull! pull! pull! pull! pull!) (The music-boat lifts up and flies away. Tiny Clanger and the Hoot-planet have stopped.)
There she is! There's Tiny Clanger!		(The Cloud arrives and supports Tiny Clanger.)
She doesn't seem to be hurt.	S.C.	Are you safe Tiny?
Yes, she's all right!	T.C.	Yes, I am fine.
Small Clanger's giving that planet a good telling off. Well, it should pay attention, not go hoisting Clangers about like a crane.	S.C.	The rotten planet! Hey you! Hoot-planet! You are rotten! You pinched the organ and hooked up Tiny Clanger and gave all of us a terrible fright...
	T.C.	No... look.
er what?	S.C.	What?
	T.C.	Look all around!
Ooh look! Look at all those! What a peculiar collection of heavenly bodies. I wonder why they have all come here.	S.C.	Ooh!.. oh I say! (He sees the other planets.)

I know, they've come to make music!

Ah here comes Major Clanger, looking a bit puzzled. Er, Tiny.
No time for talking.

Very good, very good.
And when you've quite finished deafening the whole of creation with the music of the spheres we'll go home.
Ah yes, the pump organ is staying with the hoots. It'll be happier with them.
Goodbye hoots, goodbye all you other musical planets and goodness knows what. Time to go home. And home they go.
Major Clanger, Small Clanger and Tiny Clanger and the Cloud and the music boat. Away through the silent emptiness of space to their own planet and green soup for supper.
Goodbye.

T.C. All right, let it down!
(The Hoot planet lowers the organ to the cloud.)
T.C. Right, start the pump.
S.C. O.K. Right. All ready?
(She taps and conducts an enormous music of the spheres. At the end Major Clanger claps.)
Mj.C. (claps)
Mj.C. Very good, very good. Now, if you've quite finished deafening the whole of creation, we will go home!
T.C. Right-ho! Take it up! Hoots!
(The Hoot planet raises the organ.)
T.C. (Goodbye Hoots. Goodbye everybody.
S.C. (Goodbye, goodbye!
(Major Clanger has thrown a rope. The music-boat tows the Cloud away back to the Clangers' planet.)

Clangers II music. page.6.

Episode 11. This has a theme which recurs later as the big orchestral piece in Episode 13. so think them out together.

~~11.A.~~ ✓ play 3 notes on high ~~oboe~~ clarinet as if trying out 3 ~~pan~~ pipes. play 2 more. pause (play some more if necessary) pause. Then play them as a scale. (they are the basic notes of the theme)

~~11B.~~ ✓ Tiny Clanger plays one note on ~~two~~ one of her pipes (high ~~oboe~~) clarinet. 7 275 432
The glow-flowers reply the same note. (~~G~~ soft vibe) they are lovely like singing
T.C plays another note. The glowflowers repeat it
T.C plays three notes together. The flowers repeat that.
T.C plays the theme. The flowers repeat it. (these last about 10 secs)
T.C and the flowers play the tune in unison.
T.C and the flowers play it three times with variations and parts.

5 482 498

~~11.C.~~ ✓ T.C and the flowers play the theme once very happily and then it becomes orchestral over the end captions.

~~11.D.~~ ✓ 3 notes on Harp answered by 3 notes on vibe, 11E 3 notes of theme 11E 3 notes harp only. 7 057 098

Episode 12.

~~12A.~~ ✓ Hoot planet has hove to above. It drops two Hoots on strings. They play the flowers theme. Then T.C. flowers and hoots sing it together

6 510 534

0 hoots descend. 4. hoots play flower theme 14. T.C flowers and hoots play it together 24.

~~12B.~~ ✓ T.C is ~~tuning~~ trying out her pipes against notes from the music trees. One note from harp – reply same note from ~~high oboe~~ clarinet – repeat for 5 other notes. 7 155 275 (2)

~~12C.~~ ✓ T.C fits up the broken pump as a pipe-organ with the pipes.
– play flower theme. starting slowly and speeding up as she winds handle
– play flower theme at good speed. 7 432 458

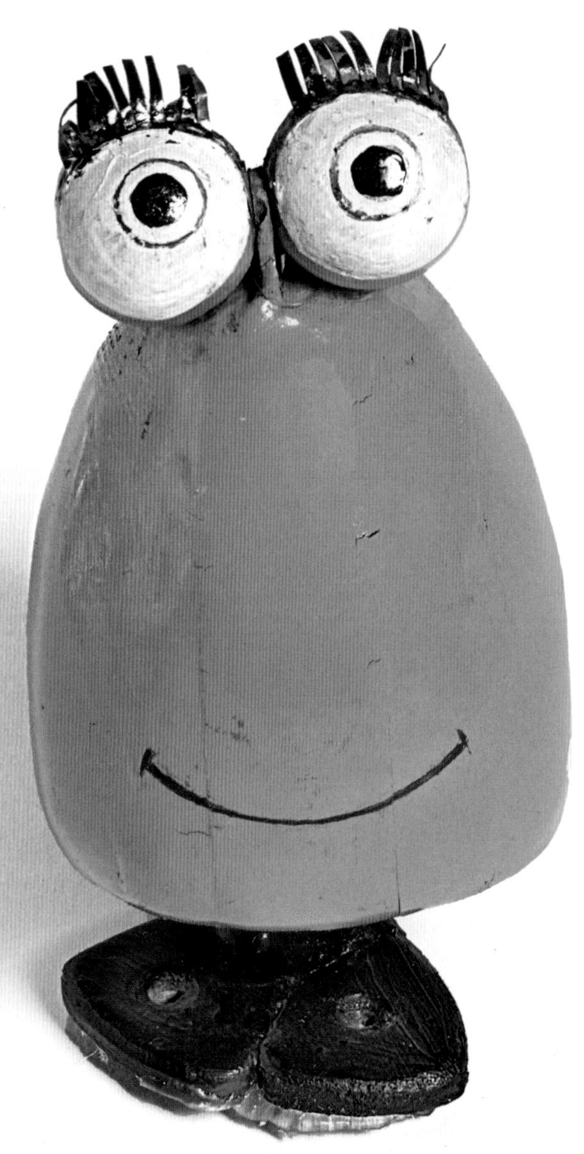

Vote for Froglet

It is early 1974 and Britain is going to the dogs while the two main political parties are preoccupied with thumping chunks out of each other.

Oliver Postgate is concerned. He was in Germany after the end of the Second World War, delivering spadefuls of honey from a large barrel to desperate villagers, so he knows a thing or two about the dangers of societal collapse. Before the first general election of that year he secures a slot on BBC Radio 4's Woman's Hour to air his views on how the electorate needs to vote for the Liberal Party in order break the detrimental deadlock of the two-party system.

At a Q&A on Smallfilms, Oliver and Peter were asked: 'Where are the Clangers now?' Oliver replied with a wistful flutter of his hand that they were somewhere up there, in space, living out their quiet, peaceful lives on their little blue planet. At which point a grinning Peter Firmin intervened to say, 'No, they're not. They're in a metal trunk under my desk.'

The election is inconclusive and another is booked for later that year. Another election, another chance for Oliver to express his views. He decides that this time his powers of persuasion are best expressed through the medium he knows best: single-frame animation. The metal trunk is pulled from under the desk, and the Clangers are released once more!

'Vote for Froglet' was made in three days, just in time for it to be aired on the BBC on election night. The Clangers ultimately abandoned their own election as, naturally, it proved to be unpleasantly divisive, and retired to their caves to continue their happy lives as an autonomous collective. The British, however, struggled on as best as they could with democracy.

Election Clanger 2nd draft 15 9 74. Oliver Postgate

M/ S Earth in space

(Sound over)

Deep montage of selected election speeches. A general hubbub in which certain Gems like "You know it makes makes sense,"You never had it so good"and"Let the militants know they are defeated!" can be picked out.

7 mins

about 15 seconds still then T/O

Fade sound to half and add echo as camera tracks out

Narrator Hmm. Sometimes our planet is a bit noisy in places. It must seem odd to other creatures on other planets. The Clangers for instance. I wonder what they make of it all.

pan L to L/S Clanger planet.
cut into close shot of Clangers by a hole, looking to Right.

Major Clanger. What on earth is going on?

Major Clanger looks at camera and opens his arms

Narrator What is going on?
That is the sound of Democracy at work. That is the proudest moment of the British people...A Parliamentary Election.

Mother C. A Parliamentary what?

Narrator An Election. The people of Britain are about to choose some six hundred men and women to sit in the House of Commons and decide the best way to run the affairs of the country.

Clangers. Oooooh
Major C But what is all the noise about?
Narrator The noise? That is the Election Campaigns of the political parties.
Major C. Political parties? What are they?

Narrator Political parties? Well...er... How shall I explain? They are a part of democracy I suppose. Where two or three people of like mind are gathered together and think that a particular policy is in their/or the country's best interests they form a political party. /own

Major C What for?

Narrator What for? Well obviously so they can be a force. They have unity and loyalty and faith in a cause. They can act together to defeat other political parties and get what they want. Do you understand?

Clangers No No

Narrator I wonder how I can explain. Look. Who is in charge of the Clangers' planet. You know, which of you tells the others what to do.

Clangers In charge? I don't know, What's in charge? You must be in charge I have no idea (ad lib)

Narrator Come on, somebody must be in charge. Don't you know?

Clangers No, we don't know

Narrator Well there you are then! There's the cause of all your trouble. In our country we have a

	Narrator (cntd)	government. They make the laws and tell us what to do
	Major C.	Who chooses the government?
	Narrator.	A good question. I'm glad you asked me that. Who chooses the government? That is where democracy comes in. The people choose the government by holding an election.
	Small C.	An election?
	Narratbbr	Yes, that's right...look, suppose you decide to have a government. You could choose cl the government of the Soup dragon for instance.
	Soup dragon	A government of the Soup dragon oooh yes.
	Narrator	Or the government of the Froglets. Are there any Froglets there?
	Froglet	Yuk.
	Narrator	Oh, only one. Well, one will do so long as he has the support of a strong political party who will campaign for him.
	Major C	How will they do that?
Soup Dragon and Froglet into place	Narrator.	How? I'll show you. The Froglet stands on the left and the Soup-dragon on the right... Good, that's right. Now, we need a policy. A manifesto, a statement of policy.
	Soup D.	A statement of policy?
	Narrator.	That's right. You tell us all the good things your government is going to do to make life better for everybody on the planet.
	Soup D	Better? But life is marvellous!
	Narrator	Oh, come now. There must be some way you can improve it. There must be progress. You can't be a government and be in charge of everything if you haven't got a policy. There must be something you want.
	Soup D	Hmm oh, hmmm...The soup wells. Close the soup wells one day a week.
	Narrator	Close the soup wells one day a week. Good. Even a soup dragon is entitled to rest.
	Soup D	Yes. Yes.....And those Froglets go splashing about in the soup wells. I say No Froglets in the soup wells!
	Narrator	No Froglets in the soup wells.
	Soup D.	Yes, and from now on soup must be paid for!
	Narrator	Soup must be paid for. Hey, but what with? you don't have xxx money.
	Soup D.	Oh ..er..well er I know. Free soup for all!
	Narrator	Free soup for all. That should catch the votes. Free soup for all!
	Soup D	Free soup for all..Except Froglets!
	Narrator	Free soup for all..Except Froglets!

Election Clanger 2nd draft page 3

	Soup Drago~~Narrator~~	Free soup for all..Except Froglets! Froglets are a nuisance Froglets are messy. Froglets hop! Free soup for all. but no soup for Froglets
	Narrator	Dear me you do learn fast. Now wait a minute. We must hear from the Froglet. Froglet. What is your policy?
	Froglet	Yuuurk.
	Narrator	Well that's just rude. Now come on. What is your attitude?
	Froglet	Whatever the soup dragon wants I'm against it.
	Narrator	Whatever the soupdragon wants he's against it.
	Froglet	Right.
Small C. runs to the Froglet	Narrator ~~right~~	Right. Now who will support the Froglet?
	Small C.	I do! I do! The soup dragon is horrid to froglets ... Poor Froglet
	Froglet	Yurrrk.
	Narrator.	There. Now you are a political party. It is your job to persuade the electors to vote for Froglet.
Small C. goes to the other Clangers and pushes them about	Small C	Vote for Froglet. Vote for Froglet. You know it makes sense. Come on. vote for Froglet Vote foo Froglet
	Clangers	(reply ad-lib, mild pandemonium)
Major.C crosses to soup.D who is looking dejected.	Major C	Don't worry Soup Dragon, I am on your side
	Narrator	Major Clanger. You are on the soup dragon's side. Would you mind telling me why.
	Major C	The soup-dragon is my friend.
	Narrator	The soup dragon is your friend. Well, we're all friends I hope. What about the policy?
	Major C.	We don't pay for soup anyway. So things stay as they are.
	Narrator	Yes! a very good point. ~~X~~ You don't pay for soup anyway, so free soup for all means things stay as they are. You would like things to stay as they are?
	Major C.	Yes! Yes! Free soup for all That's what we want.Free soup for all!
Major C.Goes to the others and exhorts them	Soup D.	Free soup for all Except for Froglets.
	Major C.	Free soup for all. Vote for the Soup Dragon Free soup for all. Down with Froglets!
	Small C.	Don't be damn stupid, Vote for Froglets Vote for Froglet.
... and Major ...t eachother	Clangers	(join in excitedly. Angry pandemonium)
	Narrator	Hold it hold it! That'll do. Stop arguing. Now you have heard the campaigns of the two political parties. It is time to cast your votes. You must choose. Froglet or soup dragon. The one with the most votes

Election Clanger xaxaxd 2nd draft page 4

Narrator (contd.) will have the duty of being the government and will make the laws. Now, we can't have a secret ballot here, so you all just go below and then come up one by one and join the Froglet or the Soup dragon.

They go below.
Small looks out

Clangers (ad lib) Down we go, come on everybody.

Small C. Ready?

Narrator Yes, ready. One at a time please.

Small Clanger leaps out and runs to Froglet

Small C I vote for Froglet

Froglet Yurk yurk

Small C. Froglet! Froglet for ever!

Major C. climbs out and crosses to the soup dragon

Major C. I give you my wholehearted support.

They shake hands

Soup D Thankyou very much Free soup for all!

Major C Free soup for all

Tiny Clanger comes out

Major C Tiny, come over here.

Small C Come with us, Tiny.

Tiny Clanger hesitates

Major C. Come here at once

Tiny Clanger moves slowly to Soup dragon

Small C That's not fair!

Major C. Shut up Frogface!

Uncle Clanger comes out

Small C. Vote for Froglet(ad lib.)

Major C. Vote for free soup for all (ad lib.)

Uncle Clanger sides with Small Clanger.

Narrator There now. A swing to the left and it's level pegging. Who is to give the casting vote?

Mother C. looks out

Mother C. Is it me now?

Narrator. Mother Clanger. Yes. It is time to vote.

There is hush as she slowly inspects each side.
She is overcome with doubt.

Mother C. Must I?

Narrator Yes, you must.

Mother C But I don't want to choose.

Narrator. Can't help that. It is your civic duty to vote.

Mother C. Oh dear Oh dear Oh dear

She weaves about and in the end dumps herself by the soup dragon and sits dejected.

Major C. Congratulations Soup dragon Hooray

Narrator Yes. By two votes to three I declare that the soup dragon is duly elected to form the government of this planet.

Small C. Its not fair Not fair!

Narrator Not fair? Of course it's fair. What could be fairer than an election? The soup dragon has a majority of three to two. He has the right to impose his policies.

Election Clanger page 5.

Small C. No It isn't fair. Mother Clanger didn't want to choose. Nor did Tiny Clanger.
Major C. Shut up, it was fair
Tiny C. Yes it was
Major C. Free soup for all!

Clangers (ouch Yarooh Gerroff)

They come to blows
Only Mother Clanger sits still.
She jumps up — Mother C Stop. Stop at once. Stop
She wades in and stops the fight
Mother C I have changed my mind.

Narrator. No, no, You can't change your mind. The election is over.

Soup D. Yes she can. I don't want her vote.
Narrator It doesn't matter what you want. You are elected to carry out the policies you promised. No soup for froglets.
Soup D. But I want to give soup to Froglets. I like Froglets. Soup for Froglets.

Narrator You can't do that. That is betraying your own party.

Soup D But Froglets will be hungry without soup.

Narrator True. Froglets will be hungry without soup. But you should have thought of that before. The whole thing is settled now. No soup for Froglets.

Mother C. Oh rubbish fiddlededee! get stuffed!

Narrator Rubbish? That's party politics.

Mother C. Stuff and nonsense. Come on everybody, sit down here..Now, soup dragon will you give soup to Froglets?
Soup D. Of course of course. I always do.
Major C. I think that's a good idea. What was all the fuss about?

Clangers talk softly together
Narrator Hey, wait a minute, Mother Clanger. You can't go setting up an opposition now.

Mother Clanger Oh sod off!

Narrator. Look I was only trying to show you how we do things on our planet. It is all right for Clangers to sit down together and settle their arguments but people can't do that.

Clangers ignore the camera

Mother Clanger Can't they? Why not?

Narrator No..well. I suppose people can. In fact people on their own can be as loving and generous and tolerant as Clangers. They can welcome sacrifice and compromise for the common good but political parties can't. Anything like that is just weakness in a political party....listen. I mean whoever heard of Political Generosity? It's a contradiction. Party politics is a struggle for power. Hey, are you listening to me?

The Clangers talk among selves. They e and one by one

Clanger shakes his head
Major C. ...No...Goodbye
clangs shut.

A Note on the Authors

Oliver Postgate was one of the greatest children's storytellers of the modern era. His work, which includes *Clangers*, *Ivor the Engine*, *The Pogles*, *Noggin the Nog* and *Bagpuss*, is beloved by generations.

Daniel Postgate is an award-winning author and illustrator of over 50 children's books. He was a freelance cartoonist for the *Sunday Times*, *Radio Times*, *The Biochemist* and *Loot*, and is now a BAFTA-winning scriptwriter.

Unbound is the world's first crowdfunding publisher, established in 2011.

We believe that wonderful things can happen when you clear a path for people who share a passion. That's why we've built a platform that brings together readers and authors to crowdfund books they believe in – and give fresh ideas that don't fit the traditional mould the chance they deserve.

This book is in your hands because readers made it possible. Everyone who pledged their support is listed below. Join them by visiting unbound.com and supporting a book today.

Ian Abbott, Tom Abell, Susan & Rob Acton-Campbell, Abi Adam, Nick Adams, Robin Adams, Wyndham Albery, Richard Alcock, John Alderson, Deborah Allen, Louise Allen, Sarah Allen, Mike Allum, Fran Anderson, Mark & Diane Anderson, Gina Anderson-Besant, Martin H. de T. Andrews, Bernard Angell, Alice Angus, Anji, Kirk Annett, Jenna Appleseed, Malcolm Apps, Philippe Ariaudo, Neil Arlett, Jo Armes, Tracey Armes, Keith Armstrong, Hilary Armstrong x, Sabrina Artus, Abigail Ashton, Adrian & Zoe Ashton, Janet Askari, John Aspinall, Carol Atack & Alex van Someren, Joe Austin & Andrea Hilton, Nicola Awdry, James Aylett, Jamie Badminton, Clare Baguley, Martin Bailey, Chris Baker, Helen Baker, Kath Baker, Nigel Baker, Steve Baker, David Baldacci, Elsa Baldwin, Jason Ballinger, Cherrie Barber, Kevin Barber, Jenni Barclay, Adam Bard, James Barker, David Barlow, Ruth Barlow, Joods Barnard, Catherine Barnes, Gavin Barnes, Steve Barnes, Jane Barney, David Barraclough, Kevin David Barratt, Andrew Barrett, Robert Baskerville, David Bates, Andrew Baxter, Bazille, Michael Bearpark, Jane Beaufoy, Roden Beckwith, Harold & Alfred Bedwell, Dylan Beech, Mark Beecham, Francesca Bekker Graham, Lou Bell, David Benn, Greg Bennett, Phil Bennett, Phillip Bennett-Richards, Janet Bentley, Lily Bentley, Liz Bentley, Paul Bentley, Alison Berrett, Donna, Fraser & JJ Berry, Anna Best, Wendy Bevan-Mogg, Andrea Bick, Deborah Bick, Andrew Biggs, Chris Biggs, Ian Billingham, Nige Billings, Marian Bingham, Joe Binks, Paul Bird, Matt Bishop, Simon Bisson, Dave Black, Simon Black, Heather Blake, Rob Blake, Rupert Blakeley, Graham Blakelock, Bridge Blankley, Steven Blevins, Arthur Boden, Hilda Bodley, Simon Boggis, Gary Boller, Muriel Bonner, John Bonney, Nick Bonny, Serena Booth, Alexander Borg, KJ Boswell, Tim Bourne, Bruce Bowie, Tony, Karen, Alice, Daisy, Fred, Ben & Arthur Boydell, Jos Boys, Caitlin Bracken, Tom Bradley, Simon Bradshaw, Julia Bramble, Barbara Brannigan, Kal Breadmore, Allyson Breeds, Nick Breeze, Benita Brett, Miles Brewis, Steve Brickell, Beverley Bright, Andrew Brignell, Alice Broadribb, Richard Brook, BrotherRock, Jim Broughton, Nicky Brown, Tony Brown, Rebekah Browning, Simon Browning, Brian Brunswick, Angie Bryant, Sandra Bryant, Amelia Buchanan, Pauline Buchanan Black, Ellen Buck, Jennifer Buckie, Jason Buckley, Victor Buckley, Ann Budd, Claire Budd, Duncan Budd, Geoffrey Budd, Tamsin Budd, Samantha Bull, Erica Bullivant, Jackie Bullock, Gillian, Hann & Tony Bunn, Julie Burgess, Christine Burns, Sarah Burnside, Roger Burrows, Amber Burton, Andrew M Butler, David Butler, Rob N Byrne, Ric Caesar, Susi Caesar, Liam Cahill, Lorna Cairney, Nicholas Cairns, Clare Campbell, John Campbell, Julie Campbell, Nick Campbell, Sarla Campbell, Maria Carlton, Jonathan Carr, Morwenna Carr, Christopher John Carroll, Ciarán Carter, Michael Carter, Antony Cartlidge, Amy Cartmell, Kathy Cartmell, Anna Chambers, Lorraine Chamen, Julian Champion, Agnes Chandler, Jude Chandler, Shirin Chandy-Welham, Janet Chaney, Julia Chanteray, Stuart Chapman, Luke Charles, Suz Chate, Neil Chavner, Paul Cheeseman, Sally Cherry, Michael Child, Jonathan Childs, Nick Childs, Ben Chipps, Samantha Jayne Chisnall, Paul Chisnell, Juan Christian, Peter Christian, James Clancy, Alison Clapham, David Claridge, Alexia Clark, Anthony Clark, Charlotte Clark, Jan Clark, Steve Clark, Jason Clarke, John Clarke, Sarah Clarkson, Peter Clary, Chris Claxton, Ann and Doug Cleaver, Helen Cliffe, Jen Coates, Angela Coburn, Sam Cocking, Michael J Codd, Edward Cole, Andrew Coleman, Janis Coles, Stevyn Colgan, John Collar, Sam Collett, Christopher Collingridge, Louise Collins, Tim Collins,

Penelope Colman, Michael Comeau, Catherine Congreve, Jez Conolly, Ilka Cook, Luna Cooling, Porl Cooper, Ray Cooper, Steph Cooper, Stephen Edwin Cooper, Denis Copeland, Percy Copley, Peter Corrigan, Janet Costello, Katy Costello, Ashley Costin, Justin Costley, Teresa Cotterell, Cath M. Cotton, Frank Cottrell-Boyce, Simon Coward, Peter Cowin, Pippa Cowin, Stewart Cowley, Elizabeth Joyce Cox, Susheila Cox, Sheena Coxhead, Fiona Coyle, Imelda Cracknell, Donald Craig, Paul Craigie, John Crawford, Stuart Crawley, Douglas Crighton, Roi Croasdale, Peter Crocker, Yvonne Crocker, Gary Crockford, Robert Croft, Ruth Croft, Louise Crook, Nic Crosbie, Amanda Cross, Jane Cross, Malcolm Cross, Simon "Bawdy Monkey" Cross, Stephen Cross, Janet Crossley, Rob Crow, Julian Cruft, Eileen Cullen, Polly Cumming, Graham Curtis, André Michael Czausov, L. Dactyl, Pam Dalby, Chris Dale, Dales, Anna Dallow, Sally Dallow, Frank Danes, Evelyn Danson, Larry Darby, Michael Darvell, Elinor Dautlich, Alan W Davidson, Harriet Davies, Nia Davies, Pete Davies, Rhys Davies, Mick Davis, Jon Davison, Karen Dawson, Sarah Day, Jane De Moratti, Anuree De Silva, Denise De-Foe, Michael Dean, Ronan Deazley, Joanne Deeming, Esther Deidun, Kirsty Delahunt, Clair Delmege, Sian Denereaz & Joe Cruddas, Nick Dennerly, Oliver Densham, Greg Dewar, Robin Dewar, Pat Dibben, Nikki Dix, Steve Doherty, Manir Donaghue, Kevin Donnelly, Mr Doo & friends, Louise Dop, Barry Doughty, Linda Doughty, Francesca Douglas, Paul Douglas, Philip Drake, Stuart Draper, Nigel Drury, Edmund Duffy, Hazel Duhy, Andrew Dunford, Rory Dunleavey, Sheila Dunn, Steve Dunn, Sheila Dunscombe, Jane Dunster, Cairo Durham Loveall, Rosie Dutton, Sarah Dyer, Melanie Dymond Harper, Jan Dzieminski, Peter Earl, Lorna Easterbrook, Christine Eddowes, Simon Edmondson, Paul Edwards, Sandi Edwards, Gregor Egan, Ruth Elkins, Catriona Elliott Winter, Debra Elsdon, Jerry Elsmore, Phillip A. Emery, Verna Emery, Bob English, Ian Ericson, Edwin Evans, Keith Evans, Mick Evans, Phillip Evans, Steve Evans, Val Evans, Victoria Evans, Sarah Evans & Mike Chamberlain , Victoria Ewart, Sue Facey, Grark family, Kersey family, Mary & Adrian Farmer, Rebecca Farrar, Andy Farrell, Salar Farzad, David Faulkner, Lisa Feinson, Ann Fenton, John Fenton, The Fergs and Laura, Verity Ferguson, Professor Cathy Fernandes, Stuart Ffoulkes, Momo Field, Michelle Fillmore, Gareth Finch, Duncan Finlyson, Maureen A Firth, Sam Fisher, Anton Fishman, Roy & Lesley Fishwick, Simon Fitch, Indira Flack, Helen Flanagan, Sarah Flanagan, Molly Fletcher, Paul Flynn, Clan Fodor, Lesley Foot, Jim Foster, Rosalind Fowler, Myszka Fox, Richard Fox, Rose-Anna Frankenberg, Hugh Franklin, Janet Freeman, Adrian Friedli, Derek Frood, Adrian Fry, Dominic Fry, Oliver Fulton, Ruth and Jem Gadlington, Ian Gair, Alison Garner, Lula Garner, Rob Garrett, Jo Garton, Deborah Gatty, Caroline Gent, Francesca Georgia, Daniel Gerhardt, Amelia Gersema, Sarah Getliff, Warren Getty, Jude Gibbons, Matthew Gibbons, David Gibbs, Julian Gibbs, Andy Gibson, Lyn Gibson, Julie Gilbert, Julie Giles, Rachel Giles, Richard Gillin, Martin Glassborow, Tina Glassenbury, Richard Glover, Bruce Goatly, Sue Goddard, Jake Godfrey, Sarah Godsell, Jan Goffey, Tim Goodier, Paul J. Goodison, Paul Goodman, Kashi and Emily Gorton, Jane Gow, Jon Graeme, Bullet Graham, Sheila Graham, Andrew Grant, Joanna Grant, Mark Grant, Anne Grauberg, Jeremy Grayson, Kathryn Green, Mark Green, Nick Green, Rachel Green, Matthew Greenburgh, Deborah Greensmith, Daisy Jane Greenwood, Samuel John Greenwood, Shirley Greenwood, Ollie Gregory, Louise Greig, Randi Gressgård, Tamzin Griffin, Alun Griffiths, Sarah and Andy Grigg, Andy Grimley, Jon Gripton, Elinor Groom, Beth Groves, Bill Groves,

Alan M Gruber, Dr Pete Gubbins, Emma Gubbins, Genevieve Guise, James Gunn, Nicola J Guy, Margaret Gwilliam, Owen Gwilliam, Christine A Gwynn, John Gwynne, John Hackett, Pip Hackett, Edward Hadden, Ion Hadden, Angela Hague, Tim Haillay, Laura Hailstone, Lesley Haines, Iain Halket, Alice Hall, Eileen Hall, James Hall, Claire Hamer, Stephanie Hamer, Clive Henry Hamilton, Cherry Hamlett, Roger Hamlett, Louisa Hamper, Jacquie Hampton, Gillian Hanhart, John Hankinson, Audrey Lucie Hannaford, Guillaume Hannaford, Maud Ellen Hannaford, Irene Hannah, John Hannawin, Elizabeth Hanson, Helen Hanson-Jarvis, Happy 40th Birthday Matthew, love Mum, Marg Hardisty, Robin Hare, Jean & Tony Harker, Pat Harkin, Christine Harper, Darryl Harper, Paul Harper, Samantha Harper, Eleanor Harris, Beverley Harrison, Mathew J Harrison, Jane Harrowing, Caryl Hart, Stephen J Hart, David Harvey, Ella Harvey, Jessamy Harvey, Liam Harvey, Mike Harvey, Paula Haselup, Simon Haslam, Darren Hatcher, Jill Hatton, Callum Hay, Caroline Hayden, Mark Hayward, Anna J Haywood, Grant Hazelton, Andrew Hearse, Beccy Heath, Martin Helsdon, Sheena Henderson, Anne Henshaw, Elizabeth Henwood, Lucy Henzell-Thomas, Nic Herriot, Erica Hesketh, Ken Hesketh, composer, Daniel Hewitt, Jenny Hewitt, Adam Hewson, Benedict Hextall, Benedict Heywood, Catherine Heywood, Wayne Hibberd, Gwyneth Hibbett, Nicola Hibon Jackson, Keith Hicks, Elaine Higgins, Joseph, Jennifer and Thomas Hill, Kathryn Hill, Robin Hill, Peter Hilliard, Robert Hills, Charlie Hinchliffe, Jenny Hinchliffe, Ralph Hinton, Ros Hiser Bach, Jon Hobbs, Philip Hobbs, Daryl "Major Clanger" Hobson, Gavin Hobson, Andrew Hoddinott, Jane Hodgson, David Holberton, Gina Holden, Matthew J Holland, Pauline Holland, Samantha Holland, Marion Holliday, Rosie Holliday, Dan Holloway, John R Holmes, Paul Holroyd, Sara Holroyd, Nigel Holt, Hazel Hope, Jan Hope-Collins, Sian Hopkinson, Simon Hopper, Kevin Horton, Philippa Hoskin, Lily Hoskins, Andrew Houston, Sue Howard, Zena Howard, Bob Howell, Julian Howells, Debby Howrie, Chris Hoyland, Mark Hunter, Nancy Hunter, Maya Hussain, Cee Hutchinson, Sue Hutton, Fran Huxley, Jonathan Hylton Clark, In memory of Monica and Cyril Laws , Pierpaolo Inga, Lucy Ingham, Carolyn Irvine, Suzanne Isaacs, Sladjana Ivanis, David Jackson, Melanie Jackson, Belinda James, Sarah James, Dorothy James-Jones, Margot Jamieson, Ian Jarvis, Robert Jarvis, Keith Jeffery, Grandad Jeffs, Lottie Jeffs, Katie Jenkins, Philip Jenkins, Julia Jewitt, Mara Joan, Meg Johannessen, Sue John, Victoria Johns, Dave Johnson, Lyndon Johnson, Wendy Johnson, Helen India Jolly, Stephen Jolly, Jane L C Jones, Ruth Jones, Rolf Jordan, Philip Joseph, Helen Josland, Joanne Joy, Joy, JP, Alison Judd, David Julyan, Alexander Justham, Tim Justham, Nick & Ros Kaijaks, Frances Kapherr, Ann Keen, Kate Keen, Mark Kehoe, Birgit Kehrer, Manda Keith, Dan Kelly, Gill Kelly, Joanne Kemp, Cathy Kennedy, Neil Kenny, Sean Keogh, Philip Keown, Isabel Kerins, Os Keyes, Prem Khanna, Dan Kieran, Capt Kim, John Edward Kind, Dominic King, Harriet King, Sarah King, Paul Kingett, Rob Kirby, Tim Kirby, Tim Kirk, Nigel Kitcher, Grant Klein, Doreen Knight, Nichola Knight, Rob Knight, Belinda Knowles, Kathie Knowles-Smith, Gary Kyle, Paul La Planche, Abhilash Lal Sarhadi, Emma 'Froglet' Lane, Gillian Lane, Samantha Lane, Maud Lang, Pete Langman, Paula Lankester, James Lark, Sheena Laurie, Morgan Law, Sara Law Bryce, Duncan Lawie, Robert Lawler, Sarah Lawrance, Sarah Laws, Elizabeth Lawson, William Layzell-Smith, Ben Le Foe, Andy Le Vien, Neil Leacy, Vicky Lear, Valérie Lechene, Glen Ledger, Mark Lednor, Elaine Lee, Andrew Christopher Leeson, Stephanie Legard, Karen Leigh, Chris Lemon, Rachel Lemon, Andy Lenthall, David Lewis, Wayne Lewis,

Ann Lill, Francis Lilley, Stephen Lindop, Matthew Ling, Steven Linnington, Lisa and Andrew, Claire Little, Maggie Livesey, Hazel Loadman, Sandra Lockwood, Dr Emma Long, James Long, Cath Longbottom, Penny Longman, Lady Lothian, Lisa Lovebucket, Catriona M. Low, Iain Lowson, Benjamin Lumbers, John Lynch, Paul Lynch, Den Lyons, Helen MacDonald, Jackie Machling, Tess & Nell Machling, Will Mackie, Clare MacLaren, Duncan MacLaren, Ian MacLennan, Shan Maclennan, Huw Maddock, Gaynor Ellen Maher, Phil Mahoney, Daryl Main, Michelle Major, Nigel Mallett, Bryce Malton, Anna Mankee Williams, Kenneth Mann, Sarah Mann-Yeager, Fran Manning, Pamela March, Sarah Markham, Jayne Marling, Charles Marriott, Eva Marriott, Jeff Marriott, Antony Marshall, Gareth Marshall, Keith Marshall, Margaret and Andrew Marshall, Oliver Marshall, Carl A H Martin, Francis Martin, Neil Masey, Alan Mason, Rachel Massey, Brenda Mastin, David Matkins, Matt & Maggie, Becca Mattingley, Graham Maughan, Richard Max, Caline May, Rhiannon May, Yvonne Maya, Neil Maycroft, Jo Mayne, Helen McAninly, Paul McAninly, Jennifer McArdle, Anthony McBride, Sue McBride, Peter McCarthy, Trevor McCarthy, John McCartney, Sarah McCartney, Yvonne Carol McCombie, Ian McDonald, Daniel McGachey, Paul McGill, Marty McGuigan, Ron McGuinness, Geoff McHugh, Joe McIntyre, Janet McKee, Kerry McKenna, Sarah McKinlay, Ian McLachlan, Alison McReath, Dionne McShane, David Mcwhirter, Fiona Meads, Paul Meads, Isobel Medcroft, Ruth Medcroft, Tina Meldon, Linda Meredith, Richard Metcalf, Jonathan Meth, George Michaelson, Greg Michaelson, Rosa Michaelson, Michelle & Lilli, Fi Miles, Frank Miles, Julie Miles, Stephanie Kim Miles, Tim Miles, Gavin Millar, David Millard, Tony Miller, Judith Milligan, Jan Millington, Simon Mills, William Mills-Wade, Sara Milner, John Mitchinson, James Moakes, Deena Mobbs, Mark Mobbs, Tes Monaghan, Linda Monckton, Alastair Monk, Janet Montefiore, Alison Moore, Jonathan Moore, Julia Morris, Yvonne Morrison, Sister Morticia, Ben Mountfield, Richard Moysey, Rebecca Mulcahy, Graham Mulholland, Jude Mulholland, Jilly Murison, Daniel Aodhan James Murphy, Elizabeth Murray, Emma Mustill, Stu Nathan & Andrea Burgess, Carlo Navato, Chris Neale, Richard Neale, David Nelmes, Paul Nethercott, Richard Newbold, Menai Newbould, Phil Newman, Catherine M. M. Newnham, Andrew Newton, Jim Newton, Karen ni Mheallaigh, Mr Mark William Niblett, Andrew Nicholas, Gary Nicol, Tiff Nield, Catherine Nisbet, Andy Norledge, Marco Norris Keiller, Ebon Northfield, Lesley Northfield, Cora Nowikow, Jeremy Nurse, Raymond O'Brien, Rebecca O'Brien, Su O'Brien, Emma O'Connell, Maggie O'Malley, Mark O'Neill, Matt O'Donovan, Ian Keith Oakeshott, Tina Oberman, Kevin Offer, Richard Ogden, Sarah Jane Ogg, Sarah Oldridge, Helen Oliver, Susan Ord, Angela Osborne, Family Osborne, Ian Osborne, Celia Osbourne, Family Oswald, Neil Ovey, Sue Owen, John Page, Andy Palmer, Colin Palmer, Mark Pangborn, Nigel Park, Nigel A. Park, Karin Parker, Terry Parker, Debbie Parker Kinch, Clive Parkes, Gary Parravani, Claire Parsons and Mark Seymour, Graham Partridge, Elizabeth Paterson, Michelle Paull, Abigail Pavitt, Sarah Peacock, David Peak, Siobhan Peal, Sarah Pearson, Stephen Pegge, Jeremy Pellatt, Bianca Pellet, Pen & Chris, Ann Penn, Nigel Pepper, Martin Percival, Emma Percy, Richard Perrett, David Perry, Paul Persighetti, Marc Petitjean, Elizabeth Phillips, Jonathan Phillips, Howard Phillis, Peter Phipps, Mr Phoenix, Mick Phythian, James Pilgrim, Simon Pilley, Jerry Pinel, Phil Pinel, David Pinney, Keith Pirie, Alicia Pivaro, Andrew Plant, Kristin Plant, Georgina Platt, Dan Pollard, Justin Pollard, Philip G Pollard, Helen Pomeroy, Victoria Poole,

Stephen Pope-Carter, Andrew Porter, Joanna Postgate, Selina Postgate, Verity Postgate-Cronbach, Iain Potter, Alan Pottinger, Dave Powell, Nigel Powell, Natasha Powers, Andrya Prescott, Mark Preston, Janet Pretty, Michael Pretty, Martin Price, Michael Price, Neil Price, Dameon Priestly, Carolynn Pritchard, Charles Pritchard, Heather Pritchard Dyer, Simon Procter, Jason Proctor, Sophie Proctor, Ioan & Seren Protheroe, Jim Proudfoot, Rachel Proudfoot, Laurence Pryke, Pup and Squiggle, Chris Purdon, Jacqui Pybus, Jonathan Pye, Andy R, Dawn Zoë Raison, Annette Ramsden, Dan Randall, Andy Randle, Helen Randle, James Raraty, Vivienne Ratter, Angela Rayson, Colette Reap, Ian Redgwell, Lily Redman, Nick Reed, Susan Reed, Mark Reeves, Helen Reid, Rebecca Reid, Bill Rennie, Adele Reynolds, Kirsten Reynolds, Cath Rhodes, Christopher Rhodes, Tom Richards, Ben Richardson, Sue Richardson, Stuart Riddle, Andrew Rigby, Steve Rigby, Steve Rigden, Andrew Rilstone, Mark Ripley, Boo Ritson, Anne Rixen, Hamish Roberton, Andy Roberts, Carolyn Joanne Roberts, Claire Roberts, Deb Roberts, Dorothy Roberts, Ozzie Roberts, Paul Roberts, Sue Roberts, Ian William Robertson, Simon Robertson and Clare Lovett, Harry Robins, Kathryn Robinson, Liz Robinson, Rod Robinson, Kate Robotham, Geoffrey Robson, Philip Robson, Andrew Rocksmith, Rachel Rodger, Jessica Roe, Jay Roff, Dr Mike Rogers, Nina & Dave Rogers, Steve Rogers, Neal Rollason, Cathy, Eb, Aidan, Colin and Catriona Rooney, Oliver Rose, Richard Rose, Chris Ross, Sally Ann Ross, Michael Rossell, Michael Rowell, Nancy Rowell, Steve Rowlands, Katherine Ruhl, Lisa Rull, Julie and Charles Runacres, Paul 'Rushy' Rush, Ruth, Katie Ryan, Sian Ryan, Kate Ryland, Karen S, Hesham Sabry, Nicola Sainsbury, Caroline Sale, Stephen Salmon, Christoph Sander, John Sanders, Sukhdev Sandhu, Gavin McCaw Sandison, Bernice Sargent, Ro and Tom Saul, Helen Saunders, Mark & Jane Saunders, Gregory Savage, Kerry Savage, Andy Sawyer, Jon Sayer, Keith Scaife, Claire Schlinkert, Schmeinstein, Rob Schofield, Jenny Schwarz, Family Scoley, Graeme Scott, Sarah Scott-Robinson, Katharine Seal, Myra Sefton, Rosemary Senior, Lily Serena, Dale Sergent, Andrew Setchfield, Anna Sewell, Debbie Seymour, Peggy Seymour, Tom Shakespeare, Martin Sharkey, Sam Sharp, Victoria Sharratt McConnell, Jane Shaw, Clare Shepherd, Dane Shepherd, Alan Sherriff, Carolyn Shier, David Short, David Shriver, Si & Jo, Chris Signore, Jonathan Silverman, David Simmonds, John Simmons, Samantha Simmons, Paul Simpson, Alan Sims, Sarah Sinsbury, SisterRainbow, Joe Skade, Deborah Skelton, James Slade, Debbie Slater, Laura Sleep, Keith Sleight, Georgia Slowe, Fran Sluman, Louise Smart, Iain Smedley, Alan Smith, Armitage Smith, Barry Smith, Caroline Smith, Derek Smith, Jennifer Nimmo Smith, Nigel Smith, Peter Smith, Papa Smurf, Chris Smyth, Ruth Solomons, Saffron Somers, Caroline Sommerville, Steve Southart, Maureen Kincaid Speller, Edward Spencer, Olivia Spencer, Graham Spencer Watkinson, Teresa Squires, Jo Squirrel, Sraddhamani, Lisa St.John, Wendy Staden, Tim Standish, Neil Stanley, Iain Stanton, Alex Steeden, E Steer, Andrew Stefaniak, Jane Stemp Wickenden, Alan Stephen, Anna Stephens, Ros Stern, Steve & Sytske, Kate Stevens, Gwyneth Stewart, Hugh Stiles, A Still, Ian Stinton, Paul Stockley, Alison Stone, Peter Strachan, Willem Strauss, Rae Streets, Frances Stroud, Harriet Stuart-Clarke, Zena Sturges, Tobias Sturt, Laurence Sumeray, Carolyn Sunners, Jim Surgeon, Our Susan, Chris Suslowicz, Jenny Sutton, Eileen Sweeney, Cathy Swift, Janine Sydenham, Bill Sykes, Louise Sykes, Matthew Sylvester, Alan Tait, Brian (Taz) Tarry, Stephen Tavener, Becky Taylor, Dave Taylor, Georgette Taylor, Karen Taylor, Kate Taylor, Louise Taylor, Nicola Taylor, Paul Taylor, Steve Taylor, Jill Tees, Amanda Tennant,

Gill Theodoreson, Julia Theulings, Caroline Thomas, Gareth Thomas, Judith Thomas, Lisa Thomas, Mari & Steve Thomas, Peter Thomas, Victoria Thomerson, Adam Thompson, Victoria Thompson, Andrew Thomsett, Gordon Thomson, Andrew Thorne, Carol Thornton, Nigel Thornton Clark, Sarah Thorowgood, Graham Thorpe, Amanda Thurman, Jill Thwaites, Tibs, Dan Tilbury, Robbie Tingey, Heather Tisdale, Kirsteen Titchener, Jonathan Todd, Pip Todd, Maggie Tolman, Alannah Tomkins, Wayne Tomlinson, Toni Tompkins, Samuel Toogood, Ian Totterdell, Susan Tottman, Ian Townsend, Karina Townsend, Sheila Townsend, Alison Trace, Richard Tracey, Simon Tracey, Samuel Trainor, Kirsteen Treacher, Tree, Ross Tregaskis, Rebecca Trembirth, Kate Trezise, K & J Trinder, Phillip Troth, Dr. Lucy J Troup, Sally Turnbull, David Turner, Dr. Andrew Turner, Ellery Turner, Melanie Turner, Sandy Turner, Cassie Tyas, Colin Udall, Helen Underwood, Jane Unwin, Jann Valenzuela, Alison Van der Linden, Berty van Hensbergen, Dennis Vaughan, Jodie Lee Vaughan & Arron Carter, Craig Vaughton, Mark Vent, Jackie Verge, Nicholas Verlaine, Dee Vick, Sue Vickers, Peter Vince, Jeremy Vincent, Sue Vincent, Gordon Von Krafft, Georgina Vye, Janet W, Jo W, Evan Waddell, Hildy Wade, Kestrel Wade, Richard Wainman, Rupert Wainwright, Christopher Wakefield, Paula Wakefield, Alison Wakeham, Hayley Waldron, Andrew Walker, Jeremy Walker, Mark Walker, Stewart Walker, Peter Walker-Birch, Dj Walker-Morgan, Karen Louise Wall, Sue Wallace, Gabriel Wallen, Louis Wallen, Robert Wallis, Annie Walters, Carole-Ann Warburton, Halina Ward, John Ward, Stephen R Ward, Emily L Warren, Peter Warren, Dominic Warwick, Beth Waters, Craig & Julie Watkins, Ian Watson, Meg Watson, Rachel & Dave Watson, Sian Watson, Andrew Weatherston, David & Helen Webb, Ted Webley, Katherine Wedell, Steve Welburn, Kevin Wellings, Robert Wells, Nicola Went, Kevin West, Lydia West, Sue Western, Tina Weston, Emma Whewell, Lisa Whistlecroft, Alan Whiston, Darren White, Elizabeth White, Esmé White, Jacky White, Nicholas White, Orla White, Rozie White, Simon Whiteside, Trevor Whittock, Darren Whitworth, Penny Wicken, Henry Wickens, David Wickham, David Wilbraham, Simon Wilcox, Stephen Wilcox, Jeff, Sue and Thom Wilkins, Anthony Wilkinson, Philip Wilkinson, Sean Wilks, Chris Willars, Peter Willatts, Jason Willbourn, Ann Williams, Bruce Williams, Charles Williams, Dave Williams, Ieuan Williams, John D Williams, Karen Williams, Martyn Williams, Paul and Pam Williams, Kate Williamson, Joanna Willmott, Edith Willow, Simon and Sheila Wills, Alexa Wilson, Dr D. M. Wilson, Stephen Wilson, Hazel Winchester, Jaye & Tony Windmill, Lucy Winter, Tim Winterburn, Alexandra Wood, Caroline Wood, Henry Wood, Jennifer Wood, Jo Wood, Jon Wood, Nicola Wood, Steve Wood, Amanda Woodfield, Fiona Woods, Julian Woods-Wilford, Peter Woolford, Stephan Work, Alec Worrall, Pamela Worrall, Alec Worsfold, Andrew Wright, Carolyn Wright, Dr Fiona Wright, Jen Wright, Rachel Wright, Joanna Wyld, Anne Young, Georgie Young, Peter Young, Andrew Zeyfert